MW01168997

VENETIAN ART GLASS

VENETIAN ART GLASS

An American Collection

1840 - 1970

Marino Barovier

ARNOLDSCHE

First Edition
June 2004

Catalog design by
Marino Barovier and Enrico Fiorese

Photographs by
John Dessarzin, New York, USA

Graphic production by
Enrico Fiorese and Nicola Ferro

Catalog edited by
Nicoletta Bertoldini

Translations
for the texts by Marino Barovier and Carla Sonego
Cristopher Huw Evans
for the texts of the catalog and the glossary
Olga Barmine

Printed by
Tipografia Rumor S.p.A., Vicenza, Italy
Printed in Italy

ARNOLDSCHE Art Publishers, Liststraße 9, D-70180 Stuttgart
(www.arnoldsche.com)

Bibliographic information published by Die Deutsche Bibliothek
Die Deutsche Bibliothek lists this publication in the Deutsche Nationalbibliografie; detailed bibliographic data is available in the Internet at *http://dnb.ddb.de.*

ISBN 3-89790-205-2

Made in Europe, 2004

Front cover
Vetro mosaico Glass, 1929-30 (see pages 90-91)

Back cover
Primavera Glass, 1924-35 (see pages 98-99)

Frontispiece page 2
Vetro mosaico Glass, 1929-30, detail (see pages 90-91)

Contents

To Elizabeth
and Mark, who
always see the
beauty in life.
With love,
Donna + Neil

Foreword

Donna and Neil Weisman

We have always loved Italy and the passion and spirit of the Italian people. During the first half of the Twentieth Century, Venetian glass blowers and designers were among the great artistic innovators. They reintroduced and reinterpreted ancient glass techniques, and experimented with new materials. Led by architects, painters and sculptors, a melting pot of Italian as well as international talent revolutionized the aesthetics of art glass.

Donna, an Italian Renaissance art major, and I, the consummate collector, are constantly browsing the world for new additions to the collection. Donna initiated our collection in the early nineties with four pieces of 1950's Italian glass, attracted to their shape and color. From there, my natural instincts as a collector gathered momentum. My main criterion became technique.

We collect glass the same way we collect art, instinctively. We are particularly attracted to Italian glass from the 1920's and 1930's, with a predilection for mosaic pieces from the 1920's.

A collection is an open-ended endeavor. When the passion to find the next addition to one's collection fades away, one is no longer a collector. Our passion remains strong, as we prepare for our second book.

Benvenuto Barovier, designs for glass vases inspired by ancient models, late 19th Century, Marino Barovier Archives.

Murano's Rebirths

Marino Barovier

The history of glass on Murano stretches back almost a thousand years and has its roots in the fertile soil of a rich material culture. Ancient knowledge, passed down from father to son, has been married with manual skills in an unbroken tradition, with its own rules and rituals, that is brought back to life every day through the extraordinary sensibility of the island's master glassmakers.

These craftsmen exploit the peculiar properties of a material whose unique chemical composition, based on silica and soda, allows it to solidify slowly from the molten state. This means that they are able to carry out complex operations with the hot material, adopting precise techniques (of which the most significant is glassblowing) which constitute the remarkable and characteristic heritage of the island in the Venice Lagoon, recognized all over the world. A heritage that has been built up over centuries, during which time the material's many possibilities have been explored, from the more strictly utilitarian ones, such as tableware and lighting, to the decorative arts.

The history of Murano glass, though largely characterized by periods of great enthusiasm, experimentation and success, has also gone through times of great difficulty which were often, in part at least, the consequence of unfavorable economic and political conditions. In particular, the beginning of the 19th Century brought a deep crisis on Murano, dealing a severe blow to the glass industry. An already delicate situation, which had seen the expansion of Bohemian crystal at the expense of Venetian glass over the previous decades, was seriously aggravated by the fall of the Repubblica Serenissima (1797), with all the political and economic upheavals that this caused. One such was the abolition of the guilds, and in particular the Arte dei Vetrai (1807), which until then had protected and promoted the craft, from the organizational as well as commercial viewpoint.

As Venice came under Austrian, French and then Austrian rule again, the local market was increasingly handicapped, partly as a result of heavy customs tariffs imposed on the import of raw materials, a measure designed to favor the products of crafts and industries located on the other side of the Alps (Barovier Mentasti 2002, p. 16).
Combined with a drastic reduction in the number of furnaces, all this led to an impoverishment of the store of technical expertise and manual skill in the lagoon area, where not much more than glass beads were produced in those years.
Toward the end of the 1830s and during the 1840s, however, sporadic attempts were made to revive glassmaking on the initiative of people like the antique dealer Antonio Sanquirico. Spending a great deal of time on the island, he commissioned reproductions of pieces made by the technique known as *filigrana a retortoli*, in which rods of colorless glass with colored or opaque white threads in the middle are twisted into spirals, which he then sold as antiques. This instilled new life into the process, which came to be known by the name of the antique dealer, transformed into *zanfirico* in the local dialect.
The *filigrana* technique attracted the attention of technicians such as Domenico Bussolin, Lorenzo Graziati and above all Pietro Bigaglia, who came up with some extraordinary interpretations of it around 1845. He created extremely refined pieces of glassware with fairly linear forms, sometimes classical in style, and characterized by brilliant colors. In fact Bigaglia used unusual polychrome rods of glass to make his *filigrana*, to which he often imparted a golden glow by the inclusion of *avventurina*. Like Lorenzo Radi after him, who made glass with a texture resembling the color-banded variety of chalcedony called agate in the 1850s, Bigaglia also set about experimenting with a new type of glass that had an appearance similar to granite.

A fundamental part in the revival and exploitation of Murano's ancient cultural heritage was played by the abbé Vincenzo Zanetti, an expert on the art of glass who in 1861 – with the support of the island's mayor Antonio Colleoni – founded the Glass Museum, setting up a school to teach apprentices the art and technique of glass the following year.
As the abbé declared: "in that period when, after over half a Century of decline, the foundations were laid for revival of the famous art, [...] three precious elements remained [on which to build this hoped-for revival]: *the classic models, the history and the technical and practical traditions of the work*" (Lorenzetti 1932, p. 562).

Given these premises the museum's collection – which was gradually enriched with antique pieces and examples of current production – and the school, where such objects were used as models for study, became the driving forces in the process of restoring vitality to a vanishing art.
Significant from the viewpoint of production was the activity commenced in 1866 by Antonio Salviati, a lawyer from Vicenza who set up a new glassworks, the Società Anonima per Azioni Salviati & Co. He did so partly with British capital, a reflection of the renewed interest in Murano glass shown by foreign markets, especially on the other side of the English Channel.
In 1872 it was renamed the Venice and Murano Glass and Mosaic Company Limited (Salviati & Co.), and then came to be known as the Compagnia Venezia e Murano.
Present on Murano since 1859, when he had opened a large and soon famous mosaic workshop, Salviati ran the new furnace for the production of lightweight blown glass, turning to the best craftsmen and technicians on the island, men like Antonio Seguso, Vincenzo Moretti, Andrea Rioda and the brothers Antonio and Giovanni Barovier. Thanks to these skilled workers, whom the entrepreneur from Vicenza sent to study at

Benvenuto Barovier, study for a plate with glass rods and *murrine*, late 19th Century, Marino Barovier Archives.

Compagnia Venezia Murano advertisement, late 19th Century, Marino Barovier Archives.

Fondamenta dei Vetrai, Murano, late 19th Century, Marino Barovier Archives.

Zanetti's school of design, the output of the glassworks stood out both for the high quality of its execution, something by which Salviati set great store, and the wide variety of its forms. Alongside objects inspired for the most part by blown glass from the late 16th Century and the baroque period, glassware with enamel decorations was produced and several attempts at imitating antique glass were made.

Following disagreements among the partners, Salviati left the company in 1877 to set up two new businesses: Salviati & Co. specializing in mosaics and Salviati Dr. Antonio, where he was still able to count on the skills of the technician Andrea Camozzo and the Barovier brothers to produce blown glass.

Along with excellent copies of antique glassware, chiefly from the Renaissance, the master

glassmakers continued to diversify the range of products with their own personal interpretations, sometimes showing off their remarkable dexterity by making objects of great fragility. Nevertheless, for the first years after the split at least, the styles were fairly similar to those of the Compagnia Venezia e Murano (run by Alessandro Castellani from 1877 onward), as was evident at the Universal Exposition held in Paris in 1878 (Dorigato 2002, p. 206). Among the objects presented on that occasion, where the two glassworks tried to outdo one another in the quality of their production, were pieces inspired by archaeological finds, including imitations of early Christian glass with engraved gold leaf and so-called *murrini* (murrhine glass), based on the mosaic glass of the ancient Romans.
Mosaic glass had already attracted the attention of the technicians and craftsmen on Murano at the beginning of the 1870s, when fragments of the characteristic material found in archaeological excavations had been brought to the island first by Salviati and then by Augusto Castellani, a Roman jeweler and antique collector who donated them to the Museum.
Encouraged by Salviati, numerous attempts were made to reproduce this type of glass. Initially (ca. 1871) Salviati's own craftsmen made it by blowing glass, which was not the technique used in Roman and Alexandrian times. In fact the objects they produced were pieces of blown glass covered by sections of canes, called *millefiori*, which were then embedded in the wall.
The finest practitioner of this ancient technique was Vincenzo Moretti, who worked for Salviati until 1877 and then moved to the Compagnia Venezia e Murano. Overcoming the great difficulties entailed in the preparation of the glass pastes, he succeeded, after the mid-seventies, in creating extraordinary objects without blowing the glass. He did so by layering sections of glass canes and then heating them until they fused together. The material was then shaped in special molds and finally ground and polished.
This glass was shown for the first time in 1878, earning praise from Zanetti among others. The fact that he called them *murrini* led to this philologically incorrect term being used for any mosaic glass made from sections of canes. In his *Naturalis Historia*, Pliny the Elder had applied the expression *vasa murrina* (murrhine vases) to multicolored objects fashioned from a semiprecious stone of Eastern origin, perhaps fluorite, which the Roman glass masters were able to imitate. So the failure to identify either the mineral or, above all, its reproduction in glass stimulated the imagination of the glassmakers on Murano, who from then on used *murrino* as a name for mosaic glass (Sarpellon 1990, pp. 103-4).
After this remarkable success, Moretti took his research further, producing exact copies of antique murrhine glass or his own interpretation of it. This set the tone for much of the production of the Compagnia Venezia e Murano, where he worked until 1900, the year he moved with his sons to a new glassworks.
At Salviati Dr. Antonio too the interest in antique glass and especially Roman murrhines continued to grow, although this production consisted chiefly of *millefiori* glass made by blowing, an art at which the Barovier brothers excelled, along with their sons Giuseppe, Benvenuto and Benedetto, who were also working in the furnace during those years.
When Salviati withdrew from the glassworks in 1883 to devote his time to running his stores, it was they who took over the firm, while continuing to work exclusively for the entrepreneur. Known on Murano as the Artisti Barovier, they did not change the original name of the furnace until several years after Salviati's death, when they set up the company Artisti Barovier & Co. in 1895.
This was the year that the best of Murano's products were put on show at the *Terza Esposizione di Scelti*

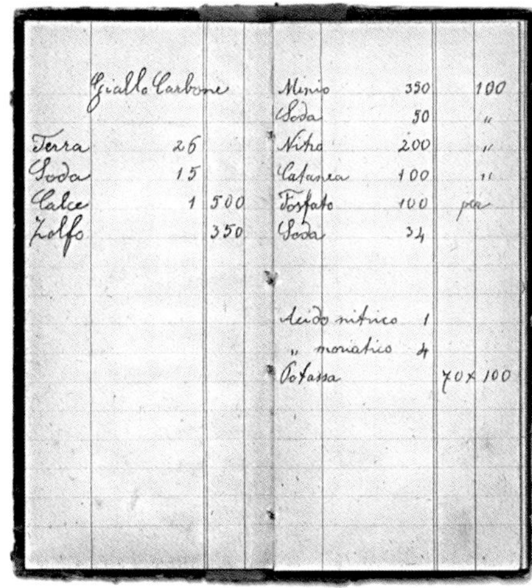

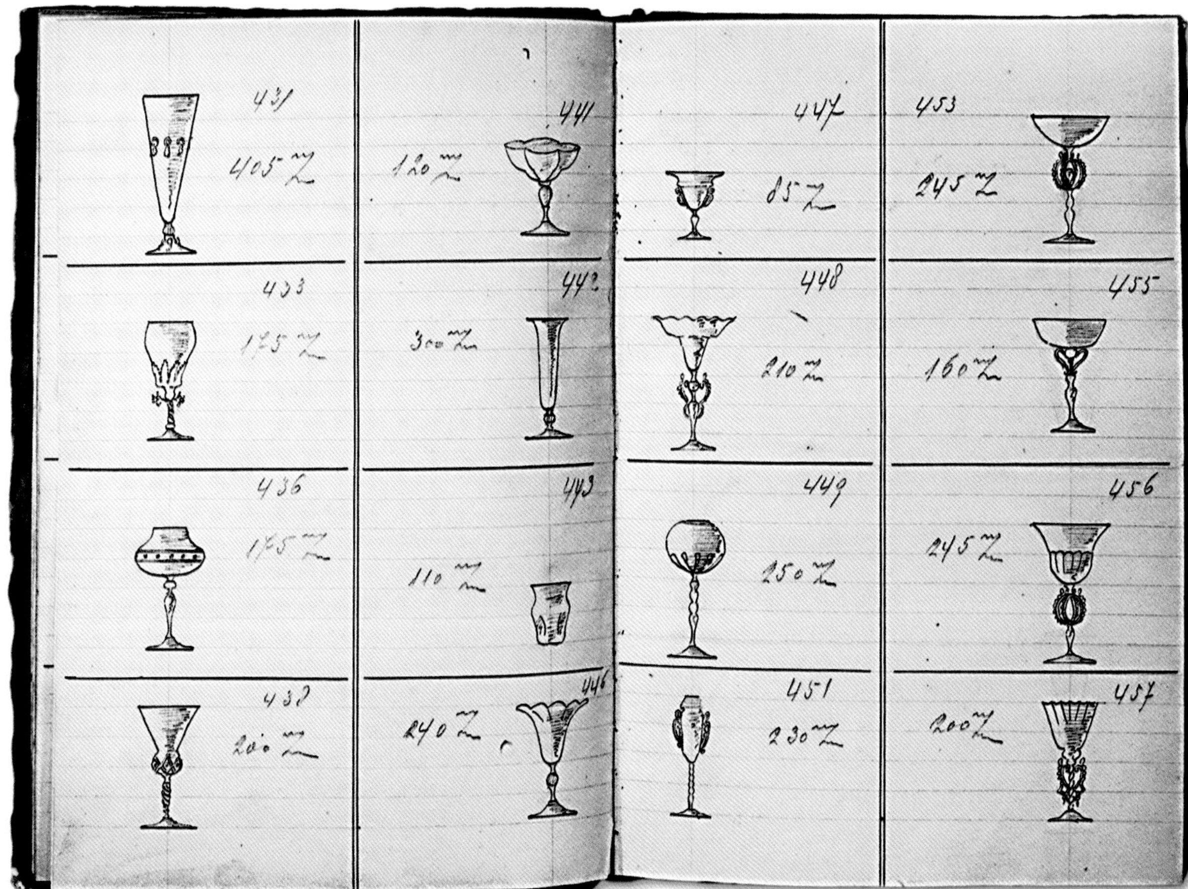

Benvenuto Barovier as a youth, sitting at the work bench while working glass, second half of the 19th Century, Marino Barovier Archives.

A page from the book of *partie* (recipes for glass colors) from the Artisti Barovier glassworks, late 19th Century, Marino Barovier Archives.

Models produced by Artisti Barovier around the end of the 19th Century, Marino Barovier Archives.

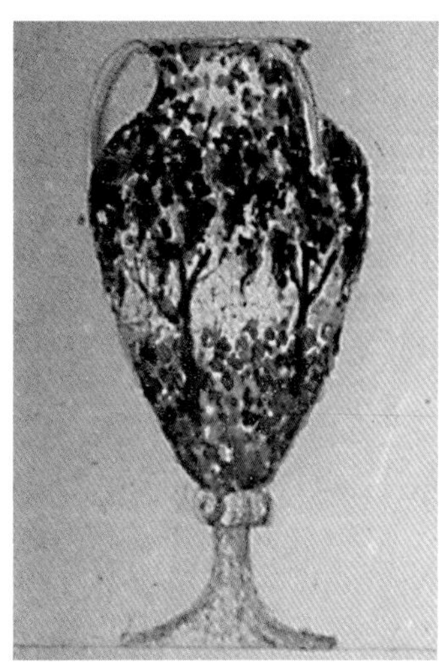

Benvenuto Barovier, models for vases in *a murrine* glass, late 19th - early 20th centuries, Marino Barovier Archives.

Benvenuto Barovier with his wife Elisa and their eleven children. Among them on the far right stands his son Ercole and behind their mother, brothers Diego and Nicolò, first decade of the 20th Century, Marino Barovier Archives.

Vetri Artistici ed Oggetti Affini, staged on the island to coincide with the first Venice Biennale. To a great extent this reflected the state of glassmaking in the last decades of the Century, characterized by the predominance of a sterile virtuosity and by a constant harking back to the styles of the past. While these had brought new vigor to production after the middle of the Century, they now represented a severe limitation.

The island's industry proved essentially impervious to innovation, which was linked in those years – especially in the field of decorative arts – to the emergence of the Art Nouveau style. While elsewhere, and in the rest of Europe in particular, glassmaking was going through a truly innovative phase thanks to designers like the Frenchmen Gallé, Daum and Lalique and the American Tiffany, Murano was not very receptive to the new modernist ideas, and when it did take them up, it was in a rather fragmentary and episodic manner.

On that occasion the only timid attempt to respond to the new stimuli consisted of "a few modern objects", including lithe goblets with spiral stems and feet made by the Artisti Barovier, although most of their output was still along "traditional" lines.

It was not just a suspicion of innovation on the part of Murano glassmakers that contributed to this situation, but also the local market, consisting largely of wealthy tourists who purchased much of the production and wanted articles that could be described as "Venetian" in character.

In those years, around the end of the 19th Century and the beginning of the 20th, the technique of murrhine glass started to be more widely adopted on the island. A glance at some of the catalogs of the time reveals the significant variety of *a murrine* blown glass produced by furnaces such as Ferro Toso, founded in 1901, or by highly skilled craftsmen like Vittorio Zuffi. Presumably it was he who introduced the process to Fratelli Toso, a company that had been active since 1854 and was known chiefly for its ordinary glassware, but which established a reputation in this new sector during the first few decades of the 20th Century (Junck 1998, pp. 26, 38-42).

The forms were drawn mostly from an eclectic repertoire, often embellished with elaborate frills, while the appearance of the glass itself was diversified by more or less complex combinations of murrhines, distributed uniformly over the surface or arranged in alternating rows or checkerboard patterns, often associated with vertical canes of *avventurina* glass.

This type of production, which really began to catch on in the second decade of the Century, can be said to have played an important role in the interpretation, albeit a belated one, of Art Nouveau, or the Liberty style as it was called in Italy, and its adoption on Murano.

On the one hand the use of murrhines representing individual flowers or floral motifs, however simple, may have favored a move in this direction, as the subsequent production of Fratelli Toso, for example, would suggest.

On the other hand the skill and original handling of the technique by craftsmen like Giuseppe Barovier – who presented several of his own murrhine glass pieces along with the famous *murrina del pavone* under his own name at the Ca' Pesaro Exhibition in 1913 – aroused the interest of "Sezessionist" artists like Teodoro Wolf Ferrari and Vittorio Zecchin, who wanted to try their own hand at this technique.

In fact the same year, with the help of the Artisti Barovier, the two painters from the group based around Ca' Pesaro created a small but distinctive series of objects in glass mosaic, shown first in Munich and then at the 1914 Venice Biennale.

By adapting the technique of execution to new expressive requirements, the collaboration between Wolf Ferrari and Zecchin and the Barovier brothers proved that it was possible to apply

Artisti Barovier showroom, Murano, ca. 1919, Marino Barovier Archives.

Vetreria Artistica Barovier showroom, Murano, ca. 1928, Marino Barovier Archives.

Compagnia Venezia e Murano Pauly & Co showroom, Venezia, ca. 1930, Marino Barovier Archives.

OMNIS·ARS·IMITATIO·EST·NATVRAE

pictorial schemes of "Sezessionist" inspiration to the material and produce surprising results, taking the art of glass to a high level by freeing it from the constraints of tradition.
Thanks to the contact with these artists, who came from the lively anti-academic circles of Ca' Pesaro, the world of glassmaking began to open up, belatedly, to the research of the avant-garde. A significant contribution also came from the work of the ceramic artist Hans Stoltenberg Lerche, who between 1911 and 1914 used the techniques of hot decoration in new ways at Fratelli Toso to make innovative glass pieces in fluid and sinuous shapes and iridescent colors, producing results that were comparable with those attained outside Italy.
After these first, sporadic experiences, the glassworks became increasingly aware of the need to revitalize their production by taking on board contemporary artistic ideas. All this was to lead, in the Twenties and Thirties, to enduring collaborations between the furnaces and artists or architects and to the emergence of the new figure of the designer, who has played, and still plays, such an important part in raising the quality of glass production.
So sometime around the middle of the second decade the activity of the Artisti Barovier, regarded as the best furnace of the time, was more or less directly influenced by the brief experience with Zecchin and Wolf Ferrari in this new climate of experimentation. Up until the beginning of this decade the Barovier brothers had continued to rely on mosaic glass to produce studied decorative compositions, in some cases utilizing sophisticated "Sezessionist" motifs that can make attribution of the pieces difficult. Taking an innovative approach, the murrhine lost its figurative autonomy in these works and was treated instead as *a tessera*, as a more or less elaborate part of a true mosaic created by the juxtaposition of many pieces of glass to form a single design.
One of the earliest known examples is the small range of glassware produced around 1914 for the Salviati stores, now run by the heirs of the founder, and presumably intended for an elite market.
In addition to their considerable size, what is striking about these articles, generally set on a flared foot and the product of undeniable technical and manual skill, is the structure of the glass body, made up of murrhines arranged in a more or less geometric pattern. In the extremely precious production of the next few years (ca. 1915) and the period immediately after the war, what could be described as naturalistic themes predominated, with extraordinary transparent mosaics, forming the walls of the objects.
Moreover, as Lorenzetti recalled, they were "pieces of glassware simple in form but glinting and sparkling with the most splendid and daring palette of colors; [...] the most varied and opulent shades of color appeared in strange and fantastic combinations of plants, flowers and animals [...]" (Lorenzetti 1921, p. 1094).
Similar polychromy can be seen in several works resulting from a collaboration between Umberto Bellotto and the Artisti Barovier around 1920, in which objects made of mosaic glass were combined with elaborate supporting structures of wrought iron. These were the famous *connubi ferro e vetro* (unions of iron and glass), in some cases created with the help of the Fratelli Toso, and a belated example of Venetian Art Nouveau.
A decidedly floral version of this style was maintained in the postwar production of glassworks like the Fratelli Toso and the one run by the Barovier brothers, which in 1919 was renamed the Vetreria Artistica Barovier & Co. following changes in the structure of the company. Such articles, presumably aimed at a wider public, developed solutions that had already been presented at the *Mostra dei Fiori* in 1914, where the Artisti Barovier won first prize in the short stem category of the contest for "memorial vases".

Umberto Bellotto, *murrine* vases and the *connubi ferro e vetro vases*, ca. 1923.

The Cappellin store, ca. 1927, Marino Barovier Archives.

Following their example, the vases were embellished with floral murrhines embedded in the wall of the glass during its manufacture, along with polychrome threads of glass imitating branches and twigs, which took on a distinctly expressive quality in the glassware produced by Barovier in the Twenties.
It was around the middle of that decade, however, that a new interpretation of mosaic glass emerged from the Barovier furnace, although one that still had echoes of late Art Nouveau. It was created by two members of the new generation: Ercole and Nicolò, the sons of Benvenuto Barovier.
This series of vases, often of considerable size, was decorated with stylized motifs, still based on floral designs, in general produced by the juxtaposition of special colored murrhines with an amethyst border and a colorless core. They stood out against a grid of clear murrhines ringed with pale colors, creating singular chromatic effects through the transparence and luminosity of the shades. This effect is particularly evident in some of the glassware made by Nicolò, in which more abstract decorations are accompanied by tesserae with segmented patterns, arranged irregularly so as to produce an unusual texture that renders it highly expressive. Despite the extraordinary quality of these pieces, they did not suggest any new directions and to some extent represent a belated return to a style that had already come to the end of its life several years earlier.
Instead the direction to be taken for a revival of Murano glassmaking was indicated by a new furnace, V.S.M. Cappellin Venini & Co., founded in 1921 by Paolo Venini from Milan and Giacomo Cappellin from Venice, who brought in Vittorio Zecchin as art director to carry out their "courageous modern reform" (Lorenzetti, 1932, p. 572).
After the earlier experience with the Barovier brothers, he had turned his attention to the material again around 1919, working on his own and producing blown glass decorated with enamels and gold engraved with typically "Sezessionist" motifs. Placed in charge of the new furnace, Zecchin designed very light pieces of blown glass in soft colors, sometimes inspired by the Renaissance glassware depicted in the paintings of Titian, Veronese and others. Thus Cappellin Venini glassware, abandoning the late 19th Century legacy of superfluous virtuosity still to be found in the output of the time, was distinguished by the extreme elegance and cleanliness of its lines, showing itself to be truly in the vanguard.
It proved a great success at the major exhibitions of decorative art held during that period, and in particular at the Paris Expo in 1925, although this resulted in disagreements between the two partners and their separation.
Cappellin and Venini went on to found the Maestri Vetrai Muranesi Cappellin & Co. and the Vetri Soffiati Muranesi Venini & Co. respectively, which at the outset went on producing transparent blown glass of extreme refinement that set a benchmark for the whole of the island's industry.
Giacomo Cappellin renewed his collaboration with Zecchin, who worked at the M.V.M. until 1926, the year his place was taken by the young architect Carlo Scarpa. Able to rely on the best craftsmen employed by the furnace at the time, Scarpa pursued the line of research initiated by the painter from Murano.
After the early transparent glassware, he created many models at the end of the twenties that were characterized by essential forms and by the quality of the glass textures: these were sometimes produced by traditional Murano techniques that had fallen into disuse, such as *a reticello* and *a decoro fenicio*. At the beginning of the Thirties Cappellin's glassware, repeatedly published in specialist magazines like Gio Ponti's *Domus*, achieved a significant success with its "wonderful *paste vitree* in the most refined and precious

colors" and its "exquisite *lattimi*" (Lorenzetti 1931). However, imprudent management of the company's finances, aggravated by the economic slump, forced Cappellin to close down in January 1932.
Paolo Venini, on the other hand, when he opened his new glassworks in 1925, entrusted its artistic direction to the sculptor Napoleone Martinuzzi, at that time director of the Glass Museum, who worked with V.S.M. Venini & Co. until the early Thirties. Although initially influenced by Zecchin's work, Martinuzzi started to experiment with the material at the end of the second decade of the Century, inventing a characteristic opaque glass called *pulegoso*, whose distinctive feature was the innumerable tiny bubbles embedded in the thick walls.
As early as 1928 V.S.M. Venini & Co. presented its *pulegoso* glassware at the Venice Biennale, for which the sculptor chose archaic forms in imitation of ancient amphorae and goblet, sometimes of large size, in various shades of dark green as well as blue, and with variants in white glass. In addition to this series of articles, accompanied by unusual and highly sculptural cacti made of *pulegoso* glass, Martinuzzi produced a new range of glassware in another opaque material, *incamiciato* (cased) glass, in brilliant colors. In this way he played an active part in the debate over the nature of Murano glass that took place at the beginning of the Thirties, between defenders of its traditional lightness and transparence and advocates of the innovative use of heavy and opaque *pasta vitrea* glass. In particular he showed a preference for the latter even in his later work when, after leaving Venini, he characterized the production of Zecchin-Martinuzzi, the glassworks he founded in 1932, with vivid pieces of *incamiciato* glass and *pasta vitrea* glass in bright tones.
For his new artistic director, Paolo Venini then turned to the Milanese architect Tommaso Buzzi, who collaborated with the glassworks until 1933. In this manner Venini cemented his practice of repeatedly

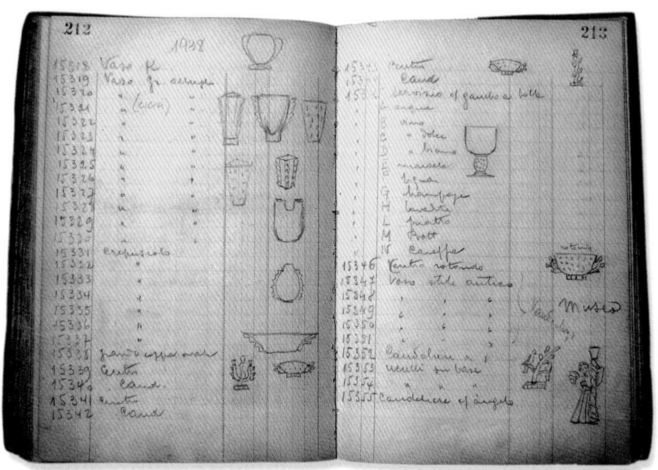

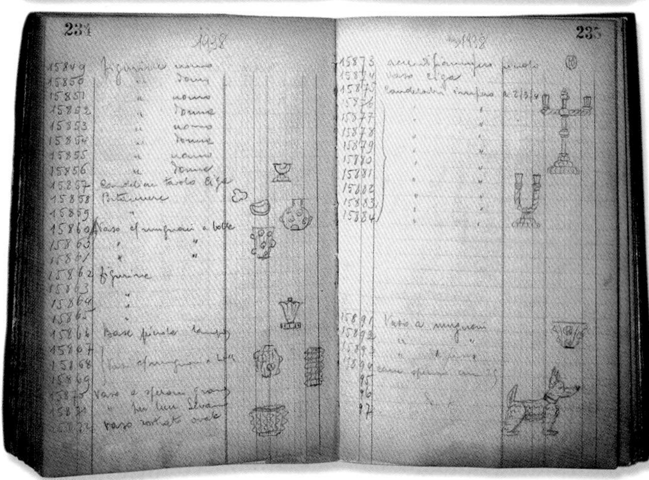

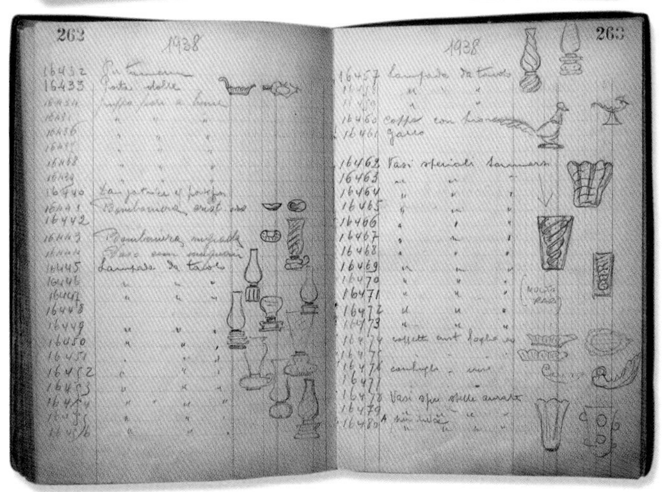

establishing fertile relationships with the artists and architects of his time, showing himself to be aware of and open to the new ideas that helped to enrich and enliven 20th Century glass.
Buzzi created extremely refined pieces, made primarily from *incamiciato* glass, a technique that he gradually made his own, creating a series of vases with several layers of glass in delicate shades of color, adorned with gold leaf and graceful applied trimmings.
The range was presented at the 5th Milan Triennale in 1933, which was proving to be the best platform for Murano glass, along with the Venice Biennale, where a special pavilion was devoted to the decorative arts from 1932 onward.
Thus the two events served as recurrent opportunities for comparison and up-to-date showcases of the best contemporary production.
In particular, the establishment of a single space dedicated to this sector at the Biennale, the pavilion of decorative arts, opened a constant window on the level of activity on Murano.
Hence its inauguration made it possible to assess the situation in the early Thirties, enlivened by the work of such furnaces as Venini, Zecchin-Martinuzzi and the historic Fratelli Toso, among others.
Another of the firms that stood out was the S.A.L.I.R., active since the mid-Twenties, which was attaining a degree of success thanks to the engraver Franz Pelzel and above all Guido Balsamo Stella. In fact the latter, as Lorenzetti pointed out, had "revived the technique of engraving on the lap and the wheel and given it a modern interpretation, not exempt from exotic tendencies, adorning the limpid crystalline surfaces of vases, dishes and goblets with figures drawn from the imagination or features of modern life and customs" (Lorenzetti 1931).
Nor did the Vetreria Artistica Barovier & Co. fail to set itself apart from other Murano glassmakers, presenting, alongside several vases, stylized animals as an example of the furnace's versatility.

Ercole Barovier, pages from the hand-written catalog with models from the years 1936 and 1940, Barovier & Toso Archives.

The production of the glassworks was now under the direction of Ercole Barovier, who progressively assumed the role of indefatigable designer and shrewd entrepreneur, taking a personal interest in questions of technique and execution as well.
"Ercole is a peculiar glassmaker since he does not blow glass" (Dorigato 1993, p.17). Yet he acted out of a deep understanding of the material, to which he was to devote himself constantly up until 1972.
Abandoning the murrhine technique, the glassworks came out with the extraordinary *primavera* series in the early Thirties, characterized by a crackled, milky appearance that was the product of the first experiments carried out in the furnace.
The remarkable success he achieved with this particular material, unfortunately the result of fortuitous circumstances that made it unrepeatable, probably induced Ercole Barovier to make the new experiments that led to the creation of the technique of *colorazione a caldo senza fusione* (hot coloring without fusion).
By introducing substances that did not have time to melt into the vitreous mixture, he succeeded in producing a characteristic glass with unusual chromatic properties. In 1934-35 he used this to make pieces with very thick walls, which were given the names *autunno gemmato*, *laguna gemmata*, *marina gemmata* and *crepuscolo* in relation to their colorings.
These pieces, which were shown at the 1936 Biennale, were often decorated with bold applications of *cristallo* glass that emphasized their plasticity, an aspect of which Barovier was particularly fond and which was to typify much of his production from the mid-Thirties until the end of the next decade.
During those years, in line with the research of the time, not least that conducted at Venini, he showed a preference for thick *cristallo* glass, as is evident in the various series described as *con applicazioni*, *rostrati* and *a mugnoni* produced in 1937 and 1938,

as well as the series *a lenti*, *a grosse costolature* and *a stelle* in 1940 and 1942. Alongside these, he made objects in unusual colors such as the *a spirale* and *oriente* pieces of 1940, again in rather thick material, or the *rugiadosi* ones, also of 1940, with an unusual rough surface.
At Venini, from 1934 up to the outbreak of the Second World War, Paolo Venini was able to count on the inexhaustible creativity of Carlo Scarpa who, thanks to the climate of open-mindedness and readiness to experiment, was able to investigate traditional techniques of glassmaking and adapt them to his own purposes in order to renew the furnace's production. In the Thirties, falling in line with the fashion for thick glassware, he created the successful series of *sommersi* (1934-36), followed by the heavy *corrosi* (1936), decorated with applied knobs or bands and produced in several versions. The following decade was a particularly fertile one, with Scarpa creating numerous models and showing a distinct preference for intense colors and innovative textures. Among the latter, one unusual type was developed to produce the *battuti* pieces which, after finishing on the lap when cold, had an irregular surface similar in appearance to that of hammered silverware.
Scarpa's work at Venini made a fundamental contribution to the vitality of Murano glass in the 20th Century and left behind a significant legacy for the furnace run by the Milanese entrepreneur. This was profitably exploited when activity resumed after the war, through the collaboration of various artists and designers, including Gio Ponti, Tyra Lundgren (already present on Murano at the end of the Thirties), and Eugène Berman, who wanted to explore the possibilities of glass and designed some decidedly sculptural objects. Another regular collaborator was Fulvio Bianconi, who created the extremely popular series of *pezzati* (1950-51), as well as pieces decorated with polychrome bands (1950 and 1953) that were characterized by unusual pictorial cadences. In a significant revival of processes from the past, Venini himself dabbled in design, reinterpreting the techniques of *filigrana* and *murrina* (1954). The latter was also used by Tobia Scarpa for some glassware produced in 1962. On the death of Paolo Venini (1959), his son-in-law Ludovico Diaz de Santillana took over the company but continued along the same lines as his predecessor, repeatedly showing himself open to new collaborations. This led him to work with, among others, American artists like Benjamin Moore and James Carpenter in the Seventies.
The postwar period also saw the relighting of Ercole Barovier's furnace, which, after a series of revolutions in the structure of the company had changed its name to Barovier & Toso in 1942. Significantly, Barovier made his appearance at the first post-war Biennale with a range of glassware made from canes and murrhines, such as the *damasco* pieces, offering a possible reinterpretation of the old techniques in a contemporary key. However, this remained a limited experiment at the outset, although it did herald Ercole's interest in this line, which he would go on to investigate in a brilliant fashion, especially from the second half of the fifties up until the end of his career.
The early Fifties was characterized chiefly by research into hot coloring without fusion, which he continued to develop, for example, in the series known as *barbarici* (1951) or *graffito barbarico* (1952). In the following years he seems to have focused on developing material with completely new colors, as is demonstrated, among other things, by his interest in *opalino* glass and its variations, which allowed him to make the *ambrati* (1956). *Opalino* glass was to reappear several times in his extensive output of *a tessere policrome* glass that, combined in a variety of ways, characterized the work of the last fifteen years of his life.
Recognizable by their elegant linearity and always evocative coloring, these pieces were shown at

Carlo Scarpa, *Corrosi* vases, 1936, Marino Barovier Archives.

every Biennale up until 1970. They were a continuous demonstration of the creativity of their designer who, harking back to the tradition of his ancestors, was able to come up with extraordinary modern interpretations of the *murrina* technique. On Murano in the Fifties the need to bring traditional processes up to date induced several master glassmakers, owners of their own furnaces, to undertake experiments. One of them, Archimede Seguso, enthusiastically set about modernizing the *filigrana* technique, producing unexpected versions of it in his ethereal *merletti*, which were to form the distinctive note of his work in the following decade as well.
A completely different but no less suggestive approach was taken by the painter Dino Martens, who was art director at Aureliano Toso from the end of the war to the early Sixties. Adapting the techniques used on Murano to some extent, Martens created glass with an accentuated polychromy, for the most part through an unpredictable combination of elements. Out of this came the *zanfirici* (1951, 1957), made by the union of distinctive canes of *zanfirico*. To produce glassware like the *oriente* (1952-54) and *eldorado* (1953) series, which he often gave curious nicknames, he made use of crushed glass, along with *avventurina* and inserts of *zanfirico* and *reticello*.
In the extraordinary climate of research that held sway in the glassmaking of those years, Giulio Radi, working on behalf of A.VE.M, studied the reactions caused by the application of particular metal oxides, which produced unusual effects of light and color. But these experiments were interrupted by Radi's premature death in 1952. His place was taken by Giorgio Ferro, who designed vases with fluid forms and a highly iridescent surface. Also working on surface textures, Ermanno Nason proposed a special type of material at the Cenedese glassworks in the early Fifties. This was *scavo* glass, characterized by irregular patterns of corrosion produced by the action of acids and salts on the wall of the article during its manufacture and creating the effect of antique glass.
At the beginning of the Fifties, the Centro Studio Pittori nell'Arte del Vetro, was founded on Murano, with the aim, "according to the syllabus, of training 'a new guild of artisans who will no longer be subject to the class pride that raises a barrier of contempt between artists and craftsmen', and getting them to support one another, so that they can arrive at "the unified work, in which there will be no further distinction between high art and decorative art", just as happens in every artistically creative period" (Gasparetto 1953, p. 33).
The initiative came from Egidio Costantini, who actively promoted the school in the firm belief that it was possible to produce art with glass, to the point that he devoted much of his life to it. The project immediately received the support of many Venetian artists, including Aldo Bergamini, Virgilio Guidi and Bruno Saetti, and very soon that of such internationally famous figures as Alexander Calder, Henry Moore and Oskar Kokoschka. As early as April 1953 their work was shown at a joint exhibition which, as well as stirring new enthusiasm,

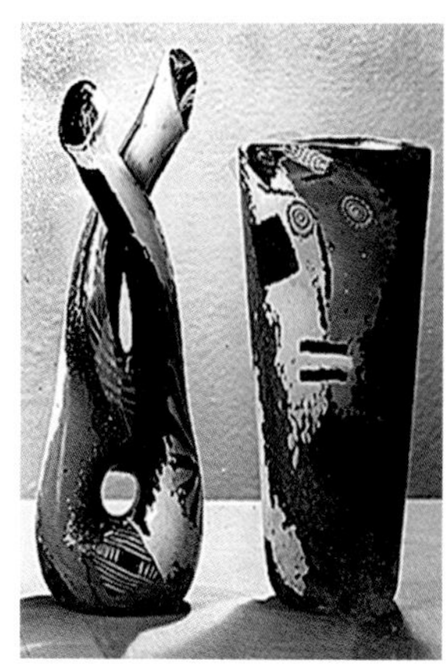

Dino Martens, *Oriente* vases, 1954, Marino Barovier Archives.

Pablo Picasso with the *Gufo* vase, Marino Barovier Archives.

roused fierce debate and anger among many Venetians.
Costantini quickly established relations with other important figures on the international art scene, above all Picasso, who sent him several designs that he was able to translate into glass through the collaboration of furnaces like Ferro Lazzarini and I.V.R. Mazzega, submitting them to the artist for approval on each occasion.
Renamed the Fucina degli Angeli by Jean Cocteau, this initiative stirred a great deal of interest among artists, but it also encountered problems – often as result of local incomprehension – that led to a stagnation in its activity. In the Sixties, with the sensitive backing of Peggy Guggenheim, Costantini and the Fucina regained their vigor and the project was expanded to bring in new artists like Jean Arp, who designed the star that was to become its symbol.
During the years of his activity Costantini also built a special relationship of trust with a number of master glassmakers who, in his own words "desired and were able [...] to throw themselves into [...] the exciting new adventure of glass" (Berruti, Serena 1993, p. 153).
So this experience contributed to the development of a new and original relationship with glass, a medium which artists were able to explore, through the skill of the craftsmen, as part of their own research into modes of expression.
Out of this came a different critical view and appraisal of an art that, while retaining strong ties with tradition, was able, especially over the course of the 20th Century, to flourish again and display a new vitality thanks to its craftsmen and to those who devoted themselves to it with passion.
This story is reflected by the works in this wonderful collection, which Donna and Neil Weisman started to put together with the same passion in 1994.
Their love of Italy and its culture brought them to the lagoon city, where their encounter with the extraordinary material that is glass has not failed to make an impact.

Portrait of Ercole Barovier, Barovier & Toso, Archives.

Ercole Barovier: A Protagonist of 20th Century Murano Glass

Carla Sonego

The year 1921, date of the foundation of Cappellin Venini & Co., marked the beginning of a new era for Murano glass: once strictly a craft industry, it was to win itself a well-earned place in the world of design over the course of the 20th Century.
In addition to indicating new stylistic trends based on monochromy and essentiality of line, the birth of this glassworks brought with it the beginnings of a different mode of working, one that entailed a clearer, and more modern, distinction of roles within the company, as was already happening in other sectors of industry.
The creative aspect in particular, hitherto to some extent the responsibility of the proprietor of the furnace, but in the main delegated to the master glassmaker, author of his own works, was now entrusted to an external designer, brought in from the world of the arts. In this case, it was the painter Vittorio Zecchin, himself a native of Murano, who was called on to act as artistic director and guide production. In this way an independent figure gradually took shape and played a decisive role in the renewal of what was still fundamentally an artisan process. In other words, what was being postulated was the existence on the one hand of a designer – and therefore of a design and a procedure antecedent to the manufacture of the object itself – and on the other of an executor, although the two figures operated in close collaboration, something indispensable in this specific area of production.
This practice was itself renewed in 1925, when the two partners, Cappellin and Venini, went their separate ways and founded companies of their own. M.V.M. Cappellin & Co. continued to make use of Zecchin, while V.S.M. Venini & Co. turned to the sculptor Napoleone Martinuzzi. This set the seal on an approach that, repeated over the years, indicated a new direction for the development of the glass industry and contributed to its vitality.
In fact the involvement of artists in this new role

and the openness of mind displayed by the entrepreneurs made it possible to achieve results of high quality, laying the foundations for a significant revival in which the two furnaces played a leading role in those years. Alongside them, and Venini in particular (in 1932 M.V.M. was forced into bankruptcy by the economic crisis), the historic glassworks run by the Barovier family also began to reassert itself, while taking another road. After the First World War (1919), it had assumed the name of the Vetreria Artistica Barovier following changes to the structure of the firm which included the entry of a new generation, in the persons of Giuseppe's son Napoleone and Benvenuto's sons Ercole and Nicolò.

It is the last two who were responsible for the characteristic production, around the middle of the Twenties, of a limited series of brightly colored glassware. To make this Ercole and Nicolò used the ancient technique of *murrina* or mosaic glass, in which their forebears had distinguished themselves in previous decades. Thus their work maintained a continuity with the extraordinary family heritage of technique and manual skill, which they attempted to reinterpret by proposing geometric or abstract motifs in addition to stylized floral decorations, although these still lagged behind the creations of the more up-to-date glassmakers. With a classical education under his belt, although one aimed at quite another career, Ercole (1889-1974)[1] was no

Piccione primavera, 1929-30, Marino Barovier Archives.

longer particularly young when he came into the furnace, something quite unusual for Murano at the time, and had immediately begun to take on board that rich store of cultural and technical knowledge, quickly developing a profound grasp of it.
"He drew and painted well and with ease",[2] recalled his son Angelo. And so, motivated in part by a keen interest in glass and by an innate curiosity, he started to design a number of objects. In addition to the aforementioned *a murrine* vases, these included animals and later on the ingenious cacti that were exhibited at the Biennale of 1928[3]. Although working with glass, he did not blow it himself, preferring technical research and experimentation. In particular he focused on preparation of the material, as is apparent from the series of *primavera* vases, with their novel milky and opalescent appearance. This glass was presumably made out of a mixture of sodium silicate and other substances which had been obtained by "chance" and therefore could not be repeated.
The series, created in 1929 and presented with success at the Monza Triennale the following year, reflected a certain late *Déco* taste and was distinguished by its unusual forms, although these were sometimes still of classical inspiration, often rounded and underlined by edgings in black glass. Along with vases and bowls on fairly essential lines, there were in fact pieces with an unusual monochrome body embellished with elaborate applications of hot glass not devoid of a certain – and perhaps wry – self-indulgence.
If on the one hand such applications can be seen as a sort of gloss on the individual objects that enhanced their form, on the other they did not conceal a virtuosity of execution typical of the Murano tradition.
Subsequently, seeking new effects, Ercole gave a highly iridescent finishing to the surface of the dark gray *acciaio*[4] glassware which, conceived in 1932, was shown at the Biennale of 1934.

Vases with polychrome decorations *"900"*, 1931, Marino Barovier Archives.

Also on display for the first time in Venice that year, where glassware by the Frenchman Maurice Marinot could be seen, just as it at the previous one, were transparent glass vases of great thickness with evocative colorings. Venini, which had now appointed Carlo Scarpa as its artistic director, proposed the *sommersi a bollicine*, in which precious chromatic effects were obtained by the superimposition of several layers of transparent colored glass and bubbly *cristallo* glass, sometimes with the inclusion of gold leaf. The *a spire argento* or *a fasce argento* vases produced by Fratelli Toso, on the other hand, owed their appearance not just to the technique of "submersion" in the case of the *a spire* vases, but also to the use of silver leaf, in some cases oxidized.
However, "on Murano, heavy glass of French origin [was] viewed with great suspicion; it seemed to be a negation of the orthodox approach to glassmaking on the island, which in the past had been celebrated for its extremely light glass."[5] So this production revived the debate over the nature of the material that had commenced at the beginning of the thirties, with the dispute over opaque glass, and that was destined to continue until the following decade with the progressive diffusion of so-called "heavy" blown glass[6].
Ercole Barovier, an attentive observer and ever more closely involved in the world of glass, did not fail to address such questions in his work. As early as 1931 the Vetreria Artistica Barovier had used colorless and fairly thick transparent glass for a number of vases shown at the exhibition in Amsterdam. All that has survived of these, described in the catalogue as *vasi trasparenti con decorazioni policrome "900"*, are contemporary photographs which, even though in black and white, still allow us to appreciate the interplay of color and transparence. Made in irregular forms, they were characterized by an abstract "polychrome" decoration produced by incorporating flattened

rods or segments of rods into the wall of the vase. But this remained a one-off episode, since in practice the inclusion of colored glass, in that period, was used only for the production of animal figures.
In the mid-Thirties the need to find new directions, perhaps partly in the light of the results proposed at the 1934 Biennale, which seem to have given Ercole Barovier food for thought (judging by the sketches in his notebooks[7]), led him to carry out further research into the material. His profound grasp of technique and his experimental bent induced him, in particular, to try out new types of coloring for glass based on oxides and metal filaments. Thus he developed the technique of *colorazione a caldo senza fusione* (hot coloring without fusion), for which he took out two patents on July 16, 1937, one for a method of making "glass containing agglomerates of oxides and metals" and another for the production of "glass containing metal filaments."
Thanks to this genuine invention he was able to create a new type of glass for Murano that owed its appearance to the characteristic stripes and specks, more or less densely packed and varying in size, which remained suspended in the thick wall of transparent glass. The chromatic effect these produced was different every time and intimately bound up with the material and the way it was made. In fact it depended on the use of substances for coloring during the manufacturing phase that did not melt, or that burned but did not have time to melt and fuse with the molten transparent glass, and that were therefore distributed in an irregular way in the object's transparent body.
In his development of the new technique Ercole may have fallen under the spell of Marinot's works, which he had probably had an opportunity to see at the Biennale, but the fact is that these supplied him with no more than ideas. Barovier conducted his research independently – there is no record of any contact between the two men[8] – and while in some cases it is possible to discern the Frenchman's influence, it is transformed by the typically Murano character of all of Barovier's works.
The first glassware made by the technique of hot coloring without fusion was shown at the Biennale of 1936, where the glassworks, known as Ferro Toso & Barovier from that year on following Nicolò's departure from the company and its merger with S.A.I.A.R. Ferro Toso, presented the *autunno gemmato* and *laguna gemmata* vases. These were joined by the *marina gemmata* and by the *crepuscolo* series, shown at the Milan Triennale the same year. It is significant that, during the exhibition, the city's Museo di Arte Applicata chose to purchase one of the vases[9].
The *gemmati*, perhaps fruit of his early experiments, were generally characterized – with the exception of the *marina* – by a fairly uneven coloring with a pattern of irregular patches that brought out the qualities of the material. The *crepuscolo*, on the other hand, were distinguished by a less marked and to some extent more abstract variegation, similar in appearance to a dense tangle of dark threads reminiscent of burnt iron wool, which was inserted between two layers of hot glass to embellish the wall of the object.
For this glassware, in his now established role of artistic director (he had become head of the firm in 1936), Ercole Barovier designed models with fairly unusual plastic forms, often with an oval, triangular or quadrangular section that was emphasized by large applications of *cristallo* glass. In many cases, in fact, the edges of the objects were underlined by bands of transparent colorless glass in relief, or by twisted threads applied by the typical *a morise* technique. Other vases, generally with more essential lines (in the shape of a sphere or a truncated cone), were distinguished by large, colorless, lens-shaped applications that, always in a deliberate contrast of form and color, accentuated

Autunno gemmato vases, 1936, Barovier & Toso Archives.

Vases by Ercole Barovier at the Mostra storica del vetro di Murano, XXVI Biennale, Venezia, 1952, Marino Barovier Archives.

Rostrati vases, 1940, Barovier & Toso Archives.

Oriente vases, 1940, Barovier & Toso Archives.

the sculptural quality of the objects themselves. This aspect, and in particular the notable figurative force of such creations, was pointed out in an article published in "Domus" in 1941[10]. Discussing the "possibilities of modern glass," this described at length one of Ercole Barovier's vases, which had a quadrangular section and was decorated with *morise cristallo* glass, identifiable as an *autunno gemmato*. "A vase like this [...]," declared the article, "is already a little monument in itself, a solid, shining monument in purple and gold glass. The fiery and brilliant opulence of the material is accompanied by the moderate breathing of the dense and animated form."

In any case, the use of the technique of hot coloring without fusion was limited in these years to a few series like the *gemmati* or the *crepuscolo*. This last was shown in Venice in 1938, together with a *zaffiro* vase in a characteristic "speckled" pattern of deep blue, as an example of that process[11]. Another variant was represented by the rare *spuma di mare* glassware, whose uniformly stippled "texture" was due to the use of sodium silicate and powdered *avventurina,* which were incorporated into the glass during its manufacture. In general, the colorings obtained at high temperature grew progressively more uniform and even, as is demonstrated not only by the last series cited, but also by the *rilievi argentati* and *rilievi aurati* bowls of 1940, the only objects of this kind to be made before the war.

In fact a large part of the production of the glassworks – called Barovier Toso & Co. from 1938 and Barovier & Toso from 1942 – was characterized toward the end of the Thirties and the beginning of the Forties by thick and transparent glass with no hint of color.

From 1937 onward, Ercole Barovier devoted himself with enthusiasm to the design of numerous "heavy" pieces of glassware, utilizing paste that was largely colorless - *cristallo* glass - or delicately tinted (pale green, *fumé*, pale amethyst). He was able to explore, manipulate and transform it through the use of bubbles, reliefs, irregular ribbing, strips and pinches, and through the application of rings, knobs, stalks, stars, etc., often with iridescent effects. New series were created with forms that were for the most part stylized and yet soft, occasionally associating various types of transparent glass (with bubbles, ribbing, etc.) that always produced different results when they were overlaid. Thus his work demonstrated the endless potentialities of glass even without a marked use of color. Exploiting the skill of the master glassmakers to the full and reinterpreting the tradition of hot working in his own way, Ercole offered a profoundly and "unmistakably"[12] Murano response to the new aesthetic and artistic demands.

One of the most successful of these works was the *rostrato* series, made up of transparent pieces of thick glassware whose entire surface was covered with small prisms on a square base set on strips of glass in horizontal rows. In general they were made out of *cristallo* glass, sometimes given an iridescent finish on the surface or replaced on the inside by glass containing bubbles or gold leaf in order to amplify the characteristic effects produced by the incidence of the light on the object's many facets. Because of these characteristics this *rostrato* or *prismatico* glass a procedure patented in February 1939, was also used in the lighting and furnishing sectors, as was apparent at the 7th Milano Triennale (1940), where among other things a bed with posts made of pulled glass was exhibited[13]. *Rostrato* glass was also employed in the fitting of the S.C.A.E.M. store in Milan by the architect Reiner Adami (ca. 1941), who used it to make elements of support, illuminated from the inside, for the plate-glass shelves[14].

A variant of this series was the so-called *a lenti* glass, where the prisms were replaced by small hemispheres. In particular, some of these objects,

shown at the 1940 Biennale, were characterized by a transparent core colored with applications of gold leaf that, covered entirely by hemispheres of *cristallo* glass, generated precious chromatic effects. In the same way the massive *a spirale* glass, also from 1940, represented a new attempt by Barovier to combine heavy transparent glass with color, which had come back into fashion in glassmaking.
This is clearly seen in the multicolored *oriente* series, which was exhibited that year in Venice and Milan along with the popular *rugiada* glassware[15], which had thick walls and a rough ("refractive") surface with grains of gold-leaf glass, the fruit of Ercole Barovier's fertile experimentation with hot working and vitreous material.
This confirmed the predilection of Murano glassmakers for thick glass, which continued to characterize the prewar activity of Barovier & Toso and which Ercole himself recognized as playing a decisive part in the renewal of the island's production. Since – as he declared – "it is heavy glass that has penetrated and made itself an intimate part of the spirit of the new architecture. And just as the new modern style of architecture has employed new materials [...] heavy glass has found precious and hitherto unknown decorative elements and has made the most of new and original colorings, with interesting glass pastes that would certainly not have been obtained by limiting creative activity to light blown glass."[16]
His almost alchemical research into the "precious material"[17] was not confined to the "new and original colorings" and "interesting glass pastes" created in the Thirties and Forties, but continued after the war, when he took the reins of the company again with new enthusiasm, as the sole, but prolific, inventor of models and formulas. When the furnaces were at last relit Paolo Venini chose once again to draw on the services of a variety of collaborators from the world of design and art, and his example was followed by other glassworks on Murano. But Ercole went on working in his own, independent way, remaining in charge of production until the early Seventies.
"His ambition was to create twenty-five thousand models",[18] a number that, however exaggerated, represented his passion and love for a material whose endless potential he, with his profound understanding of its possibilities, was able to exploit from both the formal and the technical viewpoint. At the base of his work, in fact, lay the considerable expertise built up over time by someone who "who had never worked in the furnace [but] who had always personally supervised the execution of his works from beginning to end at the side of the master glassmaker."[19]
"The artist," asserted Barovier, "must know, when he sets out to produce a design on paper, whether it can be realized using the technique of the glassmaker. The designs also have to be perfectly feasible: their imprecise reproduction would be a disservice to the designer and to the glassmaker."[20]
Thanks in part to this rich store of material culture, accumulated and absorbed over the previous years, he was able to take his research further, especially in the Fifties, but in the following decade too. It led him on the one hand to employ the technique of hot coloring without fusion with considerable assurance and to propose new chromatic solutions, and on the other to revive ancient techniques like murrhine glass, in its updated version using tesserae, that was to characterize his work up until the beginning of the Seventies.
The technique of coloring without fusion was employed to create a series of objects that differed greatly in appearance, thereby revealing its extraordinary "versatility" in obtaining a wide variety of effects.
For example the *eugenei* series (1951), from the Greek for "well born" as his son Angelo recalls, had a surface treated to make it iridescent, distinguishable by an even and markedly pearly

A *Lenti* vases, 1940, Barovier & Toso Archives.

Millefili vases, 1956, Barovier & Toso Archives.

coloring that was enhanced by the tones chosen for its realization. The *barbarici* (1951), on the other hand, had a rough texture, with dense bluish stippling that suggested the effects of time on the objects, as did the vivid speckled coloring of the *aborigeni* (1954). Bowing to the figurative demands of the period, these series were in fact modeled on archaic and primitive forms that were at times extremely close to the world of ceramics, as in the case of the *barbarici*, which are reminiscent of contemporary works by Gambone[21]. In any case "Ercole Barovier considered – perhaps instinctively – design to be at the service of the material and the technique invented,"[22] something that is evident in the intimate connection of form and material in all his creations.

At the Biennale of 1948 Ercole had started out with several extraordinary series of objects (*damasco, murrino*, etc.), made from rods and murrhines, which laid the foundations for a contemporary interpretation of traditional techniques. However, the theme did not resurface and was not developed until the middle of the Fifties, when the production of Barovier & Toso was characterized by new glass made with polychrome tesserae. This was accompanied by an extreme simplification of forms and a new approach to the material, used now to compose refined geometric patterns in delicate and suggestive colors, including *opalino* glass.

Significantly, model 21689 of the Barovier & Toso *millefili* series was singled out, along with two lamps designed by Vignelli for Venini, at the third award of the Compasso d'Oro prize in 1956[23], and thus recognized as a genuine product of design.

Ercole Barovier, artist and designer, had arrived in this world at the end of a passionate journey on which he had been propelled by an "impelling need [to bring] the new into the channel of the old tradition, but in an up-to-date atmosphere and conception."[24]

1 For biographical notes see in particular *Biografia di Ercole Barovier* in A. Dorigato (edited by), *Ercole Barovier 1889-1974, vetraio muranese,* Venezia 1989, pp. 130-131.

2 A. Barovier, *Cenni biografici su Ercole Barovier*, typewritten manuscript, June 1989.

3 For participation by the glassworks in Venetian events, see in particular in M. Barovier, R. Barovier Mentasti, A. Dorigato (edited by), *Il vetro di Murano alle Biennali 1895-1972*, Venezia 1995.

4 See among others A. Dorigato, *I Barovier ovvero la tradizione rinnovata* in M. Barovier (edited by), *L'arte dei Barovier vetrai di Murano 1866-1972*, Venezia, 1993, p. 18.

5 A. Gasparetto, *La rinascita di Murano*, in A. Gasparetto (edited by), *Vetri di Murano 1860-1960*, Verona 1960, p. 21.

6 On this subject, see G. Dell'Oro, *Il rinnovamento della produzione del vetro muranese*, in "Le Tre Venezie", November-December 1943, pp. 407-409.

7 See the page of notes by Ercole Barovier published in A. Dorigato (edited by), *Ercole Barovier...*, op. cit., p. 11, where below right two models of the *a fasce argento* by Fratelli Toso are redrawn.

8 See A. Dorigato, *Ercole Barovier 1889-1974, Vetraio Muranese*, in A. Dorigato (edited by), *Ercole Barovier...*, op. cit., p.18.

9 See G. Mori, *La collezione di vetri moderni del Castello Sforzesco acquisiti negli anni venti e trenta*, in AA.VV., *Tra creatività e progettazione. Il vetro a Milano 1906-1968*, Milano 1998, pp. 66-67.

10 *Possibilità del vetro moderno*, in "Domus", February 1941, p. 54.

11 The same year saw the series of animals *arabesco verde* made with hot colouring without fusion. See A. Barovier, *Cronologia delle opere*, typewritten manuscript, June 1989, pp. 8-9.

12 See A. Gasparetto, *La rinascita...*, op. cit., p. 21.

13 M. Chirico, *Vetro 'come', vetro 'dove' alle Biennali di Monza/Milano*, in AA.VV., *Tra creatività e progettazione...*, op. cit., pp. 33, 35.

14 C. Daniele, *Andar per vetro: un itinerante a Milano*, in AA.VV., *Tra creatività e progettazione...*, op.cit., pp.73, 78.

15 The manufacturing procedure for this type of glass, which enjoyed a vast commercial success, was registered with a patent for procedure as early as December 1938.

16 G. Dell'Oro, *Il rinnovamento...*, op.cit. p. 409.

17 E. Barovier, *La preziosa materia*, in"La Voce di Murano", No. 79, 1974, p.1. 18 Ivi.

19 A. Barovier, *Ricordo di Ercole Barovier*, in A. Dorigato (edited by), *Ercole Barovier...*, op. cit., p. 9.

20 E. Barovier, *La nascita di un vetro artistico veneziano e la sua tecnica*, in A. Vettore (edited by), *Luci e trasparenze. Vetri storici di Ercole Barovier 1889-1974*, Verona, p. 8.

21 See *Gambone ceramista*, in "Domus", November-December 1950, pp. 34-36.

22 *Ercole Barovier. La materia...*, op. cit.

23 See A. Pansera, *Il vetro al Compasso d'Oro*, in AA.VV., *Tra creatività e progettazione...*, op. cit., p. 60.

24 E. Barovier, *La nascita...*, op. cit., p. 8.

The Collection

Catalog edited by Marino Barovier
Workshops edited by Carla Sonego

The collection has been ordered by grouping the objects by manufacturer in chronological order. Each object has been dated by referring to the year of its official presentation at important exhibitions and in some cases by the publication in specialized magazines of the time. As far as the names of the single pieces, we have chosen to use the original names drawn from the catalogs of the glassworks or from magazines of the time. The description of the glass pieces uses terminology specific to the furnaces on Murano, distinguished by italics and described in the glossary at the back of the book.

Pietro Bigaglia

Compagnia Venezia e Murano Salviati Dr. Antonio

Pietro Bigaglia

Pietro Bigaglia (1788 – 1876), son of Lorenzo, one of the last great furnace owners of the eighteenth Century – he had both a crystal furnace and a plate glass furnace – pursued and expanded his father's work by opening an enamels furnace to produce conterie. He is responsible, with Domenico Bussolin, for the substantial renascence of Venetian glass in the mid-nineteenth Century. An energetic researcher and experimenter, he dedicated himself to the creation of elegant glass pieces in filigrana with unusual polychrome finishes and linear forms. He often used avventurina, and was the first to shape it into rods. In his research, he sought to create vitreous textures which imitated the texture of stones such as granite or oxydian, which he used to produce classical-style vases, some of which are conserved today at the Glass Museum in Murano. He also produced "rui", round glass pieces used to compose glazed surfaces for windows.

Compagnia Venezia e Murano Salviati Dr. Antonio

In 1866 Antonio Salviati, a lawyer originally from Vicenza, opened a new glassworks, the Società Anonima per Azioni Salviati & Co., which acquired additional capital several months later from new English partners. In 1872 the company was officially named The Venice and Murano Glass and Mosaic Company Limited (Salviati & Co.). Availing themselves of the best glass masters on the island, the company won widespread acclaim at the international expositions it attended. However the separation between partners in 1877 led to the creation of two new furnaces for the production of blown glass: the Compagnia Venezia e Murano, directed by Alessandro Castellani and Salviati Dr. Antonio, directed once again by the entrepreneur from Vicenza, who also founded Salviati & Co. for the production of mosaics. The Compagnia Venezia e Murano in particular continued to rely on composition technicians such as Andrea Rioda and especially Vincenzo Moretti, who dedicated himself specifically to the study of ancient Roman and Alexandrian glass which he was able to reproduce faithfully. In addition to these and the late sixteenth Century and baroque models, the Compagnia Venezia e Murano made glass pieces inspired by Islamic, archaeological and paleo-Christian glass (glass with etched gold leaf). It closed at the end of the nineteenth Century and reopened later with a different company organization. In 1909 it was purchased by Marco Testolini and transformed into a retail showroom when he closed the furnace.
In 1877 Giovanni, Giuseppe, Benvenuto and Benedetto Barovier followed Salviati to the new Salviati Dr. Antonio glassworks and continued to produce superior quality objects still prevalently inspired by historical styles. In 1884 Salviati sold the furnace to the Artisti Barovier and devoted himself exclusively to running his shops. The name of the furnace was maintained however until the death of its founder in 1890.

1. **A reticello**
Pietro Bigaglia

1842-45

h 10" - 25 cm

Bibliography:
Gasparetto 1960, No. 1;
Romanelli, Dorigato 1982, Nos. 73-74;
L'arte del vetro 1992, Nos. 105-106, 109;
Dorigato 2002, pp. 173-179.

2. **A reticello**
Pietro Bigaglia

1842-45

Compote in *reticello* glass with interwoven polychrome rods and *avventurina*. Twisted stem in cristallo.

h 7" - 18 cm

Bibliography:
Gasparetto 1960, No. 1;
Barovier Mentasti 1978, No. 4;
Dorigato, Barovier Mentasti 1981, No. 4;
Barovier Mentasti 1982, No. 181;
Mille anni 1982, Nos. 374-376;
Romanelli, Dorigato 1982, Nos. 73-74;
L'arte del vetro 1992, Nos. 105-106, 109;
Dorigato 2002, pp. 173-179.

3. **Graffito oro e smalti**
Compagnia Venezia e Murano

1877-1900

Vessel in transparent amethyst glass decorated with *graffito* gold leaf in vegetable patterns with polychrome enamel images of ivy and harpies at the center.
The vessel is illustrated in an 1893 leaflet about the production by the Compagnia Venezia e Murano in that period.

h 6.5" - 17 cm

Bibliography:
Barovier Mentasti 1978, No. 26;
Dorigato, Barovier Mentasti 1981, No. 13;
Baumgartner 1995, No. 100;
Bova, Junck, Migliaccio 1999, No. 80;
Dorigato 2002, pp. 196.

Vase from the "Compagnia Venezia e Murano" in "L'esposizione di Parigi illustrata 1878".

4. **Iridato**
Compagnia Venezia e Murano

1877-1900

Vessel with a sphere-shaped body in heavily iridized amethyst glass, decorated with lens-shaped applications. Because of their characteristic finish, the glass pieces in this series were called *metalliformi*.

h 13.25" - 34 cm

Bibliography:
Marangoni 1927, plate 98.

Catalog drawing from the "Compagnia Venezia e Murano", late 19th Century.

5. **Avventurina**
Salviati Dr. Antonio

ca. 1880

Pitcher in thin *avventurina* glass with a large applied handle and disc-shaped foot. The handle is decorated with a lion's head at the point where it is attached.

h 11.25" - 29 cm

Bibliography:
Romanelli, Dorigato 1982, No. 88;
I Barovier 1998, No. 2;
Bova, Junck, Migliaccio 1999, No. 135, p. 199.

Model No. 201, Salviati Dr. Antonio Catalog, 1875-1900.

6. **A fruste**
Salviati Dr. Antonio

1877-83

Vase in amethyst glass decorated with irregularly applied *lattimo* threads.

The shape of the vase corresponds to model No. 171 in the Salviati Dr. Antonio catalog (1878-1883).

h 12. 5" - 32 cm

7. **A canne**
Salviati Dr. Antonio

1877-90

Vase in transparent blue glass decorated with polychrome rods, finished over the entire surface with gold leaf applications.
h 12.75" - 32 cm

Bibliography: Barr 1998, p. 75; Bova, Junck, Migliaccio 1999, No. 79.

Model No. 171, Salviati Dr. Antonio Catalog, 1875-1900.

Vittorio Zuffi

Ferro Toso & Co.

Vittorio Zuffi

A skilled glass master, he worked with Ermenegildo D'Este, Arturo and Ovidio Nason in the Società Operaja Arturo Nason & Co., a glassworks founded in 1890 and closed in 1896, which produced glass for the Fratelli Testolini establishment. He was known especially for his production of refined *a murrine* glass, for which he showed a profound understanding (and excellent craftsmanship). The most significant of these pieces featured decorations in horizontal bands, which were produced in a limited edition because of the technical difficulty they posed. After the closing of the Società Operaja, he presumably continued his work as Vittorio Zuffi & Co. for a short time, before beginning his collaboration around the turn of the Century with Fratelli Toso, where he took his baggage of knowledge about *murrine* techniques.

Ferro Toso & Co.

The glassworks was founded in 1901 by the glass master Ferdinando Ferro with Luigi Toso and the glass master Giovanni Nason. It was the only manufacturer, along with Fratelli Toso, to work on Murano in 1909. Its production was characterized by *a murrine* glass documented in a brochure on *Italian Artistic Industries* released by the Ministry of Trade in 1912. As a result of changes in the company's organization, it changed its name towards the end of the second decade to Vitrum S.A.I.A.R. Ferro Toso when it went to work in Naples, and later, when the furnace reopened in Venice, to S.A.I.A.R. Ferro Toso.

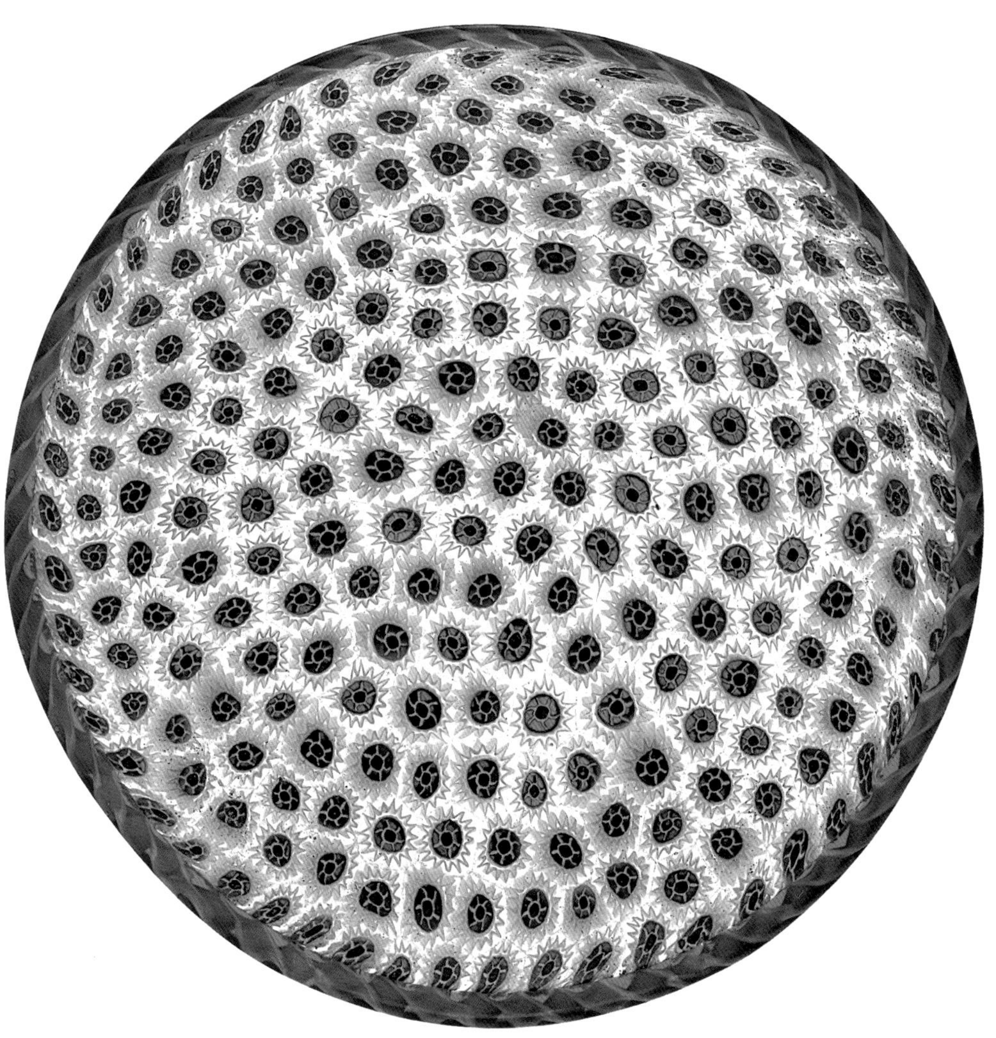

10. **A murrine**
Vittorio Zuffi

ca. 1896

Left: amphora in *cristallo* decorated with a stripe of polychrome floral *murrine*, and plate in *cristallo* decorated with a ring of polychrome *murrine* depicting butterflies.

h 4" - 10 cm; w 9.75" - 25 cm

Bibliography:
Bova, Junck, Migliaccio 1998, No. 18.

A murrine *vases, Vittorio Zuffi Catalog, ca. 1895.*

11. **A tessere e a murrine**
Vincenzo Moretti for Compagnia Venezia e Murano

1880-90

Top: glass bowl with tesserae and polychrome *murrine* laid out in a star pattern. The edge is finished with a *cristallo* and *lattimo* spiral rod applied while hot.

w 6.35" - 16 cm

Bibliography:
Gasparetto 1960, plate XIII;
Barovier Mentasti 1978, No. 40;
Barovier Mentasti 1982, No. 213;
Sarpellon 1990, p. 122;
Barovier Mentasti 1992, No. 9;
Bova, Junck, Migliaccio 1998, No. 6;
Bova, Junck, Migliaccio 1999, No. 59;
Cisotto Nalon, Barovier Mentasti 2002, p. 50.

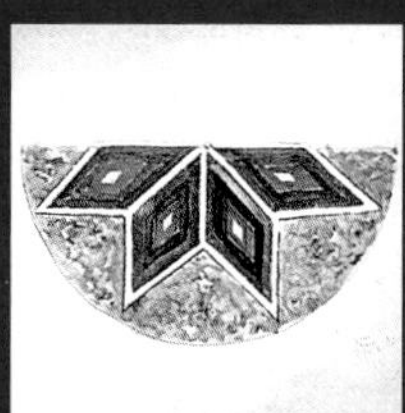

Vincenzo Moretti, preparatory drawing for a bowl in vetro mosaico*, ca. 1880.*

Artisti Barovier
Vetreria Artistica Barovier
Ferro Toso Barovier
Barovier Toso & Co.
Barovier & Toso

Artisti Barovier
Vetreria Artistica Barovier
Ferro Toso Barovier
Barovier Toso & Co.
Barovier & Toso

In 1884 Giovanni Barovier and his nephews Giuseppe, Benvenuto and Benedetto, master glassblowers previously employed in the Salviati Dr. Antonio glassworks, purchased the furnace founded in 1877 when Salviati himself withdrew from the company. On the basis of the agreement stipulated with Salviati, the glassworks kept its original name until his death in 1890, when it was changed to Artisti Barovier. Under the guidance of Benvenuto and Giuseppe the firm very soon became famous for the refined nature of its production, which revived the classical themes of 19th Century glassmaking, and later drew inspiration from floral themes, especially in the objects *a murrine*.
Artisti Barovier showed several of these pieces in a series of expositions, including the Ca' Pesaro expositions (1908, 1909, 1913), where in 1913 they also presented objects designed by Zecchin and Wolf Ferrari. After spending the war years in Livorno, where the furnace had been temporarily moved, in 1919 the glassworks acquired new partners, including Ercole and Nicolò, the sons of Benvenuto Barovier, and Napoleone, the son of Giuseppe, and changed its name to Vetreria Artistica Barovier. In 1926, Ercole and Nicolò Barovier took over the management and artistic direction of the company, creating sophisticated polychrome *a murrine* vases and unusual animals in blown glass. In 1932 Nicolò and Ercole Barovier became sole proprietors of the glassworks: Ercole in particular, was responsible for the many objects which won considerable acclaim for the company (for example the *primavera* series). A tireless creator of styles and vitreous textures, Ercole devoted himself to perfecting the hot colouring without fusion which he began to work with in the late Thirties. In 1936, after parting company with his brother Nicolò, Ercole joined S.A.I.A.R. Ferro Toso, and founded Ferro Toso e Barovier, which changed to Barovier Toso & Co. in 1939, and later to Barovier & Toso in 1942. Ercole Barovier remained the artistic director of the company until 1972, when he was succeeded by his son Angelo who already worked as a designer in the company. Since the Eighties, a long list of designers has collaborated with Barovier & Toso.

12. **A murrine e a canne**
Giuseppe Barovier
Artisti Barovier

1910-13

Vases in *cristallo* with small side handles shaped while hot, decorated with polychrome floral *murrine* and yellow *zanfirico* rods. The vases, with the exception of the one at the center, are finished with fine threads of amethyst glass. The glass pieces are part of a small series of objects similar to the ones presented by Giuseppe Barovier in 1913 at the show in Ca' Pesaro in Venezia.

h 11" - 28 cm; h 6.5" - 17 cm; h 6" - 15 cm

Exhibitions:
1913, Venezia, Ca' Pesaro.

Bibliography:
Catalogo dell'Esposizione d'Arte 1913, No. 1;
Bova, Junck, Migliaccio 1998, No. 186, p. 134;
Barovier 2001, p. 277.

Glass vase a murrine *in the* Catalogo dell'Esposizione d'Arte, *Venezia, 1913.*

13. **A murrine e a canne**
Artisti Barovier for Salviati

ca. 1914

Large glass goblet with vertical rods in *cristallo* and blue glass, and rods in red and yellow glass, decorated in the center with polychrome *murrine* laid out in a floral motif.
The bell-shaped foot is in transparent blue glass.
This object, as well as the following (Nos. 14-18) are part of a limited series of one-of-a-kind pieces crafted by the Artisti Barovier for Salviati.

Acid-stamped signature: "Salviati".
h 14.5" - 37 cm

Bibliography:
Antonio Salviati 1982, No. 77; Romanelli, Dorigato 1982, No. 99; Cerutti 1985, p. 61; De Guttry, Maino, Quesada 1985, No. 7; Barovier 1993, Nos. 35-42; Heiremans 1993, Nos. 30-31; Barovier 1994, No. 2; Deboni 1996, No. 21; Barovier 2001, p. 283; Murano 2001, Nos. 1-2; Heiremans 2002, No. 4.

La Nave, *vessel in glass rods and* a murrine, *ca. 1914, Marino Barovier Archives.*

14. **A murrine**
Artisti Barovier for Salviati

ca. 1914

Large glass vessel with polychrome *murrine* laid out in a floral motif. The slightly ribbed foot is in *cristallo* decorated with a spiral blue glass thread.
Acid-stamped signature: "Salviati".

h 15.75" - 40 cm

Bibliography:
Antonio Salviati 1982, No. 77;
Romanelli, Dorigato 1982, No. 99;
Cerutti 1985, p. 61;
De Guttry, Maino, Quesada 1985, No. 7;
Barovier 1993, Nos. 35-42;
Heiremans 1993, Nos. 30-31;
Barovier 1994, No. 2;
Deboni 1996, No. 21;
Barovier 2001, p. 283;
Murano 2001, Nos. 1-2;
Heiremans 2002, No. 4.

Glass vase a murrine on the shelves of the Pauly showroom in Venezia, ca. 1924, Marino Barovier Archives.

15. **A murrine**
Artisti Barovier for Salviati

ca. 1914

ribbed in *cristallo* with trim in blue glass.
Acid-stamped signature: "Salviati".

Romanelli, Dorigato 1982, No. 99;
Cerutti 1985, p. 61;
De Guttry, Maino, Quesada 1985, No. 7;
Barovier 1993, Nos. 35-42;
Murano 2001, Nos. 1-2;
Heiremans 2002, No. 4.

16. **A murrine**
Artisti Barovier for Salviati

ca. 1914

Large glass vessel with polychrome floral *murrine* applied in vertical stripes. Foot in slightly ribbed *cristallo* finished with a blue glass thread.
Acid-stamped signature: "Salviati".

h 17" - 43 cm

Bibliography:
Antonio Salviati 1982, No. 77;
Romanelli, Dorigato 1982, No. 99;
Cerutti 1985, p. 61;
De Guttry, Maino, Quesada 1985, No. 7;
Barovier 1993, Nos. 35-42;
Heiremans 1993, Nos. 30-31;
Barovier 1994, No. 2;
Deboni 1996, No. 21;
Barovier 2001, p. 283;
Murano 2001, Nos. 1-2;
Heiremans 2002, No. 4.

Glass vases a murrine, ca. 1924, Marino Barovier Archives.

17. **A murrine**
Artisti Barovier for Salviati

ca. 1924

Large glass goblet with polychrome *murrine* and glass rods laid out to form four flowers on a stem. Foot in transparent blue glass and ribbed sphere in *cristallo*.

h 18.75" - 48 cm

Bibliography:
Antonio Salviati 1982, No. 77;
Romanelli, Dorigato 1982, No. 99;
Cerutti 1985, p. 61;
De Guttry, Maino, Quesada 1985, No. 7;
Barovier 1993, Nos. 35-42;
Heiremans 1993, Nos. 30-31;
Barovier 1994, No. 2;
Deboni 1996, No. 21;
Barovier 2001, p. 283;
Murano 2001, Nos. 1-2;
Heiremans 2002, No. 4.

Glass vase a murrine, *ca. 1915-20, Marino Barovier Archives.*

18. **A murrine**
Artisti Barovier for Salviati

ca. 1914

Large glass vase made of polychrome floral *murrine* with lightly ribbed transparent blue glass foot.

h 15.5" - 39 cm

Bibliography:
Antonio Salviati 1982, No. 77;
Romanelli, Dorigato 1982, No. 99;
Cerutti 1985, p. 61;
De Guttry, Maino, Quesada 1985, No. 7;
Barovier 1993, Nos. 35-42;
Heiremans 1993, Nos. 30-31;
Barovier 1994, No. 2;
Deboni 1996, No. 21;
Barovier 2001, p. 283;
Murano 2001, Nos. 1-2;
Heiremans 2002, No. 4.

19. **A murrine**
Giuseppe Barovier
Artisti Barovier

1918-19

Top and left: glass vase with polychrome *murrine* laid out in a floral motif. On the walls of the vessel one can observe butterflies with open or closed wings among the flowers.
Signed with a glass tessera bearing the initials "AB" above which rises a crown.

h 9.5" - 24 cm

Exhibitions:
1920, Venezia, Bevilacqua La Masa.

Bibliography:
Barovier Mentasti 1992, No. 38;
Barovier 1993, No. 48;
Barovier 1994, No. 1;
Deboni 1996, No. 19;
Heiremans 1996, No. 5;
Barovier 1999, p. 93;
Venini Diaz de Santillana 2000, p. 10.

20. **A murrine**
Artisti Barovier

1918-19

Glass vases with *murrine* and polychrome glass rods composed in the design of a landscape with trees and birds. Near the mouth are three small handles in *cristallo*.
Signed with a glass tessera bearing the initials "AB" above which rises a crown.

h 8,5" - 22 cm

Bibliography:
Antonio Salviati 1982, No. 76.

Glass vase a murrine *in "Le Vie d'Italia", October 1921.*

21. **A murrine**
Artisti Barovier

1918-19

Glass vase with *murrine* and polychrome rods in a design depicting a landscape with trees in bloom.

h 7.5" - 19 cm

Bibliography:
Antonio Salviati 1982, No. 76;
Venetian glass 2000, No. 1;
Murano 2001, No. 3.

22. **A murrine**
Giuseppe Barovier
Artisti Barovier

ca. 1915

depicting a garland of flowers. The edge is finished with a rod in amethyst glass and the foot has a joint made of transparent *paglierino* glass threads.

Bibliography:
Sarpellon 1990, Nos. 1075-1058;
Barovier 1993, No. 43.

23. **Vaso**
Benvenuto Barovier
Artisti Barovier

middle by a series of parrots obtained by applying fine polychrome frit while hot.

Bibliography:
Barovier 1993, No. 56;
Deboni 1996, No. 22;

25. **A murrine applicate**
Artisti Barovier

ca. 1918-19

Vase in *cristallo sfumato* into green, decorated with a floral motif in relief, obtained by applying polychrome *murrine* while hot. Signed with a glass tesserae bearing the initials "AB" above which rises a crown.

h 11.5" - 29 cm

Bibliography:
Barovier 1993, Nos. 56-57.

26. **A murrine avventurina**
Artisti Barovier

1918-19

Vases in transparent yellow glass with star-shaped *murrine* in *avventurina*, and with an *avventurina* glass lip wrap.

Signed with a vitreous tessera bearing the initials "AB" above which rises a crown.

h 6" - 15 cm; h 8.75" - 22 cm

Bibliography:
Barovier Mentasti 1992, No. 37;
Barovier 1993, No. 54;
Heiremans 1996, No. 7;
Bova, Junck, Migliaccio 1998, Nos. 175-176;
Dorigato 2002, p. 239;
Heiremans 2002, No. 3.

27. **A murrine**
Benvenuto Barovier
Vetreria Artistica Barovier

ca. 1920

Glass vase with green, red and *lattimo* floral *murrine* with *avventurina* glass inclusions.

h 9.5" - 24 cm

Bibliography:
Barovier 1993, No. 63;
Bova, Junck, Migliaccio 1998, No. 187;
Barovier 1999, p. 99;
Dorigato 2002, p. 254.

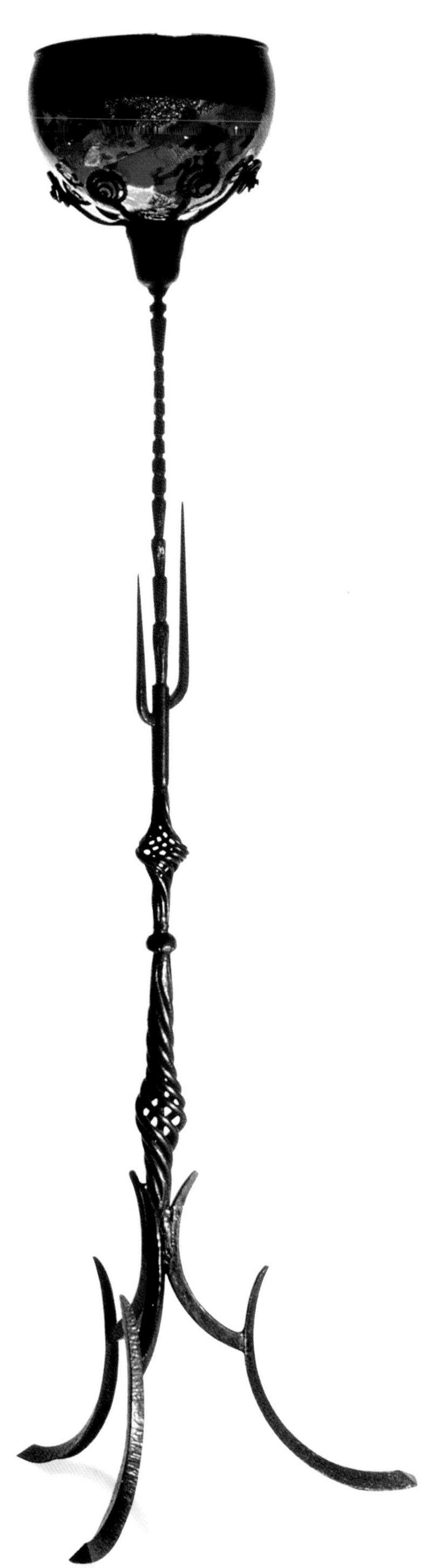

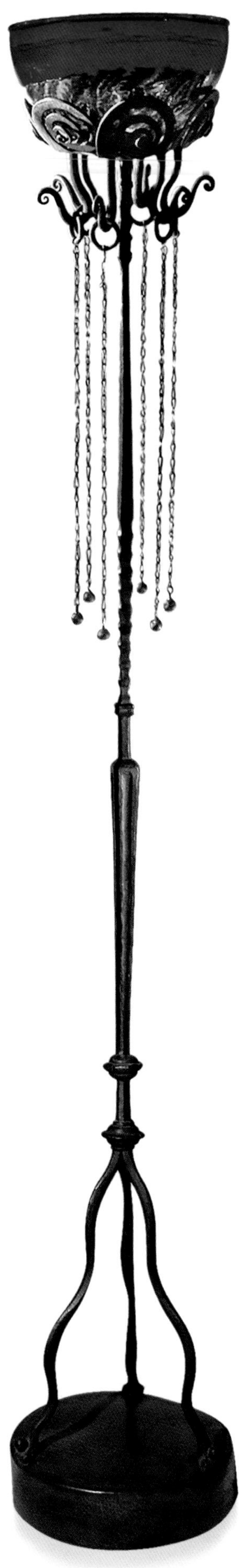

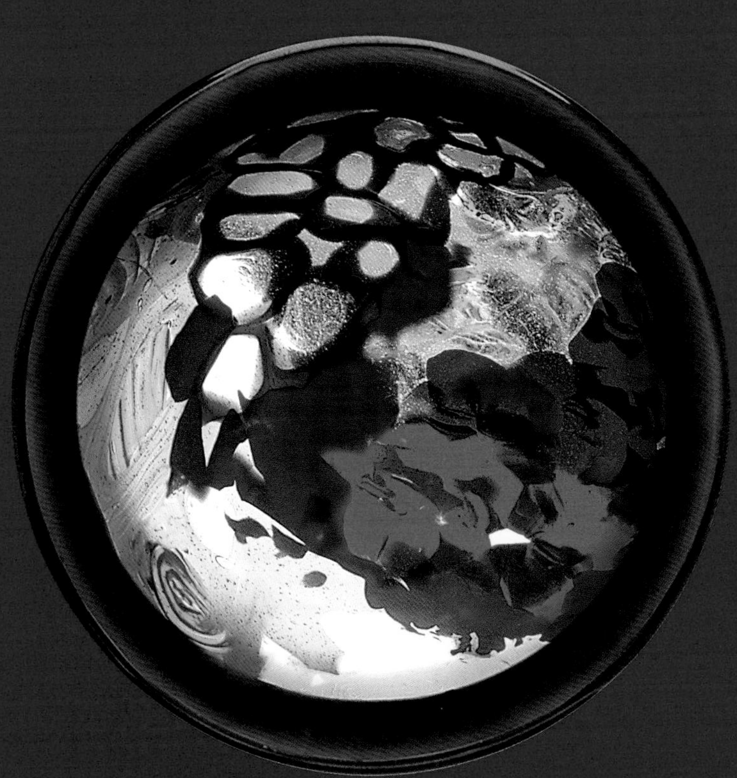

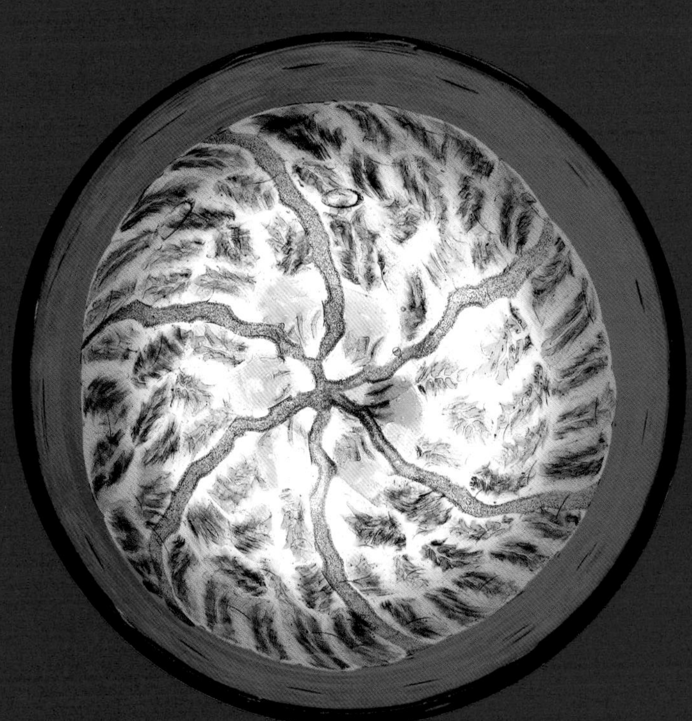

28. **Coppe su stelo**
Umberto Bellotto
Vetreria Artistica Barovier

1920

Bowls in *vetro mosaico* with polychrome tesserae on wrought iron stem.

h 52.75" - 134 cm;
h 54.25" - 138 cm

Bibliography:
Pozzi 1924, p. 31;
Dorigato 1985, pp. 65-66;
L'arte del vetro 1992, No. 298;
Barovier Mentasti 1992, No. 30;
Barovier 1993, Nos. 60-63;
Heiremans 1993, No. 32;
Barovier, Barovier Mentasti, Dorigato 1995, p. 26, No. 10;
Deboni 1996, No. 26;
Barovier 1999, p. 97;
Barovier 2001, p. 287;
Dorigato 2002, p. 245.

At side: bowls in vetro mosaico *with polychrome tesserae (detail).*

29. **Vaso su stelo**
Umberto Bellotto
Vetreria Fratelli Toso

ca. 1920

Vase in transparent blue glass decorated with applications in polychrome glass, on wrought iron stem.

h 43" - 109 cm

Bibliography:
Pozzi 1924, p. 31;
Dorigato 1985, pp. 65-66;
L'arte del vetro 1992, No. 298;
Barovier Mentasti 1992, No. 30;
Barovier 1993, Nos. 60-63;
Heiremans 1993, No. 32;
Barovier, Barovier Mentasti, Dorigato 1995, p. 26, No. 10;
Deboni 1996, No. 26;
Barovier 1999, p. 97;
Barovier 2001, p. 287;
Dorigato 2002, p. 245.

31. **A murrine floreali**
Vetreria Artistica Barovier

ca. 1920

Vase in transparent *fumé* glass decorated with branches of flowers made with vitreous threads, and polychrome *murrine* in the shapes of daisies and leaves.

h 10.5" - 27 cm

Bibliography:
Bova, Junck, Migliaccio 1999, No. 174.

32. **A murrine floreali**
Vetreria Artistica Barovier

ca. 1920

Vase in transparent yellow glass decorated with sprays of flowers made with glass rods and polychrome *murrine* in floral and leaf motifs.

h 10" - 25 cm

33. **A murrine floreali**
Probably Vetreria Artistica Barovier

ca. 1920

Vase in transparent yellow glass, with disc-shaped foot and small side handles, with body decorated in floral *murrine* and irregularly applied polychrome glass threads.

h 11" - 28 cm

34. **A murrine floreali**
Vetreria Artistica Barovier

ca. 1920

Vase in amethyst glass with star-shaped *avventurina murrine* and decorated with floral *murrine*.

h 12" - 30 cm

Exhibitions:
1921, Venezia, Esposizione d'Arte, Circolo artistico.

Bibliography:
Neri 1921, p. 118.

35. **A murrine floreali**
Vetreria Artistica Barovier

ca. 1920

Vase in transparent blue glass decorated with polychrome sunflower *murrine* and irregular green glass threads.
Compote jar and vase in amethyst glass decorated with polychrome floral *murrine* and irregular green glass threads.

h 9.25" - 23 cm; h 14.5" - 37 cm; h 11" - 28 cm

Bibliography:
Deboni 1996, No. 16;
Bova, Junck, Migliaccio 1999, Nos. 178-179;
Barovier 2001, p. 286.

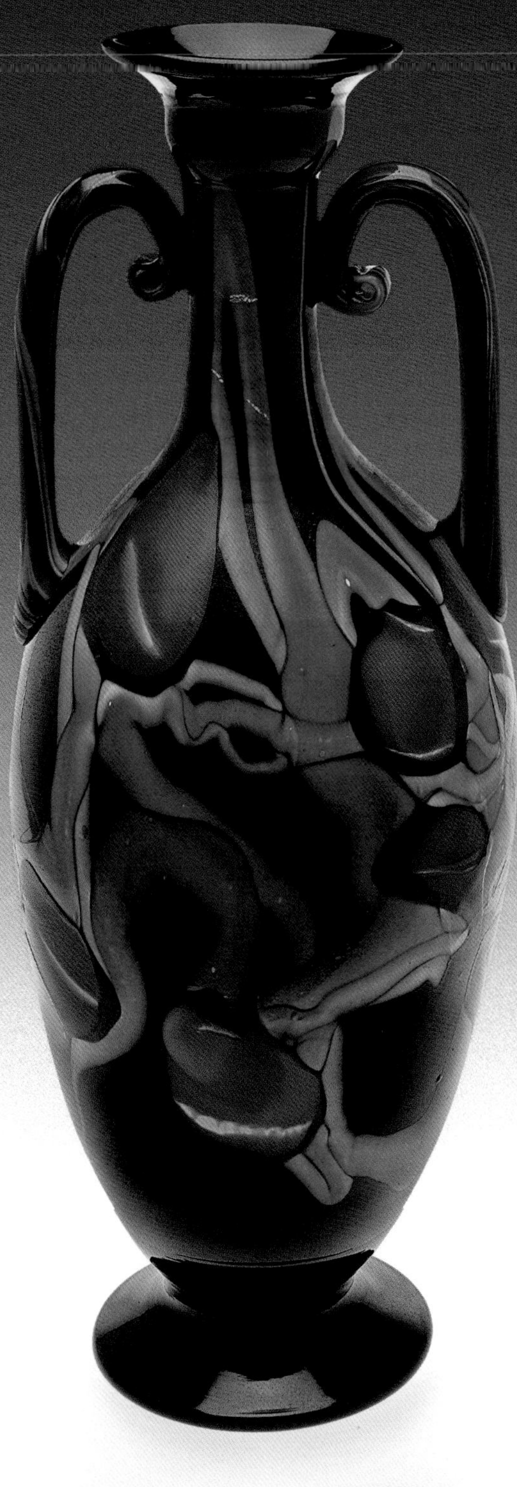

36. **A murrine floreali**
Vetreria Artistica Barovier

ca. 1920

Vase in amethyst glass, with side handles, decorated with red *murrine* and irregularly applied turquoise and *lattimo* threads.

h 12.5" - 32 cm

Glass vase a murrine floreali, ca. 1920, Marino Barovier Archives.

37. **A murrine floreali**
Vetreria Artistica Barovier

ca. 1920

Vase in amethyst glass decorated with polychrome floral *murrine* and irregularly applied *lattimo* and turquoise glass threads.

h 11.5" - 29 cm

Bibliography:
Bova, Junck, Migliaccio 1999, No. 178;
Barovier 2001, p. 286.

38. **A murrine floreali**
Vetreria Artistica Barovier

ca. 1920

Vase with side handles in transparent blue glass decorated with polychrome rose and leaf *murrine*.

h 8.75'' - 22 cm

Bibliography:
Barovier 1993, No. 58.

39. **A murrine floreali**
Vetreria Artistica Barovier

ca. 1920

Vase with side handles in transparent blue glass decorated with polychrome floral *murrine* (of daisies and pansies) and irregular green glass threads.

h 9" - 23 cm

Bibliography:
Bova, Junck, Migliaccio 1999, No. 178.

40. A murrine floreali
Vetreria Artistica Barovier

ca. 1920

Vase in *lattimo* glass cased in blue glass with side handles in *cristallo*, decorated with polychrome floral *murrine* and irregular green glass threads.

h 12.5" - 32 cm

Bibliography:
Bova, Junck, Migliaccio 1999, No. 178.

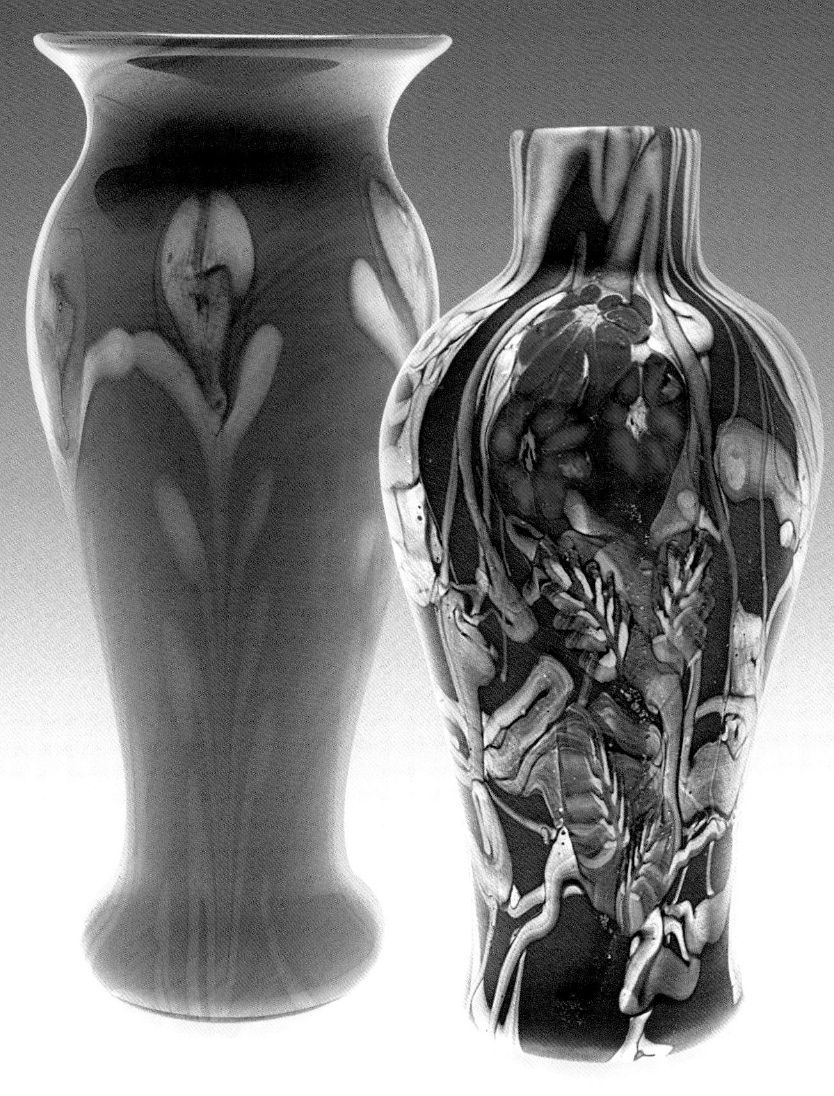

42. **Vetro mosaico**
Ercole Barovier
Vetreria Artistica Barovier

1924-25

Vase in *vetro mosaico* with transparent *cristallo* tesserae edged in turquoise with inclusions of yellow tesserae edged in amethyst, and blue tesserae representing groups of flowers.
Engraved: "E. Barovier Murano".

h 14.5" - 37 cm

Bibliography:
Gasparetto 1960, No. 3;
Barovier Mentasti 1977, No. 3;
Mille anni 1982, No. 506;
Miani, Resini, Lamon 1984, p. 84;
Dorigato 1985, No. 58;
Dorigato 1989, Nos. 1, 3;
Barovier Mentasti 1992, No. 39;
L'arte del vetro 1992, No. 300;
Barovier 1993, Nos. 65, 67-68, 70, 72;
Barovier 1994, No. 5;
Barovier 1999, pp. 100-101;
Dorigato 2002, p. 254.

43. **Vetro mosaico**
Ercole Barovier
Vetreria Artistica Barovier

1924-25

Vases in *vetro mosaico* with transparent *cristallo* tesserae edged in turquoise with flowers made of glass rods and polychrome tesserae. The vase on the right has a transparent turquoise glass lip wrap. Engraved: "E. Barovier Murano".

h 8" - 20 cm; h. 10.5" - 27 cm

Bibliography:
Gasparetto 1960, No. 3;
Barovier Mentasti 1977, No. 3;
Mille anni 1982, No. 506;
Miani, Resini, Lamon 1984, p. 84;
Dorigato 1985, No. 58;
Dorigato 1989, Nos. 1, 3;
Barovier Mentasti 1992, No. 39;
L'arte del vetro 1992, No. 300;
Barovier 1993, Nos. 65, 67-68, 70, 72;
Barovier 1994, No. 5;
Barovier 1999, pp. 100-101;
Dorigato 2002, p. 254.

44. **Vetro mosaico**
Ercole Barovier
Vetreria Artistica Barovier

1924-25

Vase in *vetro mosaico* with transparent *cristallo* tesserae edged in blue, and green tesserae edged in amethyst.
Engraved: "E. Barovier Murano".

h 10" - 25 cm

Bibliography:
Gasparetto 1960, No. 3;
Barovier Mentasti 1977, No. 3;
Mille anni 1982, No. 506;
Miani, Resini, Lamon 1984, p. 84;
Dorigato 1985, No. 58;
Dorigato 1989, Nos. 1, 3;
L'arte del vetro 1992, No. 300;
Barovier Mentasti 1992, No. 39;
Barovier 1993, Nos. 65, 67-68, 70, 72;
Barovier 1994, No. 5;
Barovier 1999, pp. 100-101;
Dorigato 2002, p. 254.

Glass vase a murrine, *ca. 1925, Marino Barovier Archives*

45. **Vetro mosaico**
Ercole Barovier
Vetreria Artistica Barovier

1924-25

Vase in *vetro mosaico* with *cristallo* tesserae edged in blue and long-stemmed flowers made of rods and polychrome tesserae.

h 13. 25'' - 33 cm

Bibliography:
Gasparetto 1960, No. 3;
Barovier Mentasti 1977, No. 3;
Mille anni 1982, No. 506;
Miani, Resini, Lamon 1984, p. 84;
Dorigato 1985, No. 58;
Dorigato 1989, Nos. 1, 3;
L'arte del vetro 1992, No. 300;
Barovier Mentasti 1992, No. 39;
Barovier 1993, Nos. 65, 67-68, 70, 72;
Barovier 1994, No. 5;
Barovier 1999, pp. 100-101;
Dorigato 2002, p. 254.

46. **Vetro mosaico**
Nicolò Barovier
Vetreria Artistica Barovier

1924-25

Vases in *vetro mosaico* with tesserae bearing characteristic segments, composed in an irregular fashion to obtain a singular texture. The vase at left is made with *cristallo* and blue polychrome tesserae which compose a stylized floral pattern. The center vase is made of *cristallo* and amethyst tesserae with red and amethyst floral *murrine*. The one on the right is made of *cristallo* and turquoise tesserae with inclusions of polychrome glass rods and tesserae composed in an abstract design.
Engraved: "N. Barovier Murano".

h 12" - 30 cm; h 8" - 20 cm;
h 10.5" - 27 cm

Bibliography:
Barovier Mentasti 1977, No. 2;
Barovier Mentasti 1982, No. 255;
Dorigato 1989, No. 2;
Barovier Mentasti 1992, No. 40;
Barovier 1993, Nos. 66, 69;
Deboni 1996, No. 27;
Barovier 1999, p. 100;
Venetian Glass 2000, No. 6;
Murano 2001, No. 4.

Glass vase a murrine, *ca. 1925, Marino Barovier Archives.*

47. **Vetro mosaico**
Nicolò Barovier
Vetreria Artistica Barovier

ca. 1925

Vase in *vetro mosaico* with yellow and *cristallo* trilobal *murrine*, and inclusions of polychrome glass rods and *murrine* composed in a design which recalls the plumage of a peacock.
Engraved: "N. Barovier Murano".

h 20" - 51 cm

Bibliography:
Barovier Mentasti 1977, No. 2;
Barovier Mentasti 1982, No. 255;
Mille anni 1982, No. 504;
Dorigato 1989, No. 2;
Barovier Mentasti 1992, No. 40;
Barovier 1993, Nos. 66, 69;
Deboni 1996, No. 27;
Barovier 1999, p. 100;
Venetian Glass 2000, No. 4;
Murano 2001, No. 6.

Glass vases a murrine and a canne on the shelves of the Pauly showroom in Venezia, ca. 1924, Marino Barovier Archives.

48. **Vetro mosaico**
Nicolò Barovier
Vetreria Artistica Barovier

1924-25

Vase in *vetro mosaico* with *cristallo* and red trilobal *murrine* with inclusions of rods and polychrome tesserae composed in a characteristic "spray" motif, often used by Nicolò Barovier.

h 16" - 41 cm

Bibliography:
Barovier Mentasti 1977, No. 2;
Barovier Mentasti 1982, No. 255;
Mille anni 1982, No. 504;
Dorigato 1989, No. 2;
Barovier Mentasti 1992, No. 40;
Barovier 1993, Nos. 66, 69;
Deboni 1996, No. 27;
Barovier 1999, p. 100;
Venetian Glass 2000, No. 4;
Murano 2001, No. 6.

49. **Vetro mosaico**
Ercole Barovier
Vetreria Artistica Barovier

ca. 1926

Vase in *cristallo sfumato* into *paglierino* glass with a regular pattern of air bubbles embedded in the wall of the object. The vase is decorated on the surface with sprays of wysteria obtained by applying hot tesserae and polychrome glass rods. It belongs to a very rare series of which only a few pieces are known to exist.

Engraved: "E. Barovier Murano".

h 12.5" - 32 cm

Bibliography:
Dorigato 1989, No. 6;
Barovier 1993, No. 78.

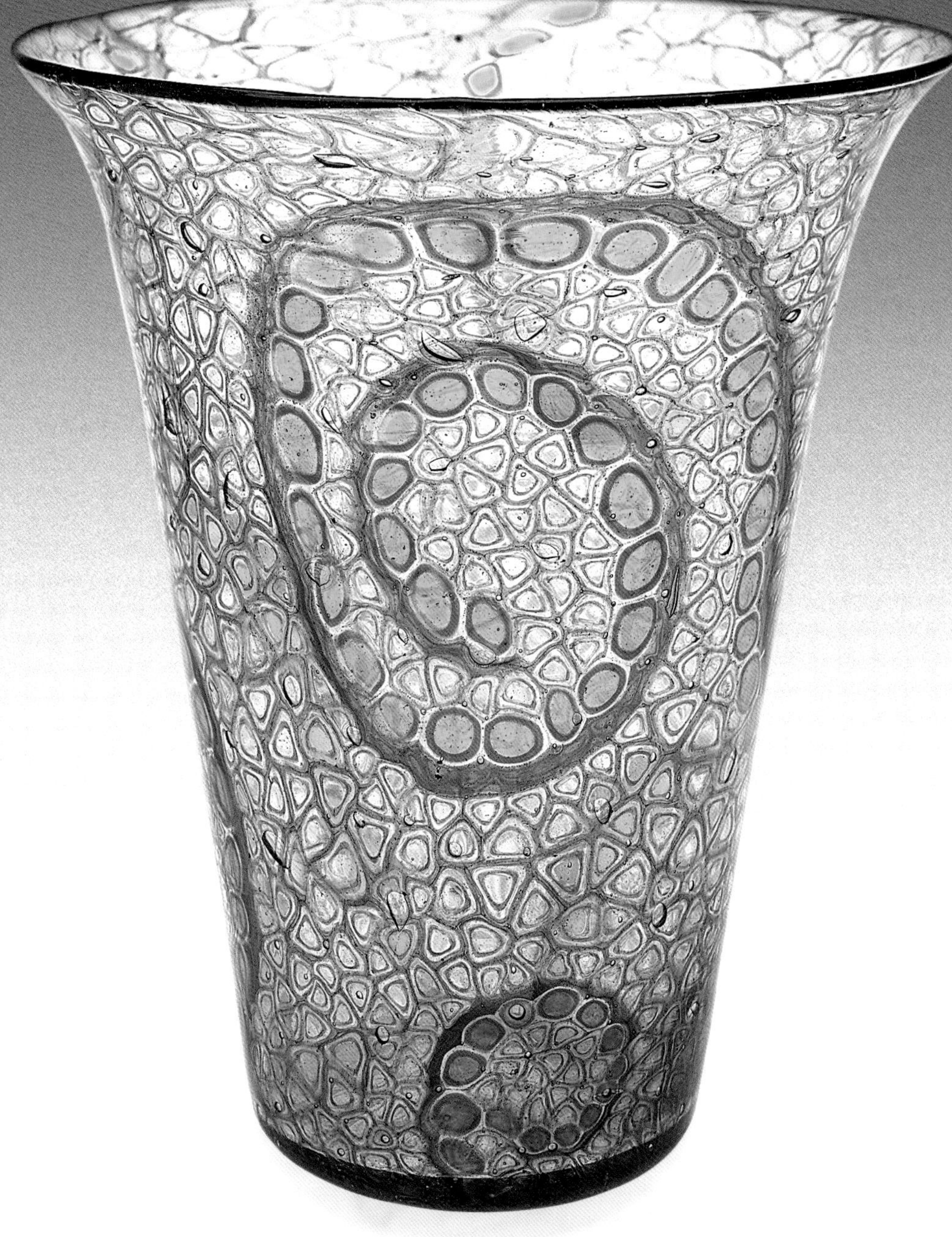

50. **Vetro mosaico**
Anna Akerdahl
S.A.I.A.R. Ferro Toso

ca. 1920-21

Vase in *vetro mosaico* with triangular tesserae in *cristallo* and yellow glass, featuring a spiral composed of purple rods and green tesserae with an orange edge.
Marked under the bottom with a vitreous tessera showing a comet.

h 8" - 20 cm

Exhibitions:
1921, Stockholm, Esposizione Italiana d'Arte Industriale e Decorativa.

Bibliography:
Barovier Mentasti 1992, No. 27;
Barovier 1994, No. 4;
Barovier 1999, p. 100.

Glass vases a murrine, ca.1921, Marino Barovier Archives.

51. **Primavera**
Ercole Barovier
Vetreria Artistica Barovier

1929-30

Vase in *primavera* glass with small side handles, mouth and foot in black *pasta vitrea*. The *primavera* glass, which appears as a seemingly *craquelé* milky white glass, derives its name from the pigeon of the same name made in the same material and presented by Ercole Barovier at the Biennale di Venezia in 1930.
h 13.5" - 34 cm

Exhibitions: 1930, Monza IV Esposizione Internazionale delle Arti Decorative e Industriali Moderne; Venezia, XVII Biennale Internazionale d'Arte.
Bibliography: "La Casa Bella", May 1930, pp. 50-51; "La Casa Bella", June 1930, pp. 56-57; "Domus", July 1930, p. 40; Neuwirth 1987, No. 119; Dorigato 1989, pp. 18-19; Barovier 1993, No. 92; Heiremans 1993, No. 34; Barovier Mentasti 1994, No. 21; Barovier 1999, pp. 129-131; *Venetian Glass* 2000, No. 7; *Murano* 2001, Nos. 10-11; Dorigato 2002, p. 272; Heiremans 2002, No. 93.

52. **Primavera**
Ercole Barovier
Vetreria Artistica Barovier

1929-30

Vase in *primavera* glass decorated at the mouth by long petals which descend the wall of the object. The petals and foot are in black *pasta vitrea*.
h 14.5" - 37 cm

Exhibitions: 1930, Monza IV Esposizione Internazionale delle Arti Decorative e Industriali Mod[illegible]; Venezia, XVII Biennale Internazionale d'Arte.
Bibliography: "La Casa Bella", May 1930 , pp. 50-51; "La Casa Bella", June 1930, pp. 56-57; "Domus", July 1930, p. 40; Barovier Mentasti 1977, No. 2; Dorigato 1989, pp. 18-19; Barovier 1993, No. 92; Heiremans 1993, No. 34; Barovier Mentasti 1994, No. 21; Barovier 1999, pp. 129-131; *Venetian Glass* 2000, No. 7; *Murano* 2001, Nos. 10-11; Dorigato 2002, p. 272; Heiremans 2002, No. 93.

Primavera *glass pieces in "La Casa bella",* [illegible]

53. **Primavera**
Ercole Barovier
Vetreria Artistica Barovier

1929-30

Branch and candlesticks in *primavera* glass with foot and trim details in black *pasta vitrea*.
The production of objects in *primavera* glass was highly successful, but quite limited because the vitreous mixture necessary to make it was the product of a fortuitous event and it proved impossible to repeat.

h 15.5" - 39 cm; h 10" - 25 cm

Exhibitions:
1930, Monza, IV Esposizione Internazionali delle Arti Decorative e Industriali Moderne; Venezia, XVII Biennale Internazionale d'Arte.

Bibliography:
Barovier Mentasti 1977, No. 2;
Neuwirth 1987, No. 119;
Dorigato 1989, p. 19;
Barovier 1993, No. 90;
Barovier, Barovier Mentasti, Dorigato 1995, No. 22;
Deboni 1996, No. 29;
Il vetro italiano 1998, No. 42;
Heiremans 2002, No. 94.

Primavera *glass pieces, ca. 1930, Barovier & Toso Archives.*

54. **Uccellini**
Ercole Barovier
Ferro Toso Barovier

1932-36

Birds in *lattimo* glass with applications of gold leaf and trim in black *pasta vitrea* on a *cristallo* branch, with a square base marked with vertical indentations.

h 8.5" - 22 cm

Bibliography:
Dorigato 1989, Nos. 27, 37.

Drawing for glass birds, ca. 1930, Marino Barovier Archives.

55. **Pesci**
Ercole Barovier
Ferro Toso Barovier

lightly iridized *cristallo* glass.

h 7.5'' - 19 cm

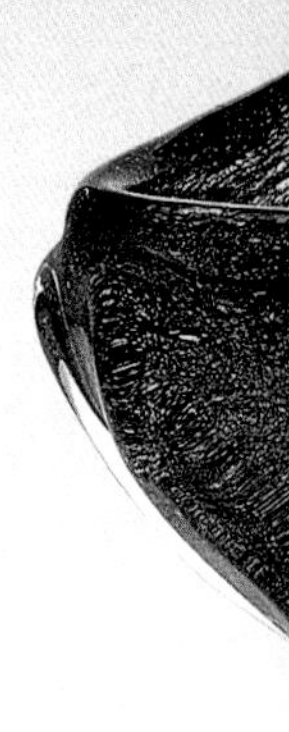

56. **Crepuscolo**
Ercole Barovier
Ferro Toso Barovier

1935-36

Left to right: plate with petals and vases from the *crepuscolo* series in *cristallo* glass with non-homogeneous brown stains obtained by using the technique of coloring while hot without fusion. To make the *crepuscolo* glass pieces, during the working process glass wool was added to the glass, so that its ashes, in suspension, would create the characteristic effect.

w 11.75" - 30 cm; h 5.25" - 13 cm; h 10.75" - 28 cm

Exhibitions: 1936, Milano, VI Triennale; 1938, Venezia, XXI Biennale Internazionale d'Arte.

Bibliography: Dorigato 1989, No. 42; Barovier Mentasti 1992, No. 70; *L'arte del vetro* 1992, No. 341; Barovier 1993, No. 101; Barovier, Barovier Mentasti, Dorigato 1995, p. 41, No. 48; Ricke, Schmitt 1996, No. 4; *I Barovier* 1998, No. 21; *Il vetro italiano* 1998, No. 69.

57. **Crepuscolo**
Ercole Barovier
Ferro Toso Barovier

1935-36

Vases from the *crepuscolo* series in *cristallo* with non-homogeneous brown stains obtained by using the technique of while hot without fusion. The vase on the top is decorated with applied *cristallo* lenses. The vase on the left, which has an oval section, is decorated with ring-shaped side handles and corresponds to model No. 14038 from the glassworks catalog. This series of thick heavy glass often presents trim and applications in *cristallo* glass.

h 14.5" - 37 cm
h 10.75" - 28 cm

Exhibitions:
1936, Milano, VI Triennale; 1938, Venezia, XXI Biennale Internazionale d'Arte.

Bibliography:
Dorigato 1989, No. 42;
Barovier Mentasti 1992, No. 70;

L'arte del vetro 1992, No. 341;
Barovier 1993, No. 101;
Barovier, Barovier Mentasti, Dorigato 1995, p. 41, No. 48;
Deboni 1996, No. 35;
Ricke, Schmitt 1996, No. 4;
I Barovier 1998, No. 21;
Il vetro italiano 1998, No. 69.

Crepuscolo *vases at the XXI Biennale Internazionale d'Arte, Venezia, 1938.*

58. **Crepuscolo**
Ercole Barovier
Ferro Toso Barovier

1935-36

Vase from the *crepuscolo* series in *cristallo* with non-homogeneous brown coloring obtained while hot without fusion. The vase, which is triangular in section, is decorated with heavy *morise* in *cristallo* applied at the corners.

h 11.5" - 29 cm

Exhibitions:
1936, Milano, VI Triennale; 1938, Venezia, XXI Biennale Internazionale d'Arte.

Bibliography:
see No. 57.

Crepuscolo *vase in "Domus", December 1941.*

59. **Crepuscolo**
Ercole Barovier
Ferro Toso Barovier

1935-36

Vessels from the *crepuscolo* series in *cristallo* with non-homogeneous brown stains obtained by using the technique of coloring while hot without fusion. Foot and side handles shaped *a morise* in *cristallo* applied while hot. The model corresponds to No.14169 of the Barovier & Toso catalog.

h 10" - 25 cm; h 9.5" - 24 cm

Exhibitions:
1936, Milano, VI Triennale; 1938, Venezia, XXI Biennale Internazionale d'Arte.

Bibliography: see No. 57.

Crepuscolo *vases, ca.1938, Barovier & Toso Archives.*

60. **Autunno gemmato**
Ercole Barovier
Ferro Toso Barovier

1935-36

Vases from the *autunno gemmato* series in *cristallo* with non-homogeneous golden brown stains obtained by using the technique of coloring while hot without fusion. The vases present *cristallo* trim details shaped while hot. In the mid-Thirties, Ercole Barovier used this technique to create, in addition to the *crepuscolo*, a series of *gemmati* glass characterized by their thickness which, depending on the diverse colorings were called *autunno gemmato* (golden brown), *marina gemmata* (light blue), *laguna gemmata* (deeper bluish).

h 5.5" - 14 cm; h 10.5" - 27 cm; h 13.75" - 36 cm

Exhibitions:
1936, Venezia, XX Biennale Internazionale d'Arte; Bruxelles, Esposizione Universale.

Bibliography:
Dell'Oro 1936;
"Domus", December 1941;
Barovier Mentasti 1982, No. 279;
Romanelli, Dorigato 1982, No. 139;
Neuwirth 1987, No. 128;
Dorigato 1989, Nos. 40, 43;
Barovier 1993, No. 102;
Barovier, Barovier Mentasti, Dorigato 1995, p. 39;
Deboni 1996, No. 34;
I Barovier 1998, No. 22;
Barovier 1999, p. 133;
Dorigato 2002, p. 290;
Heiremans 2002, No. 149.

Autunno gemmato *vases at the XX Biennale Internazionale d'Arte, Venezia, 1936.*

61. **Autunno gemmato**
Ercole Barovier
Ferro Toso Barovier

ca. 1936

Vase in *cristallo* with non-homogeneous golden brown stains obtained by using the technique of coloring while hot without fusion. Foot and side handles shaped *a morise* in *cristallo* applied while hot. These vases represent variations to the *autunno gemmato* series because of the air bubbles and *avventurina* embedded in the walls of the object.

h 12.5" - 32 cm

62. **Marina gemmata**
Ercole Barovier
Ferro Toso Barovier

1936

Vase from the *marina gemmata* series in *cristallo* with a non-homogeneous blue color obtained while hot without fusion. Foot and side handles shaped a *morise* in *cristallo*.

h 10" - 25 cm

Bibliography:
Barovier Mentasti 1982, No. 279;
Romanelli, Dorigato 1982, No. 139;
Mille anni 1982, No. 564;
Dorigato 1989, Nos. 39, 41;
Barovier Mentasti 1992, p. 80;
L'arte del vetro 1992, No. 342;
Barovier 1993, Nos. 103, 104;
Heiremans 1993, p. 45, No. 38;
Barovier, Barovier Mentasti, Dorigato 1995, No. 40;
Heiremans 1996, No. 47.

63. **Laguna gemmata**
Ercole Barovier
Ferro Toso Barovier

1935-36

Vases from the *laguna gemmata* series in *cristallo* with non-homogeneous bluish stains obtained by the technique called coloring while hot without fusion. The vases present applications and finish details in *cristallo* shaped while hot.

h 14" - 36 cm; h 6.5" - 17 cm; h 11.5" - 29 cm

Exhibitions:
1936, Venezia, XX Biennale Internazionale d'Arte.

Bibliography:
Dorigato 1989, No. 38;
Barovier Mentasti 1992, No. 70;
Barovier 1993, Nos. 103-104;
Heiremans 1993, No. 38;
Barovier 1999, p. 133.

64. **Spuma di mare**
Ercole Barovier
Ferro Toso Barovier

1938-40

Vases from the *spuma di mare* series in *cristallo* with air bubbles embedded in the greenish coloring obtained while hot without fusion. This type of glass, defined by Ercole Barovier himself as "glass with a semi-opaque and bubbly light green base" was made by using soda silicate and avventurina powder tossed into the glass during the working process.
The vases are decorated with morise in *cristallo* applied while hot. The model at the center corresponds to No. 14161 of the factory's catalog.

h 10.5" - 27 cm; h 13.5" - 34 cm; h 6.5" - 17 cm;

Bibliography:
"Domus", February 1941.

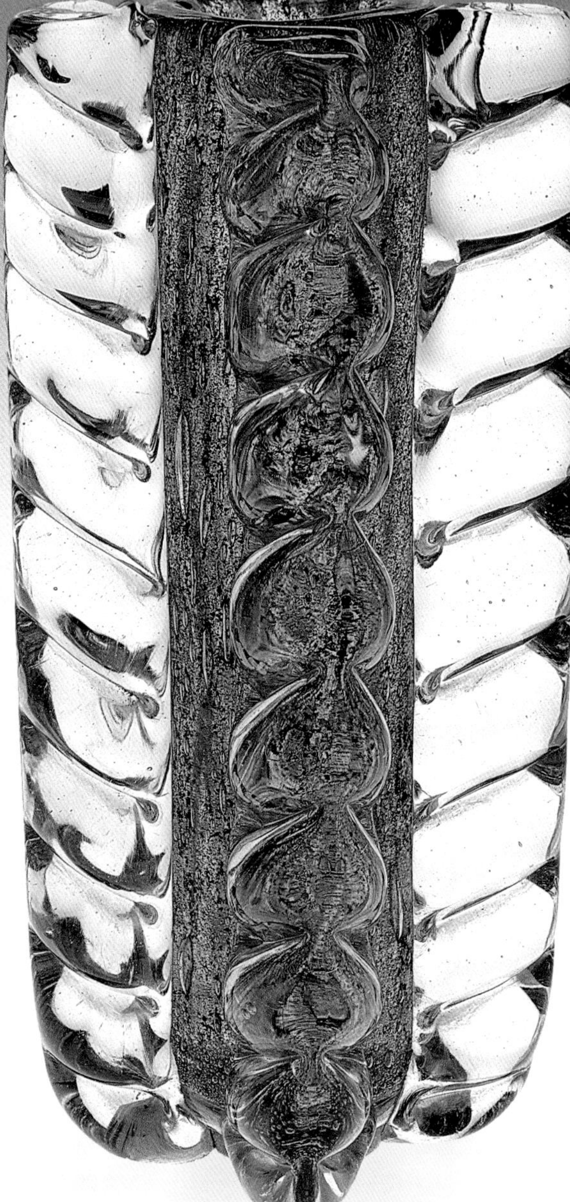

Spuma di mare *vase in "Domus", February 1941.*

65. **Con applicazioni**
Ercole Barovier
Ferro Toso Barovier

1937

First and fourth from left: vases from the *con applicazioni* series in *cristallo* with vertical ribbing decorated with vitreous ribbons bearing bubbles in relief (*spuncionae*), applied while hot in a zig-zag or spiral pattern. With a similar production, the Vetreria Ferro Toso Barovier won the Gran Prix in 1937 at the International Exposition in Paris. Second from left: vase in *cristallo* with vertical ribbing decorated with rings in *cristallo* containing embedded bubbles.

h 13.5" - 34 cm; h 8.5" - 22 cm; h 14" - 36 cm

Exhibitions:
1937, Paris, Exposition Internationale.

Bibliography:
"Domus", April 1937;
"Domus", October 1938;
"Domus", January 1941;
Dorigato 1989, No. 47;
Barovier 1993, No. 106.

66. **Con anelli**
Ercole Barovier
Ferro Toso Barovier

1938

Third from left: vase from the *con anelli* series in *cristallo* with embedded bubbles decorated with applied rings in *cristallo* and color obtained while hot without fusion. Foot in *cristallo* with vertical indentations (*a tagiol*).

h 11" - 28 cm

Bibliography:
"Domus", January 1941.

Vases with applications in "Domus", October 1938.

67. **Con applicazioni**
Ercole Barovier
Ferro Toso Barovier

1937

Vase from the *con applicazioni* series in *cristallo* with vertical ribbing decorated with glass ribbons featuring bubbles in relief (*spuncionae*), in a zig-zag pattern. This vessel also belongs to the series which won the Grand Prix at the International Exposition in Paris in 1937.

h 19" - 48 cm

Exhibitions:
1937, Paris, Exposition Internationale.

Bibliography:
"Domus", October 1938;
"Domus", January 1941;
"Domus", October 1943;
Dorigato 1989, No. 47;
Barovier 1993, No. 106.

68. **Nautilus**
Ercole Barovier
Ferro Toso Barovier

1937

Nautilus vessels in *cristallo* with embedded bubbles decorated with a vitreous thread wrapped around in a spiral. The vessels have a *cristallo* foot with vertical indentations (*a tagiol*) and are heavily iridized over the entire surface.

h 9.5" - 24 cm

Bibliography:
"Domus", April 1937;
"Domus", January 1941;
Dorigato 1989, No. 48;
L'arte del vetro 1992, No. 343;
Barovier 1993, No. 107;
Heiremans 1996, No. 50;
I Barovier 1998, No. 24.

Vases by Ferro Toso Barovier in "Domus", January 1941.

69. **Rostrati**
Ercole Barovier
Ferro Toso Barovier

1938

Left to right: vases from the *rostrati* series in very thick light green transparent glass decorated over the entire surface with diamond pointed glass ribbons, applied while hot. Right: the vessel, with a disk-shaped foot, is heavily iridized.

h 8" - 21 cm; h 9" - 23 cm

Exhibitions:
1938, Venezia, XXI Biennale Internazionale d'Arte;
1940, Milano, VII Triennale.

Bibliography:
"Domus", May 1940;
Vetri Murano 1981, No. 14;
Mille anni 1982, No. 563;
Dorigato, Barovier Mentasti 1989, No. 50;
Barovier 1993, No. 108;
Barovier, Barovier Mentasti, Dorigato 1995, p. 41;
Barovier 1999, p. 179.

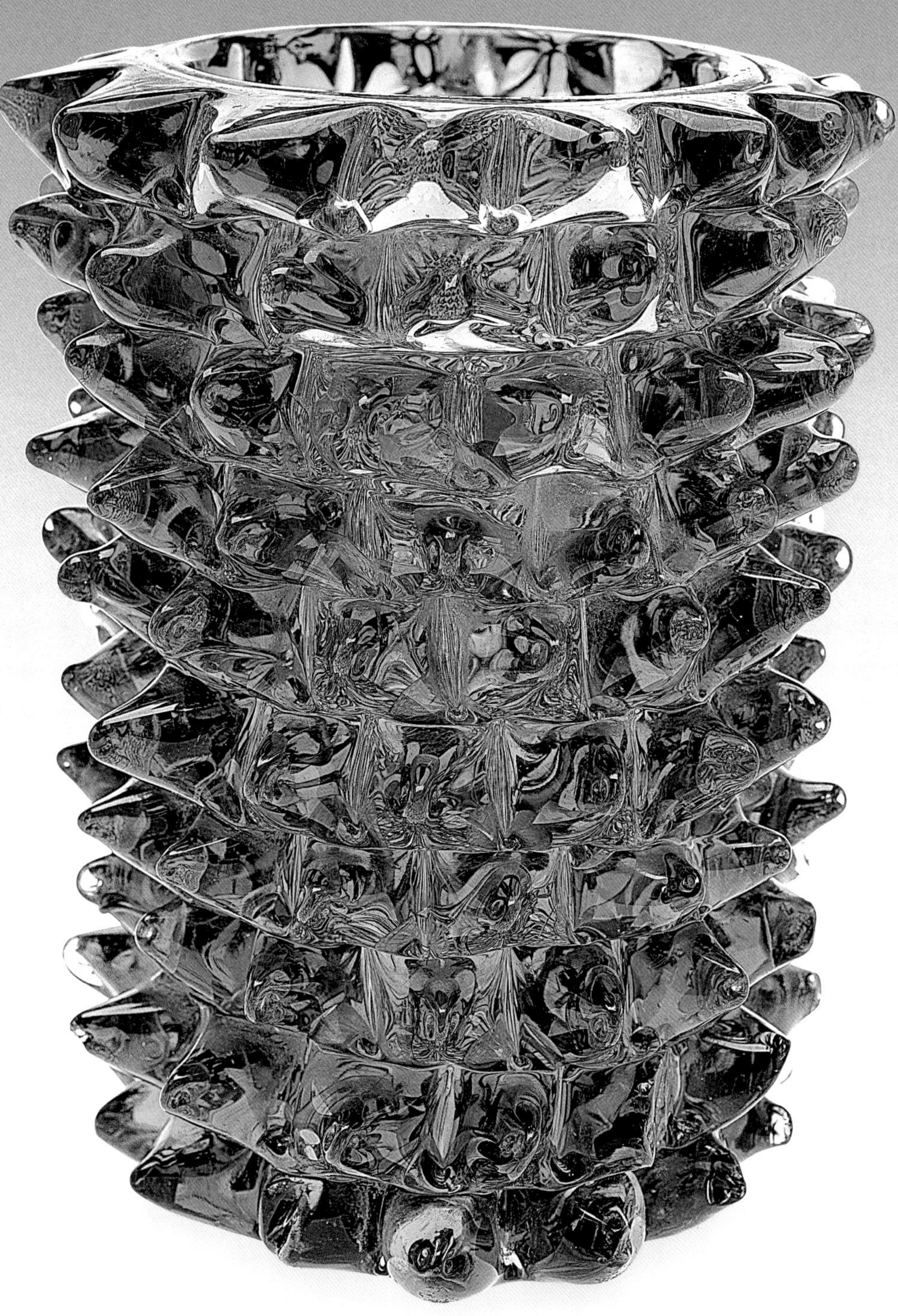

70. **Rostrati**
Ercole Barovier
Ferro Toso Barovier

1938

Vases from the *rostrati* series in very thick *cristallo* decorated over the entire surface with vitreous ribbons of diamond-head points, applied while hot.

h 10" - 25 cm; h 9.5" - 24 cm; h 7" - 18 cm

Exhibitions: 1938, Venezia, XXI Biennale Internazionale d'Arte; 1940, Milano, VII Triennale.

Bibliography: "Domus", May 1940; *Vetri Murano* 1981, No. 14; *Mille anni* 1982, No. 563; Dorigato, Barovier Mentasti 1989, No. 50; Barovier 1993, No. 108; Barovier, Barovier Mentasti, Dorigato 1995, p. 41; Barovier 1999, p. 179.

Rostrati *vases at the XXI Biennale Internazionale d'Arte, Venezia, 1938.*

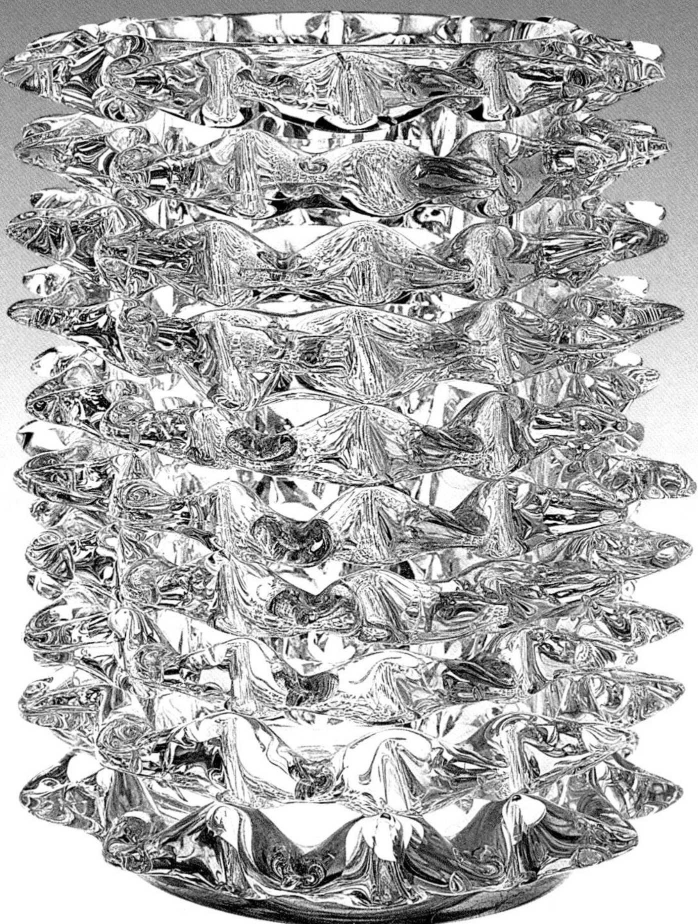

71. **A mugnoni**
Ercole Barovier
Ferro Toso Barovier

1938

Vessels from the *a mugnoni* series in very thick *cristallo* with an irregular shape, decorated with *bugne* in *cristallo* with bubbles applied while hot.
First at the left: engraved signature "Ercole Barovier".

h 14" - 36 cm; h 9.5" - 24 cm;
h 10" - 25 cm; h 14.5" - 37 cm

Bibliography:
Dorigato 1989, p. 136;
Barovier 1993, No. 109;
Deboni 1996, No. 37;
Ricke, Schmitt 1996, No. 3;
I Barovier 1998, No. 26;
Barovier 1999, p. 179;
Dorigato 2002, p. 292.

A mugnoni *vase, ca. 1938, Barovier & Toso Archives.*

72. **Medusa**
Ercole Barovier
Ferro Toso Barovier

1938

Vases from the *Medusa* series in transparent light green and *cristallo* glass decorated along the mouth and the body with vitreous barbs aligned in vertical rows. The surface of the vessels is lightly iridized. This series was created in 1938 and re-issued in 1944, and was highly successful.

h 17" - 43 cm; h 9.5" - 24 cm; h 16." - 41 cm

Bibliography:
Dorigato 1989, No. 51, p. 137;
L'arte del vetro 1992, No. 346;
Barovier 1993, No. 111;
Deboni 1996, No. 38;
Barovier 1999, p. 179.

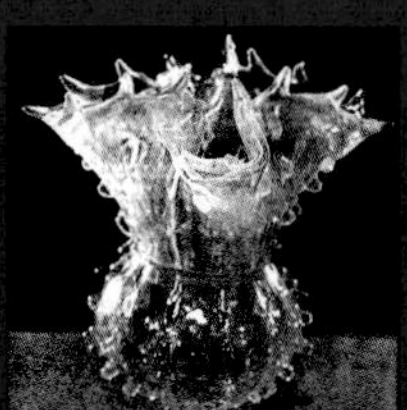

Medusa *vase, ca. 1938, Barovier & Toso Archives.*

73. **Medusa**
Ercole Barovier
Ferro Toso Barovier

1938

Vase and bowl from the *Medusa* series: vase in pink glass decorated along the edge and the body with vitreous barbs composed in vertical rows and ribbed bowl in pink glass with barbs along the ribs. Both vessels are lightly iridized over the entire surface.

h 17" - 43 cm; h 4.75" - 13 cm

Bibliography:
Dorigato 1989, No. 51, p. 137;
L'arte del vetro 1992, No. 346;
Barovier 1993, No. 111;
Deboni 1996, No. 38;
Barovier 1999, p. 179.

Medusa *vases, ca. 1938, Barovier & Toso Archives.*

74. **A lenti**
Ercole Barovier
Barovier Toso & Co.

1940

Vases from the *a lenti* series in very thick *cristallo* decorated with *cristallo* hemispheres shaped with a mold. Surface lightly iridized. The first vessel on the right corresponds to No.17045 of the Barovier & Toso catalog.

h 9.5" - 24 cm; h 8.75" - 22 cm; h 7.5" - 19 cm

Exhibitions:
1940, Venezia, XXII Biennale Internazionale d'Arte.

Bibliography:
"Lo Stile", May 1941.

A lenti *vases in "Lo Stile", May 1941.*

76. **A base gemmata**
Ercole Barovier
Barovier Toso & Co.

1940

Vases and bowl in ribbed *cristallo* with bubbles embedded in a regular pattern and foot decorated with *cristallo* hemispheres shaped with a mould (*lenti*). Left: vase with *cristallo* foot with gold leaf, whereas the other vase and the bowl, at the top, have a blue glass foot with gold leaf. A similar bowl was presented at the Biennale of Venezia in 1940.

h 12.5" - 32 cm; h 10.75" - 28 cm; h 8" - 20 cm

Exhibitions:
1940, Venezia, XXII Biennale Internazionale d'Arte.

Bibliography:
"Lo Stile", May 1941.

A base gemmata *vases in "Lo Stile", May 1941.*

77. **Oriente**
Ercole Barovier
Barovier Toso & Co.

1940

Glass bowl, bottle and vase from the *Oriente* series with intersecting polychrome glass rods, finished with applications of silver leaf over the entire surface.

h 4.5" - 11 cm; h 12.5" - 32 cm; h 12.5" - 32 cm

Exhibitions: 1940, Venezia, XXII Biennale Internazionale d'Arte; Milano, VII Triennale.

Bibliography:
Dell'Oro 1940, p. 226;
"Domus", May 1940;
Dorigato 1989, Nos. 53-55;
Barovier 1993, No. 116;
Barovier, Barovier Mentasti, Dorigato 1995, p. 45, No. 62;
Heiremans 1996, No. 61;
I Barovier 1998, No. 29;
Il vetro italiano 1998, No. 83.

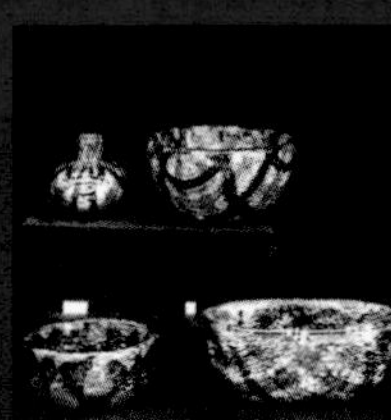

Oriente *vases at the XXII Biennale Internazionale d'Arte, Venezia, 1940.*

78. **A spirale**
Ercole Barovier
Barovier Toso & Co.

1940

Vessel with heavy ribbing from the *a spirale* series in amethyst *sommerso* glass with gold leaf inclusions, decorated with a *sommerso* spiral of black glass. The model corresponds to No. 16466 of the glassworks catalog.

h 10.25" - 26 cm

Exhibitions:
1940, Venezia, XXII Biennale Internazionale d'Arte.

Bibliography:
Barovier, Barovier Mentasti, Dorigato 1995, p. 46, No. 63;
Deboni 1996, No. 36;
Barovier 1999, p. 177.

79. **A spirale**
Ercole Barovier
Barovier Toso & Co.

1940

Sphere-shaped vessel from the *a spirale* series in amethyst *sommerso* glass with inclusion of gold leaf, decorated with a spiral *sommerso* in black glass. The surface of the vessel is finished with *cristallo* rings applied while hot.

h 8.25" - 21 cm

Exhibitions:
1940, Venezia, XXII Biennale Internazionale d'Arte.

Bibliography:
Barovier, Barovier Mentasti, Dorigato 1995, p. 46, No. 63;
Deboni 1996, No. 36;
Barovier 1999, p. 177.

A spirale *vases at the XXII Biennale Internazionale d'Arte Venezia, 1940.*

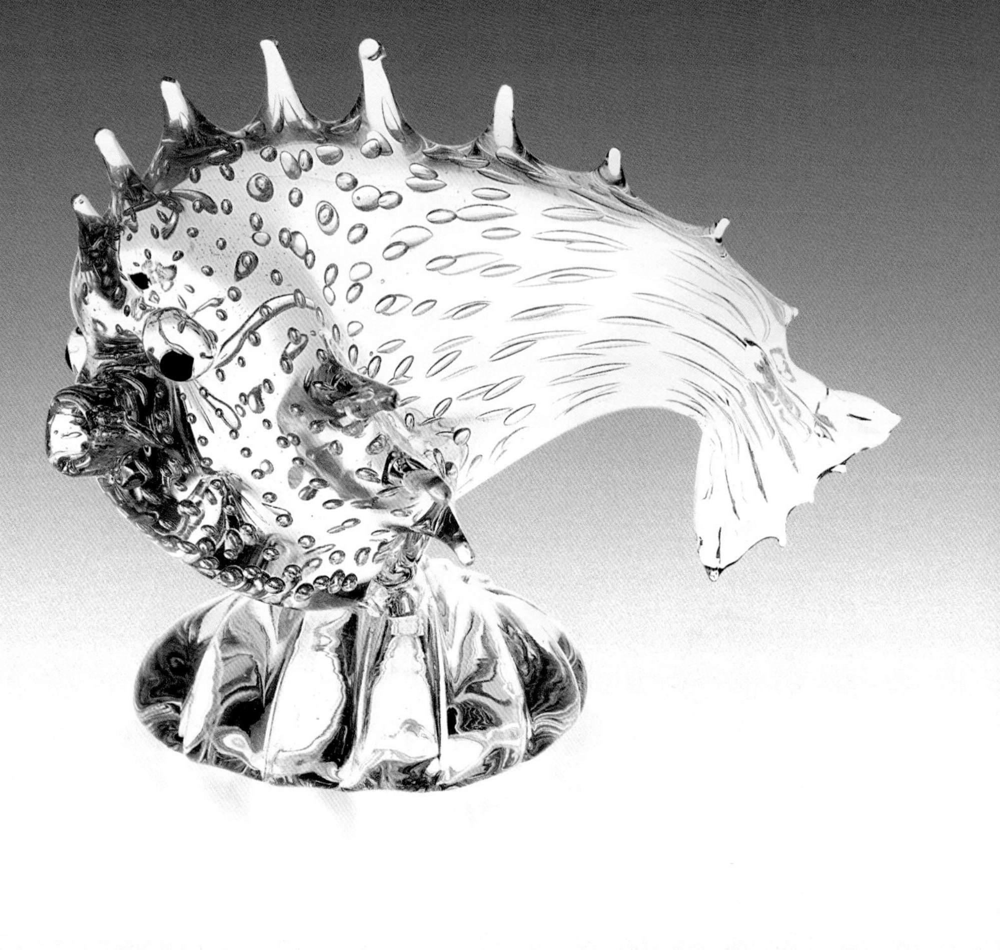

80. **Pesce**
Ercole Barovier
Barovier Toso & Co.

ca. 1941

Fish in *cristallo* shaped while hot, decorated with bubbles embedded in a regular pattern.

h 10" - 25 cm

Bibliography:
"Domus", October 1941;
"Domus", December 1942.

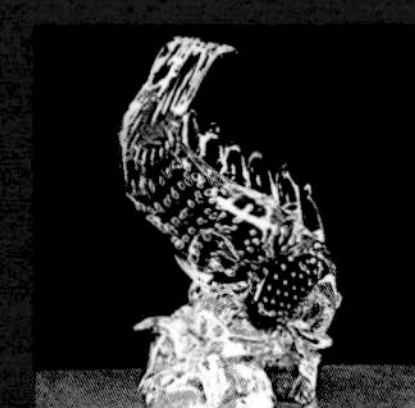

Glass fish in "Domus", October 1941.

81. **A grosse costolature**
Ercole Barovier
Barovier & Toso

1942

Bowl and vessel from the *a grosse costolature* series in *cristallo* with heavily lobed edge. The vessels, similar to seashells, are lightly iridized over the entire surface.

h 6" - 15 cm; h 12.5" - 32 cm

Bibliography:
"Domus", March 1942;
"Domus", October 1943;
Dorigato 1989, No. 68;
Barovier 1993, No. 121;
Ricke, Schmitt 1996, No. 5;
Barovier 1999, p. 179.

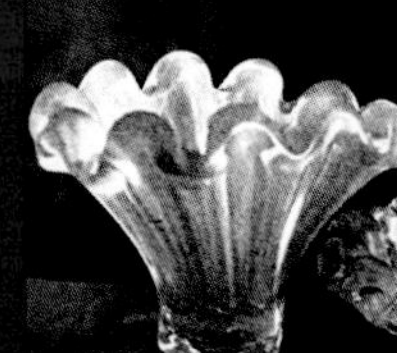

Vase with heavy ribbing in "Domus", March 1942.

82. **A stelle**
Ercole Barovier
Barovier & Toso

1942

Vases from the *a stelle* series in very thick *cristallo* with embedded pattern of regular air bubbles, decorated with stars applied while hot. Ring-shaped foot in *cristallo*.

h 11.25" - 28 cm; h 14.5" - 37 cm; h 16" - 41 cm

Bibliography:
"Domus", October 1942;
"Domus", January 1943;
Neuwirth 1987, No. 138;
Dorigato 1989, No. 69.

Vase with stars in "Domus", October 1942.

83. **Piumato**
Ercole Barovier
Barovier & Toso

1942

Vase from the *piumati* series in thick *cristallo* with a regular pattern of embedded air bubbles, and decorated with feather-like *piume* applied while hot.

h 10" - 25 cm

Bibliography:
"Domus", January 1943, p. 47;
"Domus", October 1943;
Vetri Murano oggi 1981, No. 17;
Neuwirth 1987, Nos. 137-138;
Dorigato 1989, No. 70.

Piumato *vase in "Domus", January 1943.*

84. **A canne**
Ercole Barovier
Barovier & Toso

1942

Seashell in *cristallo* with embedded air bubbles; decorated with light blue glass rods wrapped in a spiral.

h 8.25" - 21 cm

Bibliography:
Dorigato 1989, Nos. 64-65.

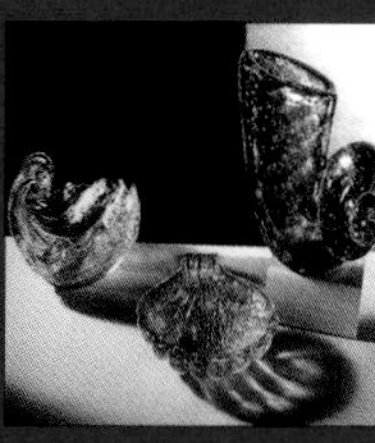

Shells, ca. 1942, Barovier & Toso Archives.

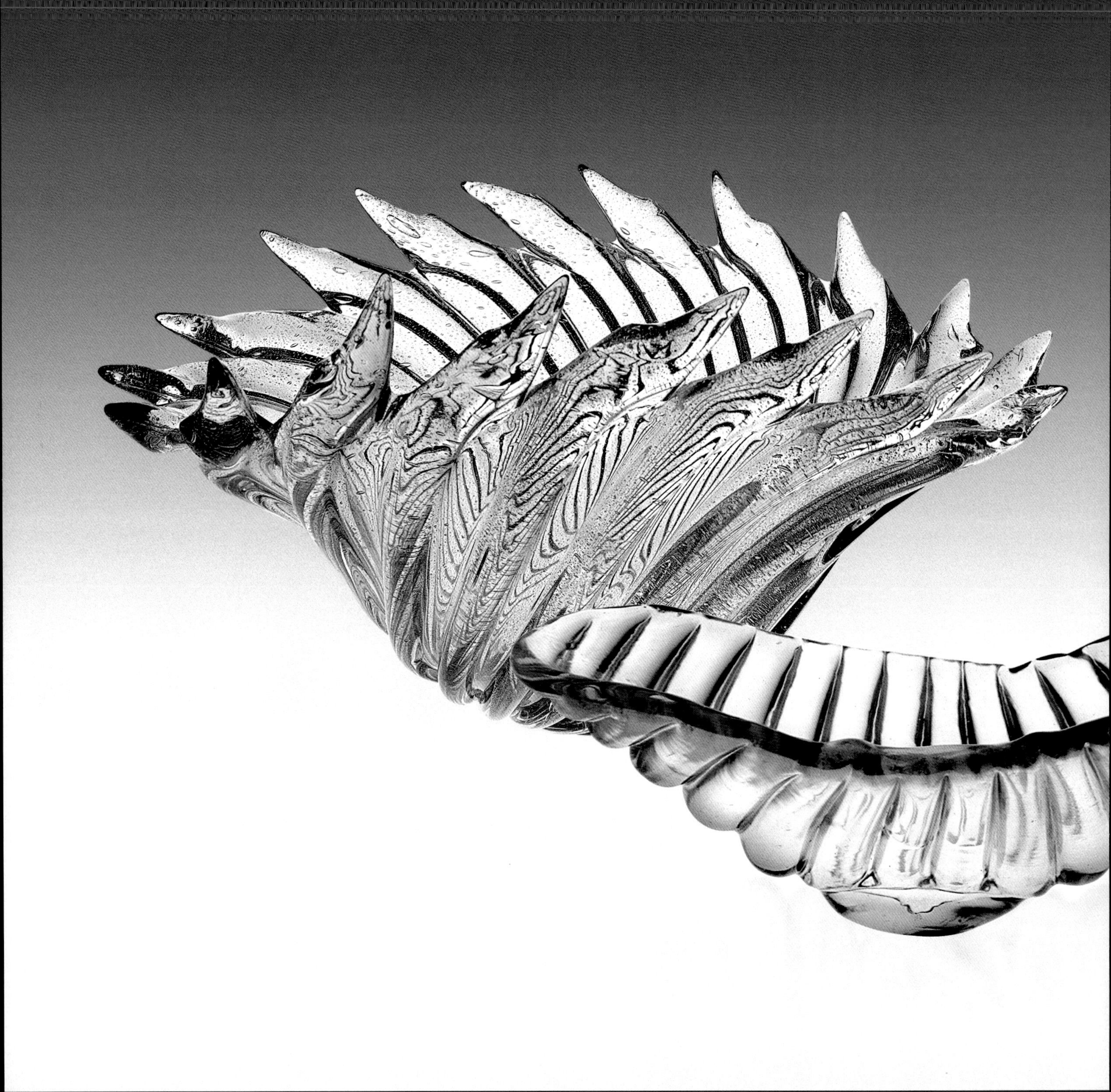

85. **A costoloni**
Ercole Barovier
Barovier & Toso

1945

Center: bowl from the *a costoloni* series in *cristallo* with parallel ribs iridized over the entire surface. Acid-stamped signature: "Barovier & Toso".

h 4.5" - 11 cm, w 12" - 30 cm

Bibliography:
"Lo Stile", October 1943; Dorigato 1989, No. 66, p. 137.

A costoloni *bowl and candlesticks, ca. 1945, Barovier & Toso Archives.*

86. **Frastagliati**
Ercole Barovier
Barovier & Toso

1945

Sides: thick heavily ribbed bowls from the *frastagliati* series in grey glass and light green glass decorated along the edge with irregular barbs shaped while hot. Heavily iridized surface.

h 8" - 20 cm, w 15.25" - 38 cm;
h 8.25" - 21 cm, w 15.5" - 39 cm

Bibliography:
Dorigato 1989, p. 137.

87. **Zebrato bicolore**
Ercole Barovier
Barovier & Toso

1949

Ribbed bowl in light blue transparent glass decorated with fine threads of gold-leaf wrapped around in a spiral.

h 5" - 13 cm

Bibliography:
Dorigato 1989, p. 138.

88. **Barbarici**
Ercole Barovier
Barovier & Toso

1951

Vases from the *barbarici* series in bluish glass and rough surface finish obtained with the technique of coloring while hot without fusion.

h 12.5" - 32 cm; h 12.5" - 32 cm

Exhibitions: 1951, Paris, Exposition Internationale du Verre; Milano, IX Triennale.

Bibliography: "Domus", September 1951; Aloi 1952, No. 25; Vetri 1952, pp. 43-45; Aloi 1955, p. 39; *La verrerie* 1988, p. 89; Dorigato 1989, No. 82; Heiremans 1989, No. 35; *L'arte del vetro* 1992, No. 374; Barovier 1993, Nos. 132-134; Barovier, Barovier Mentasti, Dorigato 1995, No. 92; Heiremans 1996, Nos. 113-114; Ricke, Schmitt 1996, No. 258; *Il vetro italiano* 1998, No. 101; Barovier 1999, p. 195; *Venetian Glass* 2000, Nos. 121-122; *Murano 2001*, Nos. 160-161.

Barbarici *vases, Barovier & Toso advertisement in "Domus", September 1951.*

89. **Damasco**
Ercole Barovier
Barovier & Toso

ca. 1948

Bowl from the *damasco* series in glass rods with threads of *lattimo* and blue edges alternated with vertical stripes of *murrine*. The surface is decorated with applications of gold leaf.

w 8" - 20 cm

Exhibitions:
1948 Venezia, XXIV Biennale Internazionale d'Arte; 1952, Venezia, XXVI Biennale Internazionale d'Arte, Mostra storica del vetro muranese.

Bibliography:
Barovier Mentasti 1982, No. 298;
Mille anni 1982, No. 580;
Neuwirth 1987, No. 144;
Dorigato 1989, No. 75;
Barovier 1993, No. 123;
Barovier 1994, No. 35;
Barovier, Barovier Mentasti, Dorigato 1995, p. 54, No. 74;
Barovier 1999, p. 193.

Damasco *bowl at the XXIV Biennale Internazionale d'Arte Venezia 1948*

90. **Saturneo**
Ercole Barovier
Barovier & Toso

1951

Glass vase from the *saturneo* series with glass rods containing threads of *lattimo* glass alternating with vertical stripes of round blue *murrine*, decorated over the entire surface with applications of gold leaf.

h 10.5" - 27 cm

Exhibitions: 1951, Milano, IX Triennale; 1952, Venezia, XXVI Biennale Internazionale d'Arte, Mostra storica del vetro muranese.

Bibliography: "Domus", October 1951; Vetri 1952, pp. 43; Gasparetto 1960, Nos. 22-23; Neuwirth 1987, No. 143; *La verrerie* 1988, p. 89; Deboni 1989, No. 42; Dorigato 1989, No. 83; Barovier Mentasti 1992, No. 88; *L'arte del vetro* 1992, No. 371; Barovier 1994, No. 35; Barovier, Barovier Mentasti, Dorigato 1995, No. 94; Ricke, Schmitt 1996, No. 260; *Il vetro italiano* 1998, No. 1103; Barovier 1999, p. 192.

Saturnei vases in "Domus", October 1951

91. **Graffito barbarico opaco**
Ercole Barovier
Barovier & Toso

1952

Irregularly shaped vases from the *graffitto barbarico opaco* series, with a festooned vitreous texture composed by alternating horizontal glass rods with gold leaf and glass rods shaped in a serpentine pattern with coloring obtained while hot without fusion.

h 16.25" - 41 cm; h 15" - 38 cm

Bibliography:
Aloi 1955, p. 34;
Neuwirth 1987, No. 142;
Dorigato 1989, p. 138;
Heiremans 1996, No. 118;
Heiremans 2002, No. 111.

Graffito barbarico *vases, Barovier & Toso Archives*

92. **Graffito barbarico**
Ercole Barovier
Barovier & Toso

1952

Vase in *cristallo* decorated with blue and *lattimo* glass rods wrapped in a spiral and segmented by ribbing, and vase in *cristallo* decorated with amethyst and *lattimo* glass rods, wrapped in a spiral and tooled.

h 13" - 33 cm; h 14.5" - 37 cm

93. **Ambrati**
Ercole Barovier
Barovier & Toso

1956

Vessels and ducks from the *ambrati* series in *opalino* glass with applications of oxidized silver leaf. Because of the singular effect of this type of glass it also came to be known as *tartaruga* (tortoise).

h 9" - 23 cm; h 6" - 15 cm;
h 8.25" - 21 cm; h 8.25" - 21 cm;

Exhibitions: 1956, Paris, Exposition Internationale du Verre de Murano; Venezia, XXVIII Biennale Internazionale d'Arte; 1957, Milano, XI Triennale.

Bibliography: Dorigato 1989, No. 88; Barovier 1993, Nos. 139 -140; Heiremans 1993, No. 46; Barovier, Barovier Mentasti, Dorigato 1995, p. 86; Barovier, Dorigato 1996, No. 101; Ricke, Schmitt 1996, No. 261; Heiremans 1996, No. 168; *Il vetro italiano* 1998, No. 137; Barovier 1999, p. 194; Heiremans 2002, No. 126.

94. **Tessere ambra**
Ercole Barovier
Barovier & Toso

1957

Glass vessels and bowl from the *tessere ambra* series with amber tesserae edged in amethyst glass, composed in pairs and alternated in a checkerboard pattern.

h 10" - 25 cm; h 2.25" - 5 cm;
h 17.5" - 44 cm

Exhibitions: 1957, Milano, XI Triennale.

Bibliography:
"Domus", January 1958; "Domus" May 1958; Barovier Mentasti 1977, No. 8; Barovier Mentasti 1987, p. 15; Neuwirth 1987, No. 90; Dorigato 1989, No. 92; Barovier 1993, No. 149; Heiremans 1993, No. 49; Ricke, Schmitt 1996, No. 262; *Il vetro italiano* 1998, No. 136; Barovier 1999, p. 195; Heiremans 2002, No. 39.

Ambrati and tessere ambra, 1956-57, Barovier & Toso Archives.

95. **Millefili**
Ercole Barovier
Barovier & Toso

1956

Glass vase from the *millefili* series with rectangular tesserae in opaline glass and rectangular tesserae with light blue glass threads, composed in a checkerboard pattern.

h 11.5" - 29 cm

Exhibitions:
1956, Venezia, XXVIII Biennale Internazionale d'Arte.

Bibliography:
"Domus", October 1956; Gasparetto 1960, No. XXXIII; *Murano Glass* 1983, No. 19; Barovier Mentasti 1987, p. 14; Dorigato 1989, Nos. 89-90; *The Venetians*, No. 40; Barovier Mentasti 1992, No. 89; Barovier 1993, Nos. 141-142; Heiremans 1993, No. 48; Barovier, Barovier Mentasti, Dorigato 1995, p. 86; Heiremans 1996, No. 177; Deboni 1996, No. 49.

Millefili *vases at the XXVIII Biennale Internazionale d'Arte, Venezia, 1956.*

96. **Pezzati**
Ercole Barovier
Barovier & Toso

1956

Vases from the *pezzati* series with horizontal tesserae in opaline glass alternated with amethyst tesserae, and vase with vertical tesserae in opaline glass alternated with brown tesserae. Both vases have a ring-shaped foot in *cristallo*. In the late Fifties Ercole Barovier created several series with glass tesserae which were highly successful in all versions.

(Nos. 94-100, 103-107)

h 10.25" - 26 cm; h 12.5" - 32 cm

Bibliography:
La verrerie 1988, p. 91;
Dorigato 1989, p. 139;
The Venetians, No. 41;
Barovier 1993, No. 144;
Deboni 1996, No. 53;
Heiremans 1996, Nos. 160-161;
I Barovier 1998, No. 43;
Barovier 1999, p. 195;
Venetian Glass 2000, No. 126;
Murano 2001, No. 164;
Heiremans 2002, Nos. 36-37.

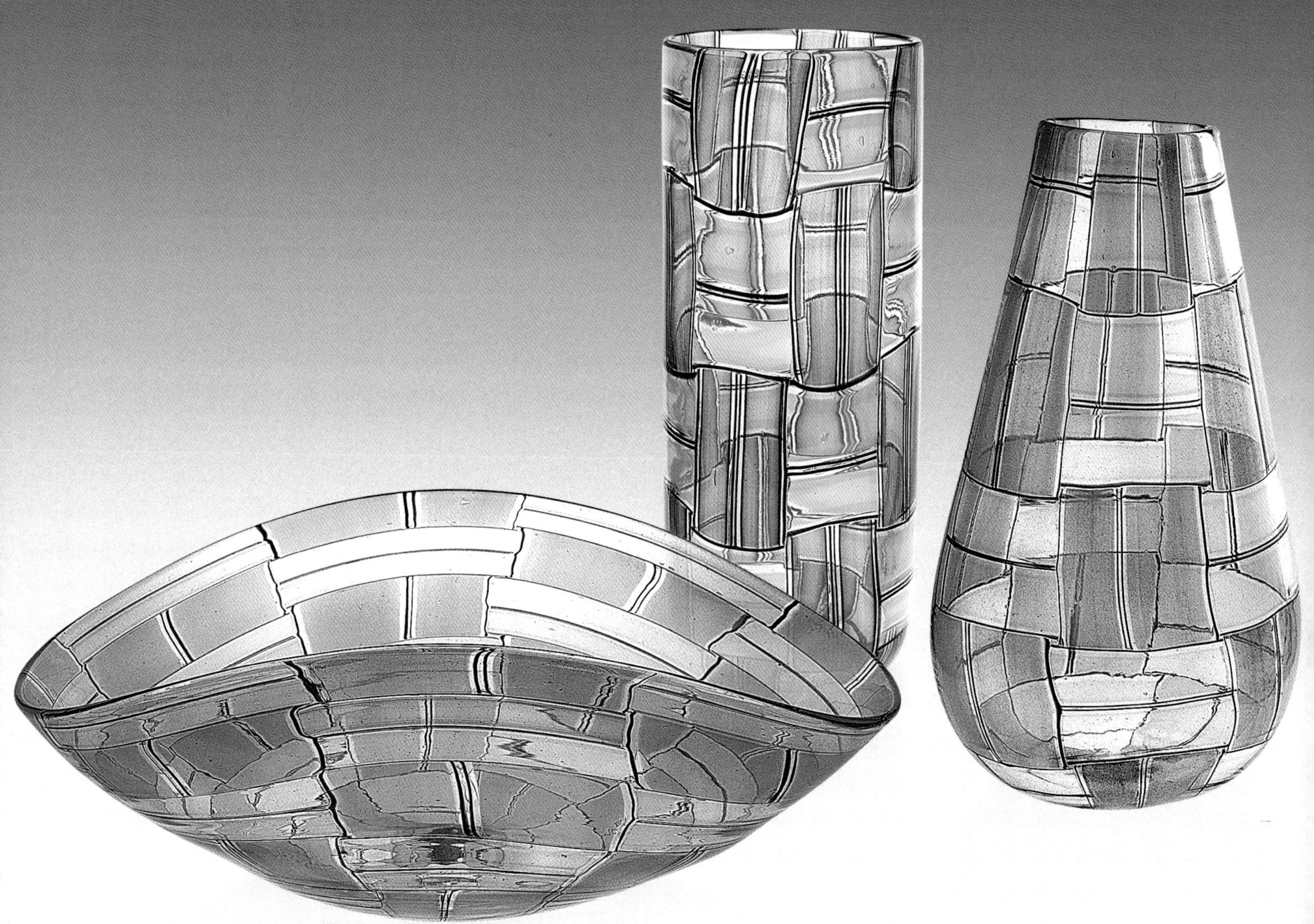

97. **Parabolici**
Ercole Barovier
Barovier & Toso

1957

Left: large bowl and vases from the *parabolici* series with tesserae in opaline or brown glass with a *cristallo* and amethyst edge, composed in a checkerboard pattern. The tesserae, laid out in pairs, are composed in an alternating vertical and horizontal pattern.

w 16.5" - 42 cm; h 12" - 30 cm; h 12" - 30 cm

Exhibitions:
1957, Milano, XI Triennale.

Bibliography:
"Domus", May 1958; Barovier Mentasti 1982, No. 299; *Mille anni* 1982, No. 582; Neuwirth 1987, No. 140; *La verrerie* 1988, p. 91; Dorigato 1989, No. 93; Barovier 1993, No. 152; Heiremans 1993, No. 50; *Il vetro italiano* 1998, No. 138.

Parabolici *vases in "Domus", May 1958.*

98. **Sidone**
Ercole Barovier
Barovier & Toso

1957

Top: plate and vase from the *sidone* series with tesserae in opaline glass and *cristallo* and amethyst edge, composed in pairs and alternated in a checkerboard pattern.

w 12.5" - 32 cm; h 8.5" - 22 cm

Exhibitions:
1957, Milano, XI Triennale; 1958, Venezia, XXIX Biennale Internazionale d'Arte.

Bibliography:
"Domus", May 1958; Gasparetto 1960, No. 40; Barovier Mentasti 1982, No. 299; *Mille anni* 1982, No. 582; Miani, Resini, Lamon 1984, p. 66; Barovier Mentasti 1987, p. 14; Neuwirth 1987, No. 86; Dorigato 1989, No. 91; Barovier 1993, No. 151; Heiremans 1996, No. 178; *Il vetro italiano* 1998, Nos. 134-135; Heiremans 2002, No. 45.

Sidone *vases in "Domus", May 1958.*

99. **Moresco**
Ercole Barovier

in amber with *cristallo* edges,
composed in a checkerboard

"Domus", May 1958;
Dorigato 1989, No. 94;

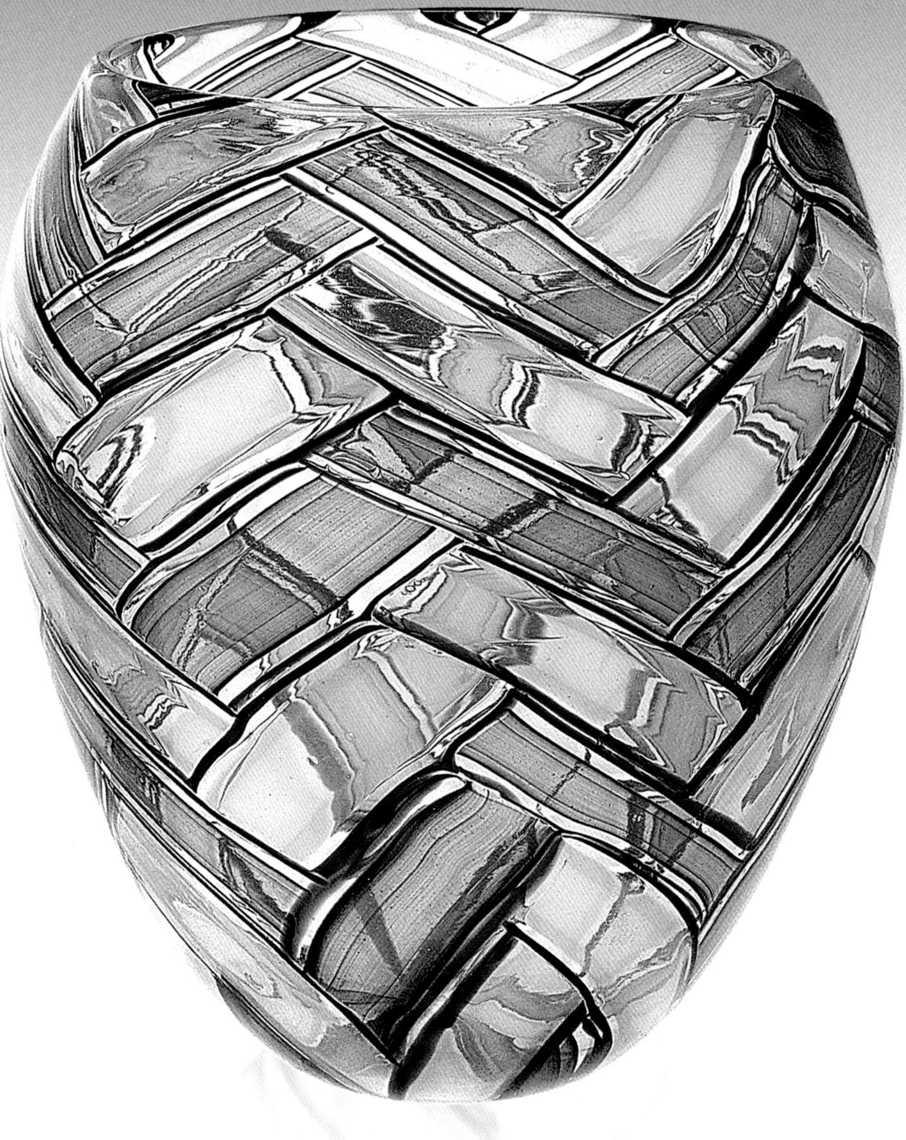

100. **A spina**
Ercole Barovier
Barovier & Toso

1958

Vessel from the *a spina* series in brown glass tesserae with *cristallo* and amethyst edge and opaline glass tesserae with *cristallo* and amethyst edge, laid down in a herringbone pattern. This series was also produced in the opaline, jade green and purple versions.

h 9.75" - 24 cm

Bibliography: "Domus", May 1958; Istituto Veneto 1960, No. 69; Neuwirth 1987, No. 88; Dorigato 1989, No. 95; Heiremans 1989, No. 55; *The Venetians* 1989, No. 40; Barovier 1993, No. 153; Barovier Mentasti 1994, No. 44; Barovier, Barovier Mentasti, Dorigato 1995, p. 89, No. 129; Deboni 1996, No. 47; Ricke, Schmitt 1996, No. 263; *I Barovier* 1998, Nos. 46-47; *Venetian Glass* 2000, No. 127; Heiremans 2002, Nos. 40-41.

A spina *vases at the XXIX Biennale Internazionale d'Arte, Venezia, 1958.*

101. **Canne policrome multiple**
Ercole Barovier
Barovier & Toso

1958

Top: bottles with stopper from the *canne policrome multiple* series in glass with vertical polychrome glass rods.

h 10.75" - 26 cm; h 10.75" - 26 cm

Bibliography:
Mariacher 1967, p. 109.

102. **Argo**
Ercole Barovier
Barovier & Toso

1959

Right: vessels from the *Argo* series with vitreous texture characterized by a grid consisting in opaline glass tesserae with a polychrome glass edge. The name of the series, reminiscent of "the mythical monster with a hundred eyes", came from the fact that if an air bubble was blown into the grid, slight bumps (*occhi*) would be formed in the *cristallo*.

h 10.5" - 27 cm; h 16" - 41 cm
h 10" - 25 cm; h 15.5" - 39 cm

Exhibitions: 1960, Venezia, XXX Biennale Internazionale d'Arte.

Bibliography: Istituto Veneto, No. 97; Gasparetto 1960, No. 39; Aloi 1964, p. 16; Dorigato 1989, No. 96; Barovier Mentasti 1992, No. 139; Barovier 1993, No. 155; Heiremans 1993, No. 58; Barovier, Barovier Mentasti, Dorigato 1995, p. 91; Ricke, Schmitt 1996, No. 265.

Argo vases at the XXX Biennale Internazionale d'Arte, Venezia, 1960.

103. **Dorico corniola**
Ercole Barovier
Barovier & Toso

1960

Left: glass bowl and vase from the *dorico corniola* series with large square tesserae in *cristallo*, *lattimo* and *corniola* glass composed in a concentric design. This series was also made in the *dorico lattimo* and the *dorico acquamare* versions so called because of the dominant colors in the tesserae.
h 15.5" - 39 cm; w 16.25" - 41 cm

Exhibitions: 1960, Venezia, XXX Biennale Internazionale d'Arte.

Bibliography: Mariacher 1967, p. 103; *Murano Glass* 1983, No. 8; Miani, Resini, Lamon 1984, p. 66; *La verrerie* 1988, p. 91; Dorigato 1989, No. 101; Cocchi 1991, No. 39; Barovier 1993, No. 161; Heiremans 1993, No. 52; Barovier 1994, p. 50; Barovier, Barovier Mentasti, Dorigato 1995, p. 91, No. 130; Heiremans 1996, Nos. 195-196; Deboni 1996, No. 53; *I Barovier* 1998, No. 49; Dorigato 2002, p. 302; Heiremans 2002, Nos. 18-19.

104. **Dorico corniola**
Ercole Barovier
Barovier & Toso

1960

Top: glass vase with large square tesserae in *cristallo* and *corniola* glass composed in a concentric pattern.

h 8" - 20 cm

Bibliography:
Barovier Mentasti 1977, No. 10;
La verrerie 1988, p. 89;
Dorigato 1989, No. 103.

Corniola *vases at the XXX Biennale Internazionale d'Arte, Venezia, 1960.*

105. **Dorico acquamare**
Ercole Barovier
Barovier & Toso

1960

Glass vases from the *dorico acquamare* series with large square tesserae in *cristallo*, *lattimo* and turquoise glass composed in a concentric design.

h 15" - 38 cm; 12" - 30 cm

Exhibitions:
1960, Venezia, XXX Biennale Internazionale d'Arte.

Bibliography:
Mariacher 1967, p. 103;
Dorigato 1989, Nos. 101-102;
Barovier 1993, p. 186-187;
Barovier 1994, p. 50;
Barovier, Barovier Mentasti, Dorigato 1995, No. 130;
Heiremans 1996, No. 194;
Ricke, Schmitt 1996, No. 266;
Deboni 1996, No. 52;
Barovier 1999, p. 241.

Dorico *vases in G. Mariacher,* I vetri di Murano, *Venezia, 1967.*

106. **Egeo**
Ercole Barovier
Barovier & Toso

1960

Vase from the egeo series with large *cristallo*, *lattimo* and green tesserae in a concentric motif and serrated edge in *corniola* glass.

h 12.75" - 31 cm

Exhibitions:
1960, Venezia, XXX Biennale Internazionale d'Arte.

Bibliography:
Neuwirth 1987, No. 213;
La verrerie 1988, p. 89;
Dorigato 1989, No. 104;
Barovier Mentasti 1992, No. 87;
Barovier 1993, p. 188;
Heiremans 1993, No. 53;
Barovier, Barovier Mentasti, Dorigato 1995, p. 91;
Heiremans 1996, No. 193;
Ricke, Schmitt 1996, No. 267;
I Barovier 1998, No. 51;
Heiremans 2002, No. 20.

Egeo *vases at the XXX Biennale Internazionale d'Arte, Venezia, 1960.*

107. **Intarsio**
Ercole Barovier
Barovier & Toso

1961

Glass vases from the *intarsio* series with inlaid tesserae obtained by cutting sheets of colored glass or *cristallo* with bubbles. Depending on the shape of the tesserae (triangular or rectangular) various vitreous textures were composed in star, zig-zag, checkerboard patterns and more. The last vase to the right is part of a rare series where the polychrome tesserae were replaced by flattened rods in turquoise glass.

h 15" - 38 cm; h 13.75" - 35 cm; h 6.5" - 17 cm; h 6.5" - 17 cm; h 6.75" - 17 cm

Exhibitions:
1962, Venezia, XXXI Biennale Internazionale d'Arte.

Bibliography:
Mariacher 1967, p. 105;
Barovier Mentasti 1977, No. 11;
Murano Glass 1983, No. 27;

Dorigato 1989, Nos. 106-107;
Heiremans 1989, No. 67;
Barovier Mentasti 1992, No. 139;
Barovier 1993, Nos. 165-167;
Heiremans 1993, No. 55;
Barovier, Barovier Mentasti, Dorigato 1995, p. 94, No. 137;
Ricke, Schmitt 1996, No. 270;
Heiremans 1996, No. 201;
Deboni 1996, Nos. 54-55;
I Barovier 1998, No. 52;
Barovier 1999, p. 238-239;
Dorigato 2002, p. 339;
Heiremans 2002, Nos. 47-48.

108 **Tessere policrome**
Ercole Barovier
Barovier & Toso

1961

Vase in *cristallo* decorated with polychrome tesserae composed in a floral motif in relief.
This vessel represents one of the first experiments by Ercole Barovier in the early Sixties, using applied polychrome tesserae and may be considered a one-of-a-kind test piece.
Engraved signature: "Ercole Barovier 1961".

h 10" - 25 cm

Bibliography:
Barovier 1993, No. 164;
Heiremans 1993, No. 54;
Ricke, Schmitt 1996, No. 268;
Venetian Glass 2000, No. 130;
Murano 2001, No. 165.

109. **Caccia**
Ercole Barovier
Barovier & Toso

1962

Glass bowl and vase from the *caccia* series in *a tessere* glass with tesserae featuring a green edge and a brown edge, concentric circles in *lattimo* glass and a nucleus in black glass. The name of the series is derived from the characteristic concentric circles motif reminiscent of a shooting range target. In the first half of the Sixties, Ercole Barovier created several glass series with tesserae decorations which enjoyed remarkable success (Nos. 109-114) The process involved preparing the composition of a vitreous pattern on a refractory slab using tesserae which would then be united by the heat of the furnace. The glass was then folded into a cylinder, closed at one end, and blown with the help of a blowpipe.

h 10" - 25 cm; h 3.75" - 9 cm

Exhibitions:
1962, Venezia, XXXI Biennale Internazionale d'Arte.

Bibliography:
Dorigato1989, No. 108;
Barovier Mentasti 1992, No. 139;
Barovier 1993, No. 163;
Barovier Mentasti 1994, No. 63;
Barovier, Barovier Mentasti, Dorigato 1995, p. 94;
Deboni 1996, Nos. 50, 53;
Venetian Glass 2000, No. 129;
Heiremans 2002, No. 26.

Caccia *glass pieces at the XXXI Biennale Internazionale d'Arte, Venezia, 1962.*

110. **Tessere policrome**
Ercole Barovier
Barovier & Toso

1964

edge and stylized motif in the shape of a flower in *lattimo*, *cristallo* and amethyst glass.
This vase is part of a rare series of which only a plate and a cone-shaped vessel are known.

Bibliography:
Dorigato 1989, No. 111;
Barovier 1993, No. 164;
Barovier 1999, p. 241.

111. **Tessere policrome** amethyst whose nucleus bears a Barovier 1999, p. 241.

112. **Tessere policrome**
Ercole Barovier
Barovier & Toso

1962-64

Glass vase from the *tessere policrome* series made with tesserae composed of a *cristallo* and *lattimo* outer edge and a triangular nucleus in red glass. Engraved signature: "Barovier & Toso".

h 9" - 23 cm

Bibliography:
Dorigato 1989, No. 110;
Barovier 1993, No. 168.

113. **Athena cattedrale**
Ercole Barovier
Barovier & Toso

1964

Glass vase from the series *athena cattedrale* with diamond-shaped tesserae edged in green, lattimo and blue glass and with a cross-shaped central motif in blue glass, and a nucleus in lattimo glass. The series was produced in a limited number and in these colors only.

h 12.75" - 32 cm

Exhibitions:
1966, Venezia, XXXIII Biennale Internazionale d'Arte.

Bibliography:
Dorigato 1989, No. 109;
Barovier 1993, No. 172;
Barovier, Barovier Mentasti, Dorigato 1995, p. 100, No. 185;
Heiremans 1996, No. 224;
Deboni 1996, No. 56;
Heiremans 2002, No. 27.

Athena cattedrale *vases at the XXXIV Biennale Internazionale d'Arte, Venezia, 1968.*

114. **Siderei**
Ercole Barovier
Barovier & Toso

1966

Bowl and vase from the *sidereo* series in *cristallo* decorated on the surface with a raised pattern composed of round *murrine* in sections of varying dimensions with hollow nucleus and *cristallo* and amethyst edge. Vase: engraved signature: "Barovier & Toso Murano".

h 11.25" - 28 cm; w 8.75" - 22 cm

Exhibitions: 1966, Venezia, XXXIII Biennale Internazionale d'Arte.

Bibliography: Mariacher 1967, p. 102; Dorigato 1989, No. 113; Barovier Mentasti 1992, No. 300; Barovier 1993, No. 173; Barovier Mentasti 1994, Nos. 82-83; Barovier, Barovier Mentasti, Dorigato 1995, p. 99, No. 207; Ricke, Schmitt 1996, No. 271; Heiremans 1996, Nos. 244-245; Heiremans 2002, No. 28.

Siderei *vases at the XXXIII Biennale Internazionale d'Arte, Venezia, 1966.*

115. **Graffito**
Ercole Barovier
Barovier & Toso

1969

Large vase from the *graffitto* series in *cristallo* with raised decoration consisting of opaline glass festoons with gold leaf, obtained by using a special tool to "comb" the vitreous thread previously applied in a spiral around the vessel.

h 19.5" - 49 cm

Bibliography:
Dorigato 1989, p. 138;
Aloi 1955, p. 34;
Heiremans 1993, No. 45;
Barovier 1993, No. 176;
Heiremans 1996, No. 118.

Graffito *vases, Barovier & Toso Archives.*

116. **Christian Dior**
Ercole Barovier
Barovier & Toso

1969

Bottles with stoppers from the *Christian Dior* series in polychrome glass rods, composed into a characteristic Scottish tartan pattern.
Original paper label.

h 9" - 23 cm; h 9.5" - 24 cm;
h 6.5" - 17 cm; h 9.75" - 24 cm;
h 8.5" - 22 cm, h 9.5" - 24 cm;
h 9.25" - 23 cm

Bibliography:
Barovier 1993, No. 177;
Deboni 1996, No. 57;
Ricke, Schmitt 1996, No. 269;
Venetian Glass 2000, No.131;
Murano 2001, No. 166.

117. **Rotellati**
Ercole Barovier
Barovier & Toso

1970

Top: glass vessels from the *rotellati* series with diamond-shaped tesserae in light blue and *fumé* glass with a center ring and nucleus in light blue glass.
Right: *rotellati* vessels with diamond-shaped tesserae with blue and amethyst serrate and a hollow nucleus with a *cristallo* and green edge.

h 4" - 10 cm; h 9" - 23 cm; h 13.5" - 34 cm; h 12.5" - 32 cm; w 10" - 25 cm

Bibliography:
Dorigato 1989, No.117;
Barovier 1993, Nos. 178-179;
Barovier, Barovier Mentasti, Dorigato 1995, No. 184;
Heiremans 1996, No. 255;
Barovier 1999 p. 277;
Venetian Glass 2000, No.132;
Murano 2001, No.167;
Heiremans 2002, No. 30.

Rotellati *vases, Barovier & Toso Archives*

Fratelli Toso

C.V.M.
(Compagnia Venezia e Murano)
Pauly & Co.

A.VE.M.

Fratelli Toso

Founded in 1854 by the brothers Ferdinando, Carlo, Liberato, Angelo, Giovanni and Gregorio, the glassworks initially produced glass for domestic use and medicine bottles, followed later by copies of antique glass pieces. In the early 1900's, they made objects and lamps in the floral style with the *a murrine* technique. In 1912 and 1914 Fratelli Toso presented glassware by the ceramist Hans Stoltenberg Lerche which was a huge success. In the Twenties, Fratelli Toso began to produce traditional transparent blown glass, registering a sharp change in direction for the Venezia Biennale in 1934, where it presented *cristallo* glass decorated with thick stripes of silvered glass. In 1936, Ermanno Toso became artistic director of the company: he progressively revisited the techniques of Murano glassblowing, providing a personal interpretation that won him considerable praise especially after the Second World War. During the Sixties and Seventies, a remarkably modern series of works designed by Renato Giusto and Rosanna Toso, for which they often chose to work with *cristallo* glass, was produced by the company. It closed in 1982.

C.V.M.
Pauly & Co.

Pauly & Co. was founded in 1902 by Emilio Pauly with several partners, for the production and sale of traditional Venetian glass products. In 1919 it was sold to a company from Milan which had also purchased the Compagnia Venezia e Murano, a firm which sold Venetian glass and luxury furnishings. The following year Gaetano Ceschina acquired both companies, running their mainly commercial activities parallel to one another. The new company's shops sold products from various glassworks, often marked with an acid-etched stamp bearing the initials C.V.M. beneath a crown. In 1963 Compagnia Venezia e Murano – Pauly & Co. was purchased by Luciano Barbon, whose heirs are the current owners.

A.VE.M.

See page 293.

118. **Portaprofumo**
Probably Hans Stoltenberg Lerche
Vetreria Fratelli Toso

in black *pasta vitrea*. Disc-shaped foot and stopper in *cristallo* shaped into the head of Anubis.

119. **Alzata**
Hans Stoltenberg Lerche
Vetreria Fratelli Toso

ca. 1912

Compote in *cristallo* decorated with *fumé*, blue and green vitreous threads applied casually in an irregular manner while hot, and supported by a tangle of vitreous threads.

h 8.5" - 22 cm

Exhibitions: 1912, Venezia, X Biennale Internazionale d'Arte.

Bibliography: Papini 1923, p. 58; Barovier Mentasti 1982, Nos. 243-244; Barovier Mentasti 1992, Nos. 22-24; Heiremans 1993, No. 179; Barovier, Barovier Mentasti, Dorigato 1995, p. 25, No. 3; Quesada, 1996, p. 33; Deboni 1996, Nos. 161-162; Heiremans 1996, Nos. 3-4; *Il vetro italiano* 1998, Nos. 32-33; Barovier 1999, p. 95; Barovier 2001, pp. 274-276; Cisotto Nalon, Barovier Mentasti 2002, p. 278; Heiremans 2002, No. 91; Dorigato 2002, p. 243.

Compote with threads at the XI Biennale Internazionale d'Arte, Venezia, 1914.

122. **A murrine**
Vetreria Fratelli Toso

1910-15

Glass vase with polychrome floral *murrine* in a checkerboard pattern.

h 8" - 20 cm

Bibliography:
Bova, Junck, Migliaccio 1998, p. 40;
Barovier 2001, p. 273.

123. **A murrine foreali**
Vetreria Fratelli Toso

1910-20

Vases in transparent blue glass decorated with polychrome floral

h 8.5" - 22 cm

Bibliography:
Sarpellon 1990, Nos. 1077-1078;
Barovier Mentasti 1992, No. 26;
Bova, Junck, Migliaccio 1998, No. 158.

124. **A murrine foreali**
Vetreria Fratelli Toso

1920

Vases in transparent blue glass decorated in a floral motif, with pink and white veined roses and green leaves; with polychrome floral *murrine* with six petals and green leaves; right, with yellow and white daisy-shaped *murrine* and green vitreous threads. The model of the first vase on the left corresponds to No. 1942 of the Fratelli Toso Catalog in the floral version.

h 6" - 15 cm; h 5.25" - 13 cm; h 5.5" - 14 cm

Bibliography:
Bova, Junck, Migliaccio 1998, Nos. 150, 161, 173, p. 41; Dorigato 2002, p. 241.

Model No. 1942, Fratelli Toso Catalog, ca. 1920.

125. **A murrine foreali**
Vetreria Fratelli Toso

ca. 1920

Left: vase in light blue cased glass and vase in transparent blue glass with small side handles, decorated with polychrome floral *murrine*.
Top: vase in transparent blue glass with decoration in polychrome floral *murrine* and ear-shaped side handles.
The models of the vases correspond respectively to Nos. 2118, 2173, and 1951 of the Fratelli Toso Catalog, in the floral version.

h 13" - 33 cm; h 5.25" - 13 cm;
h 9.25" - 23 cm

Bibliography:
Sarpellon 1990, Nos. 1079-1080;
Bova, Junck, Migliaccio 1998, No.155, pp. 40-41; *Kiku* 2000, Nos. 19-20, 45;
Barovier 2001, p. 284.

Model No. 2173, Fratelli Toso Catalog, ca. 1920.

126. **A murrine foreali**
Vetreria Fratelli Toso

1920

Vases in amethyst glass decorated with sprays of flowers composed of polychrome floral *murrine* and leafshaped *murrine*, and green vitreous threads. The vase on the right corresponds to model No. 1958 of the Fratelli Toso Catalog.

h 9.5" - 24 cm; h 9.5" - 24 cm

Bibliography:
Bova, Junck, Migliaccio 1998, No. 170, p. 41; Dorigato 2002, p. 240.

Model No.1958, Fratelli Toso Catalog, ca. 1920.

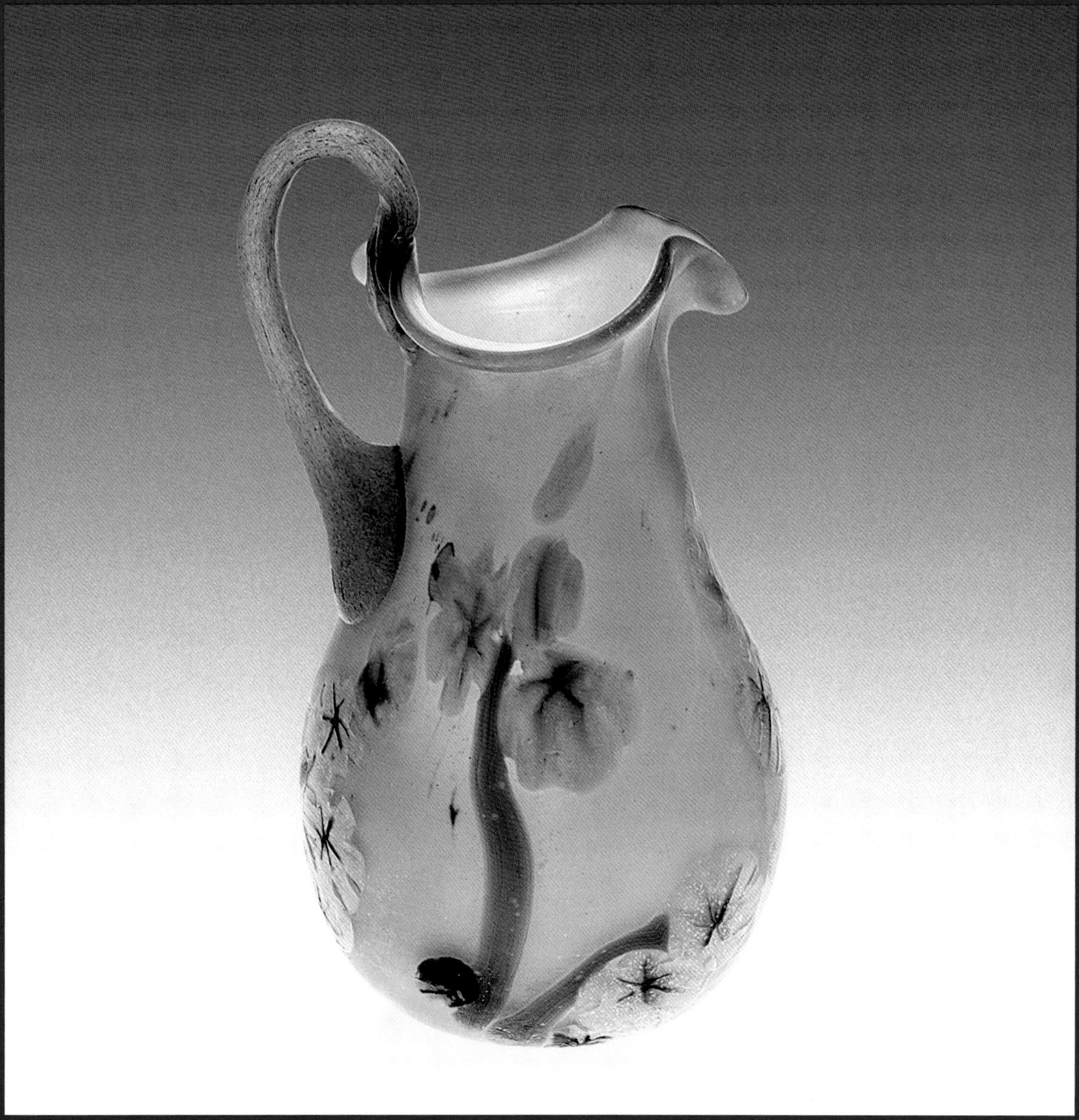

128. **A murrine foreali**
Vetreria Fratelli Toso

ca. 1920

Left: vase in transparent amethyst glass with small side handles and floral motif in *murrine* with white and amethyst roses and green leaves. Vase in transparent green glass with floral decoration made of *murrine* with daisies and leaves. Top: pitcher in green cased glass decorated with floral *murrine* with six petals and green vitreous threads. The model of the first vase from the left corresponds to No. 2165 of the Fratelli Toso Catalog, whereas the vase at the top corresponds to No. 2082 in the floral version.

h 8" - 20 cm; h 9" - 23 cm; h 5.25" - 13 cm

Bibliography:
Sarpellon 1990, No. 1080; Bova, Junck, Migliaccio 1998, Nos. 150, 164, p. 40.

Model No. 2165, Fratelli Toso Catalog, ca. 1920.

129. **A spire d'argento**
Vetreria Fratelli Toso

1934

Square glass vessel from the *a spire d'argento* series with large transparent tesserae bearing silver spiral motifs, decorated over the entire surface with applications of oxidized silver leaf.

h 9" - 23 cm

Bibliography:
XIX Biennale, Catalog, 1934, p. 226;
"Le Tre Venezie", May 1934, p. 276;
"Domus", November 1934, p. 24;
Barovier, Barovier Mentasti, Dorigato 1995, p. 37, No. 34;
Barovier 1999, p. 155.

A spire d'argento *vases at the XIX Biennale Internazionale d'Arte, Venezia, 1934.*

130. **Mutras**
Vetreria Fratelli Toso

ca. 1936

Glass vase from the *mutras* series with transparent *murrine* with spiral and square motifs in amethyst glass, *sommerso* in *cristallo*. Side handles in *cristallo* glass shaped *a morise*.

h 11" - 28 cm

Bibliography:
Heiremans 2002, No. 6.

Mutras *vase, ca. 1936, Marino Barovier Archives.*

131. **Millepunti**
Ermanno Toso
Vetreria Fratelli Toso

1955

Glass vases from the *millepunti* series with polychrome *murrine*.

The first vase to the left bears an original paper label.

h 12.5" - 32 cm; h 13" - 33 cm

Bibliography:
Kiku 2000, No. 56.

132. **Kiku**
Ermanno Toso
Vetreria Fratelli Toso

ca. 1960

Glass vases from the *kiku* series with polychrome *murrine* in a stylized floral design.

h 12" - 30 cm; h 6.75" - 17 cm

Bibliography:
Heiremans 1989, No. 163-164;
Venetian Glass 2000, No. 120;
Kiku 2000, Nos. 4, 7, 40;
Murano 2001, No. 159.

133. **Nero ossido**
Ermanno Toso
Vetreria Fratelli Toso

1952

Vase from the *nero ossido* series in amethyst glass finished over the entire surface with applications of gold leaf and decorated with bubbles of amethyst glass distributed irregularly over the surface.

h 11" - 28 cm

Bibliography:
Heiremans 1996, No. 117.

134. **Sfera psichedelica**
Giusto Toso
Vetreria Fratelli Toso

1970

Sphere from the *psichedelica* series in *cristallo* glass with embedded amethyst glass threads which create characteristic optical effects through refraction.

w 6" - 15 cm

Exhibitions:
1970, Venezia, XXXV Biennale Internazionale d'Arte.

Bibliography:
XXXV Biennale, Catalog, 1970, p.134;
Barovier, Barovier Mentasti, Dorigato 1995, p. 103, No. 180;
Barovier 1999, pp. 284-285.

Psychedelic sphere at the XXXV Biennale Internazionale d'Arte, Venezia, 1970.

135. **Trasparenti**
C.V.M. - Pauly & Co.

ca. 1923

Compote jar in transparent light green glass with trim and small handles in blue *pasta vitrea*.

h 16" - 41 cm

Bibliography:
Marangoni 1927, plate 97.

Vase from the Compagnia Venezia e Murano in the Enciclopedia delle moderne arti decorative, *Milano, 1927.*

136. **Trasparenti**
C.V.M. - Pauly & Co.

ca. 1923

Compote jars in blue transparent glass with small side handles and trim respectively in blue *pasta vitrea* and in *lattimo* glass.

h 11" - 28 cm; h 12" - 30 cm

Bibliography:
Marangoni 1927, plate 97.

Vase from the Compagnia Venezia e Murano in the Enciclopedia delle moderne arti decorative, *Milano, 1927.*

disc-shaped foot and trim in black *pasta vitrea*.
Right: goblet and stemmed vessel in *cristallo* with an embedded pattern of regular air bubbles.
The vessels, with a disc-shaped foot, are decorated with ring-shaped handles and trim respectively in blue *pasta vitrea* and in black *pasta vitrea*.

h 11.25" - 28 cm; h 12" - 30 cm; h 10" - 25 cm

Exhibitions:
1927, Monza, III Biennale delle Arti Decorative.

Bibliography:
Catalogo ufficiale della III Mostra Internazionale delle arti decorative, 1927, p. 24;
Gasparetto 1960, plate XIV;
Barovier Mentasti 1977, No. 22;
Barovier Mentasti 1982, No. 264;
Mille anni 1982, Nos. 516-517;
Mercato e travestimento 1984, Nos. 176-177;
L'arte del vetro 1992, No. 302;
Deboni 1996, Nos. 85-86;
Ricke, Schmitt 1996, p. 15;
Barovier 1999, pp. 117-119.

Bellotto vases at the III Mostra Internazionale delle Arti Decorative, Monza, 1927.

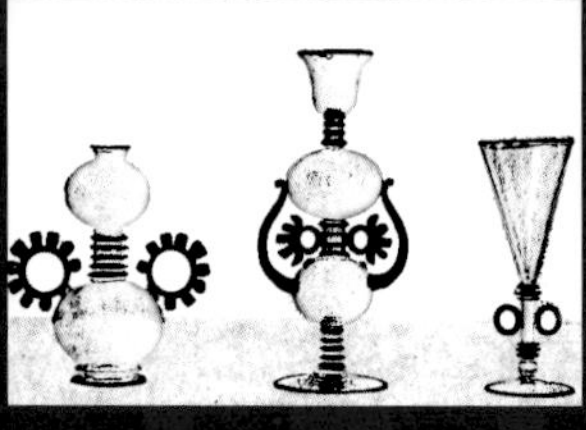

138. **Trasparente**
Unknown factory

1922-30

Vessel in transparent *fumé* glass decorated with three horizontal threads in *fumé* glass and by small handles alternated with *fragole* in transparent blue glass. The surface is lightly iridized.

h 10" - 25 cm

139. **Trasparenti**
Unknown factory

ca. 1922-30

Bottle and vase in lightly iridized *cristallo* decorated respectively with rings, applied handles and trim in transparent blue glass.

h 13" - 33 cm; h 9.5" - 24 cm

Drawing from a Carbone Catalog, ca. 1930.

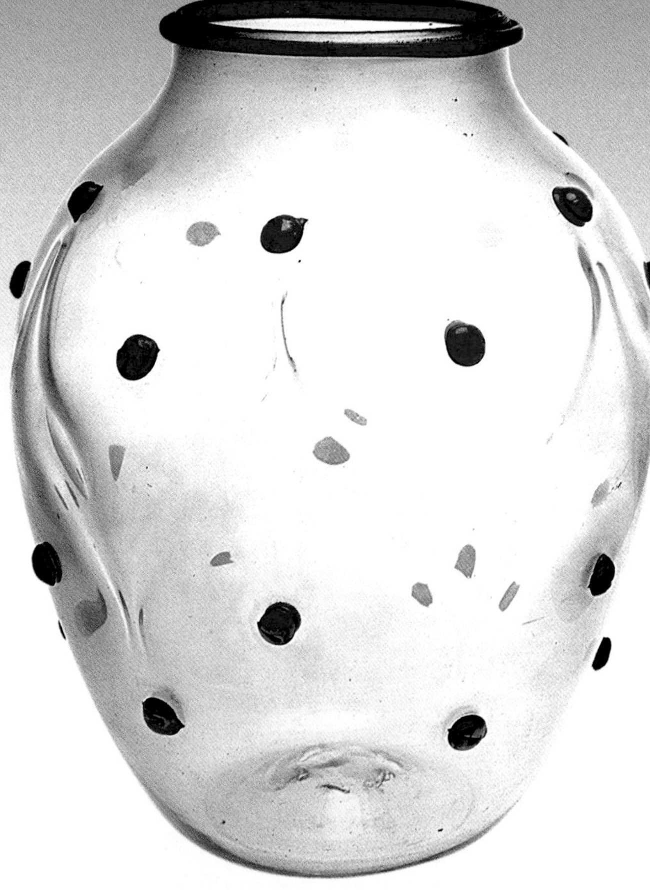

140. **Trasparenti**
Unknown factory

1925-30

Vase in transparent light green glass decorated on the neck with small *a* round applications, both in black *pasta vitrea*.
Vase in *cristallo* decorated with applications in blue transparent glass applied uniformly over the entire surface. Lip wrap in blue transparent glass. The two vases present a lightly

h 10.5" - 27 cm; h 10.5" - 27 cm

141. **Trasparenti**
A.VE.M.

ca. 1932

Vases in light blue transparent glass and in amethyst transparent glass. Both the vases are lightly ribbed and decorated at the base with irregular drop-shaped applications. The model corresponds to No.151 of the A.VE.M. Catalog.

h 13" - 33 cm; h 12.5" - 32 cm

Model No. 151, A.VE.M. Catalog.

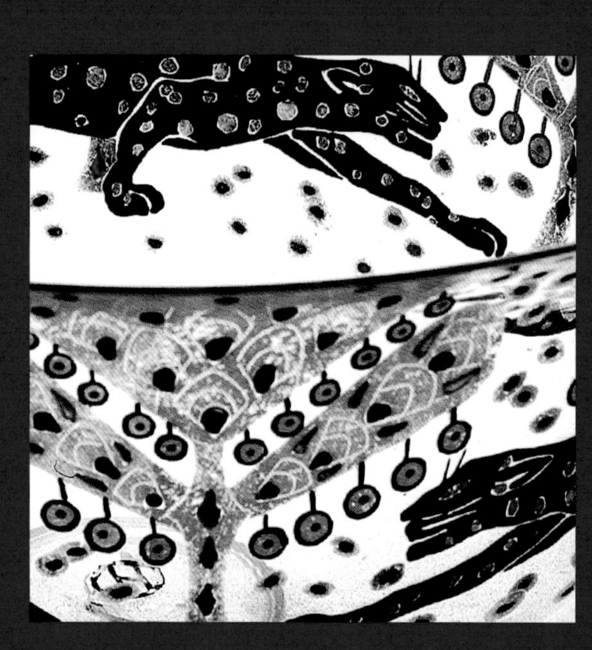

S.A.L.I.R. (Studio Ars Labor Industrie Riunite)

M.V. M. (Maestri Vetrai Muranesi) Cappellin & Co.

S.A.L.I.R.

S.A.L.I.R. was founded in 1923 by Guglielmo Barbini, Giuseppe D'Alpaos and Gino Franceschetti, decorators from the cold-work shop of the Cristalleria Franchetti, and Decio Toso. Its work mainly involved engraving (diamond, wheel, sandblasting), *intaglio*, enamel decoration and the gilding of blown glass, mirrors and decorative panels. From 1927 the firm worked with Guido Balsamo Stella and the Bohemian Franz Pelzel, the former for five years as artistic director, the latter until he retired from the business in 1968, becoming a leader of figurative engraving. Using designs by Balsamo Stella, Pelzel wheel-engraved gracious Art Déco and classical-style figures and images of every-day life. The models engraved and enameled in the Thirties were conceived by Pelzel himself, Vittorio Zecchin, Gio Ponti, Pietro Fornasetti and Atte Gasparetto. Subsequently Pelzel and his students created wheel-engraved or diamond-point glass with modern designs by independent collaborators such as Pietro Pelzel, Ettore Sottsass, Serena Dal Maschio, Riccardo Licata, Ugo Blasi, Romualdo Scarpa, Tano Zancanaro, Vinicio Vianello and Agostino Venturini. The company has been directed since 1976 by Mario D'Alpaos and Luigi Toso, respectively the heirs of Giuseppe D'Alpaos and Decio Toso and current owners of the glassworks.

M.V. M. Cappellin & Co.

The M.V.M. Cappellin & Co. glassworks was founded in 1925 by Giacomo Cappellin after a disagreement among partners led to the closing of the Cappellin Venini & Co. glassworks.

Vittorio Zecchin, a painter from Murano who had previously worked at Cappellin Venini, stayed with Cappellin, and for a short period continued to design blown glass pieces characterized by soft colors and the purest of lines. Towards the end of 1926, Zecchin left, and the artistic direction was entrusted to the young architect Carlo Scarpa. He pursued the direction adopted by Zecchin, initially creating lightweight blown pieces composed with basic geometric forms, often on a cone-shaped foot. Later, Scarpa presented fine glass pieces in *pasta vitrea* in bright colors or decorated with festoons (*fenici*). His famous production of *lattimo* pieces with gold or silver leaf was presented in 1930 at Monza, with other pieces featuring vertical glass rods and *millefiori*. Poor economic management of the glassworks forced Cappellin, who was more concerned with the beauty of his glass than the costs of production, to close the company in January 1932.

142. **A smalti e oro**
Vittorio Zecchin

ca. 1919

Le pantere bowl in *cristallo* with decoration in gold and polychrome enamels depicting panthers in the midst of stylized trees.
Signed with the initials "VZ" painted in enamel on the bottom.
Decorated by Vittorio Gazzagon.

h 6.25" - 16 cm

Exhibitions: 1919, Venezia, Ca' Pesaro, X Esposizione d'Arti e Industrie Veneziane.

Bibliography: Lorenzetti 1931, No. 20; Barovier Mentasti 1982, No. 250; *Mille anni* 1982, No. 498; De Guttry, Maino, Quesada 1985, No. 9; *L'arte del vetro* 1992, Nos. 295-296; Barovier Mentasti 1992, No. 28; Barovier, Mondi, Sonego 2002, Nos. 108, 110.

Advertisement in "Il Primato Artistico Italiano", October 1919.

143. **A smalti**
Guido Balsamo Stella
S.A.L.I.R.

Design ca. 1919
Production 1923

Giardino vessel in *cristallo* with polychrome enamel decoration depicting stylized hills with trees and birds in flight. Trim in red transparent glass.
Signed with enamel: "S.A.L.I.R."

h 8.75" - 22 cm

Bibliography:
Baldacci, Daverio 1977, No. 9;
Deboni 1996, No. 113.

Drawing for a glass vessel decorated with enamels, ca. 1919, S.A.L.I.R. Archives.

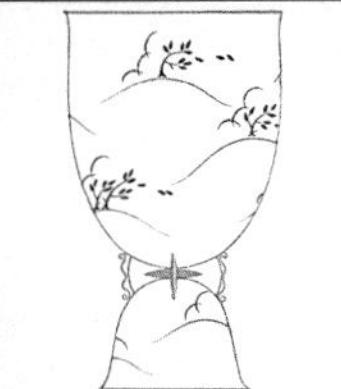

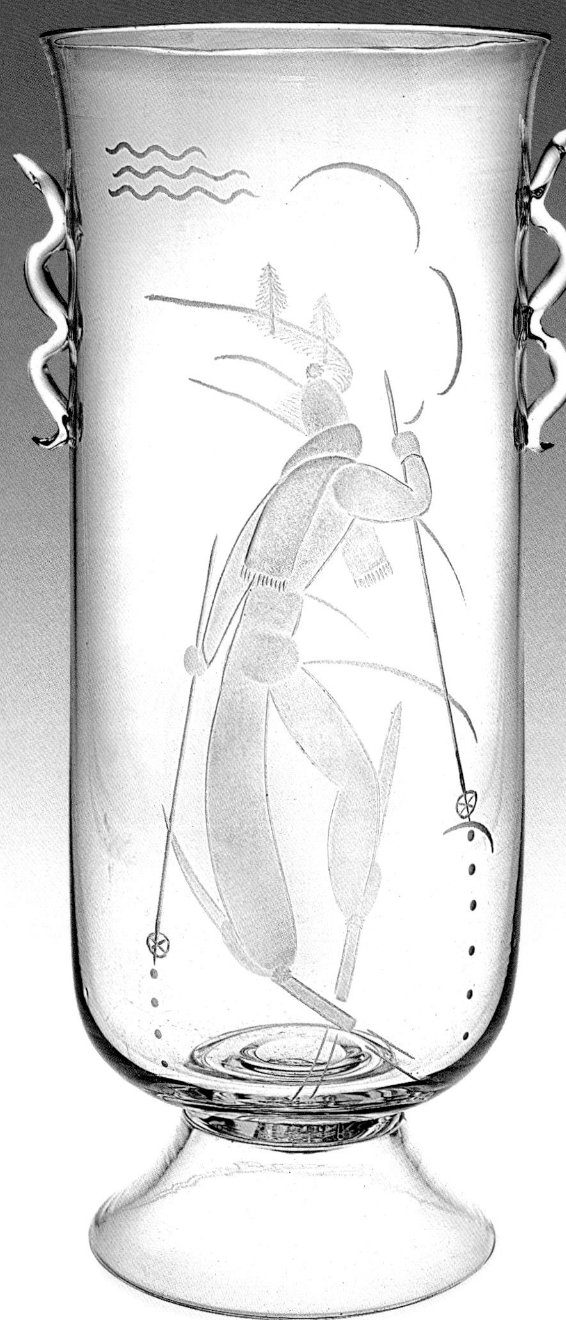

144. **Incisi**
Guido Balsamo Stella
S.A.L.I.R.

1928-30

Left to right: vessel in transparent *paglierino* glass with cone-shaped foot decorated with an engraving at the wheel depicting a dancer with veils.
Vessel in *cristallo* engraved at the wheel depicting a skier.

h 10" - 25 cm; h 9.5" - 24 cm

Bibliography:
XV Esposizione Internazionale d'Arte della Città di Venezia, 1926, p. 71;
Baldacci, Daverio 1977, Nos. 67, 68;
Romanelli, Dorigato 1982, No. 124;
Nerozzi 1987, No. 27;
Barovier Mentasti 1992, Nos. 31, 51;
Barovier, Barovier Mentasti,
Dorigato 1995, No. 19;
Il vetro italiano 1998, No. 45;
Barovier 1999, p. 121.

Sciatore vessel, *ca. 1928, Marino Barovier Archives*

145. **Inciso**
Guido Balsamo Stella
S.A.L.I.R.

ca. 1933

Vase in transparent *fumé* glass decorated with an engraving depicting a mermaid caught in a net with fish. Handles and trim in black *pasta vitrea*. The vase was made by the Vetreria Barovier Seguso Ferro.

h 11.5" - 29 cm

Bibliography:
Baldacci, Daverio 1977, No. 64.

146. **Inciso**
Peter Pelzel
S.A.L.I.R.

1932

Vase in transparent amethyst glass decorated with a copper-wheel engraving depicting fawns. A similar vessel was exhibited at the Biennale di Venezia in 1932.
Engraved signature: "Franz Pelzel".

h 8.25" - 21 cm

Bibliography:
Barovier, Barovier Mentasti, Dorigato 1995, p. 34.

Cerbiatti *vessel at the XVIII Biennale Internazionale d'Arte, Venezia, 1932.*

147. **Incisi**
Guido Balsamo Stella
S.A.L.I.R.

1930-32

Footed bowls in transparent *fumé* glass decorated with copper-wheel engravings, depicting respectively *La luna* and bathers.

h 8.5" - 22 cm

Bibliography:
Baldacci, Daverio 1977, No. 65.

La luna vessel, ca. 1928, Marino Barovier Archives.

148. **Incisi**
S.A.L.I.R.

1930-33

Left: vessel in transparent yellow glass decorated with an engraving of a female figure etched at the wheel.

The decoration was inspired by Gio Ponti's series of ceramic pieces entitled *Le mie donne*.
Right: vessel in transparent light blue glass decorated with an engraving of *Amanti*, etched at the wheel.

h 11" - 28 cm; h 12.5" - 32 cm

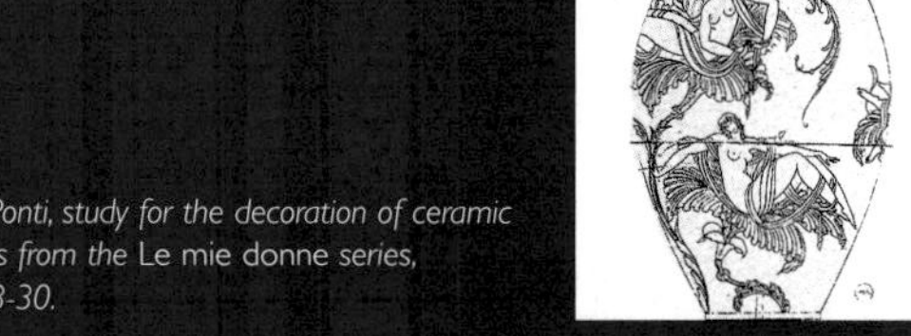

Gio Ponti, study for the decoration of ceramic works from the Le mie donne *series, 1923-30.*

149. **Mappamondo**
Ernesto Puppo
S.A.L.I.R.

1936

Sphere in transparent *fumé* glass decorated with a copper-wheel engraving and sand-blasting depicting a map of the world. Mouth in transparent *fumé* glass and cone-shaped foot in *cristallo*.

h 10" - 25 cm

Exhibitions:
1936, Milano, VI Triennale.

Bibliography:
Il vetro italiano 1998, No. 81.

150. **A smalti**
Vittorio Zecchin
S.A.L.I.R.

ca. 1938

Bowl in *cristallo* decorated with vegetable motifs in polychrome enamels.

h 4" - 10 cm, w 5.75" - 14 cm

Bibliography:
Barovier, Mondi, Sonego 2002, No. 271;
Dorigato 2002, p. 297;
Barovier Mentasti 1977, No. 31;
Romanelli, Dorigato 1982, No. 145;
L'arte del vetro 1992, No. 336;
Heiremans 1993, No. 99.

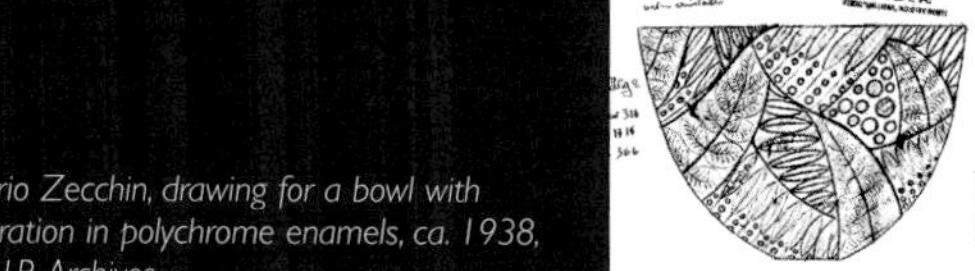

Vittorio Zecchin, drawing for a bowl with decoration in polychrome enamels, ca. 1938, S.A.L.I.R. Archives.

151. **A smalti**
Pietro Fornasetti
S.A.L.I.R.

1940

Vase in *cristallo* with polychrome enamel decoration depicting butterflies and two hands.

h 12.5" - 32 cm

Exhibitions:
1940, Milano, VIII Triennale.

Bibliography:
"Domus", May 1940;
"Lo Stile", May 1941;
Il vetro italiano 1998, No. 88;
Heiremans 1993, No. 100;
Deboni 1996, p. 54;
Le età del vetro 2003, No. 34.

Vase in "Lo Stile", May 1941.

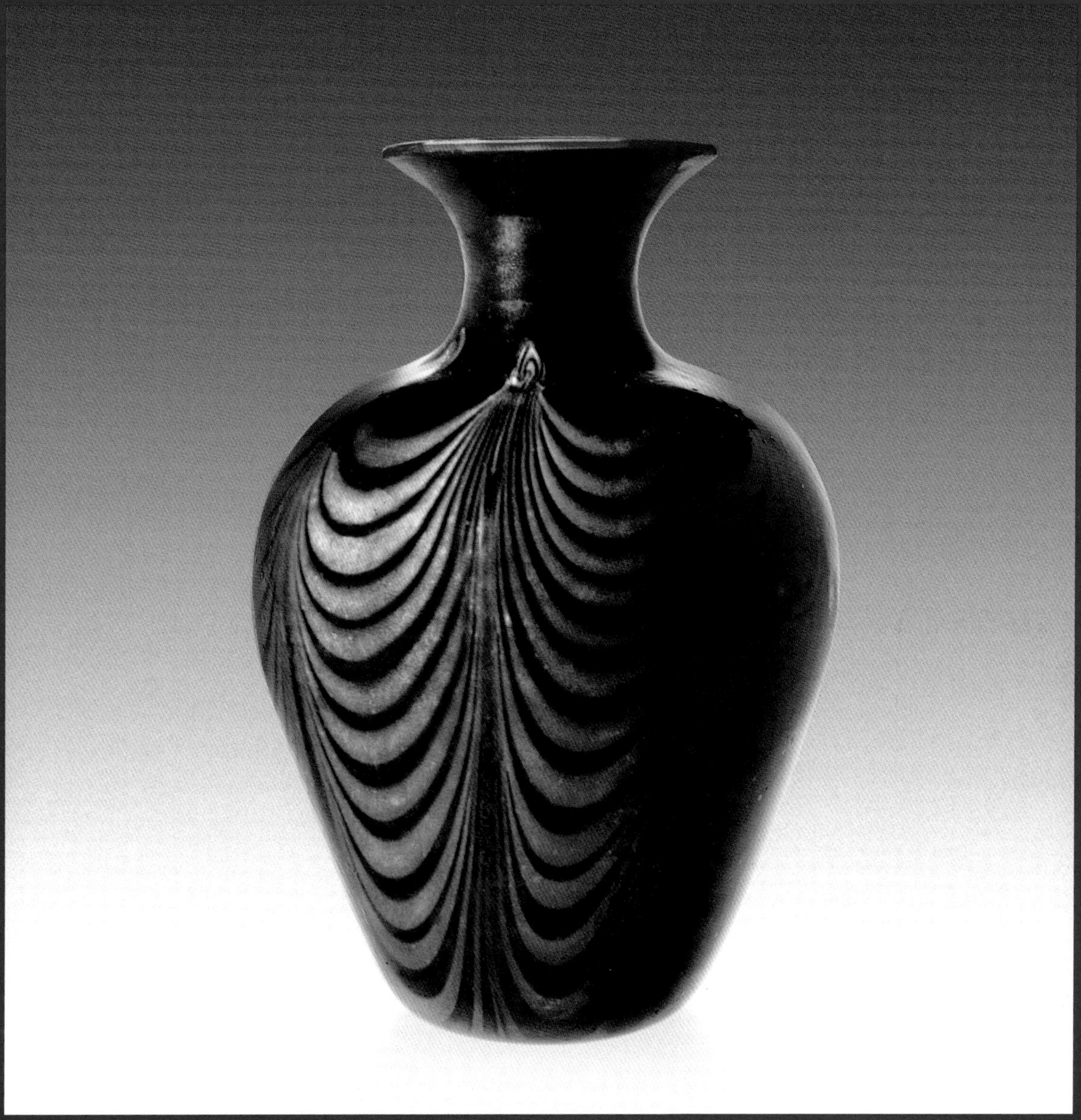

152. **A reticello**
Carlo Scarpa
M.V.M. Cappellin & Co.

ca. 1927

First and second left: vases from the *a reticello* series in glass with amethyst glass rods and *cristallo* and amethyst *filigrana*, and in *a reticello* glass with intersecting blue and *cristallo* glass rods.
Acid-stamped: "M.V.M. Cappellin Murano".

h 8.5" - 22 cm; h 4.75" - 12 cm

Exhibitions:
1927, Venezia, XVIII Esposizione dell'Opera Bevilacqua La Masa; 1927, Monza, III Mostra Internazionale delle Arti Decorative e Industriali Moderne; 1931, Amsterdam, Mostra di vetri, ceramiche e merletti d'arte moderna italiana.

Bibliography:
Heiremans 1993, No. 76;
Deboni 1996, pp. 34, 146;
Barovier 1997, p. 193;
Il vetro italiano 1998, No. 36;
Barovier 1999, p. 115;
Heiremans 2002, Nos. 51-52.

153. **Decoro fenicio**
Carlo Scarpa
M.V.M. Cappellin & Co.

1928-31

Third left: sphere shaped vase from the *fenici* series in *cristallo* with the characteristic festoon decor in transparent blue glass. Foot in *cristallo* and trim in transparent blue glass. The model corresponds to No. 6446 of the M.V.M. Cappellin Catalog.
Top: vase in black *pasta vitrea* with a characteristic festoon pattern in *lattimo* glass, heavily iridized over the entire surface. Mouth in red *pasta vitrea*. Bears an old "Pauly & Co." label.

h 8.25" - 21 cm; h 7.75" - 20 cm

Bibliography: "Domus", January 1930, p. 38; Barovier 1991, Nos. 3-4; Barovier Mentasti 1992, No. 62; *L'arte del vetro* 1992, p. 243; Glas Band 1995, p. 232; Heiremans 1996, No. 32; Barovier 1997, p. 195; *I Barovier* 1998, pp. 8-9; Barovier 1999, p. 141; *Venetian Glass* 2000, No. 23-26; *Murano* 2001, Nos. 37-40, 43; Heiremans 2002, No. 92.

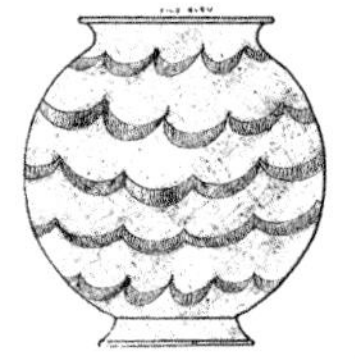

Model No. 6446, M.V.M. Cappellin Catalog.

V. S. M. (Vetri Soffiati Muranesi) Venini & Co. Venini & Co.

V.S.M. Venini & Co.
Venini & Co.

After the break-up of Cappellin Venini & Co., in 1925 Paolo Venini founded his own glassworks under the name of Vetri Soffiati Muranesi Venini & Co. Initially, under the artistic direction of Napoleone Martinuzzi, the company continued to produce pieces designed by Vittorio Zecchin, but soon the production became increasingly characterized by the original style developed by Martinuzzi on the basis of his previous experience as a *Novecento* style sculptor. In addition to his classical looking vases, Martinuzzi created cacti, often of remarkable size, in *pulegoso* glass. In 1932 the partners Napoleone Martinuzzi and Francesco Zecchin left the glassworks which changed its name to Venini & Co. For a short period, the artistic direction was entrusted to Tommaso Buzzi, an architect from Milan, who created delicately colored glass pieces. In 1934 the artistic direction was turned over to Carlo Scarpa who was responsible for most of the company's production through 1947. Beside Paolo Venini, who often intervened as a designer as well, Carlo Scarpa explored the potential of glass, using and re-inventing many traditional techniques with which, as time went on, he created objects that appeared remarkably modern.
The glass *a mezza filigrana* was followed by the first *sommersi*, the *paste vitree* which recreated the motifs of Chinese ceramics, the *corrosi*, the *battuti*, the vases *a fasce colorate*, *a pennellate*, the *variegati*, and the famous polychrome *murrine* whose surface was ground at the wheel. After World War II, Venini & Co. worked with a number of artists such as Gio Ponti, Tyra Lundgren and especially Fulvio Bianconi, who contributed significantly to the new stylistic direction taken by the glassworks.
It is important to mention the close supervision conducted by Paolo Venini, who was always beside his collaborators while their works were being developed. After the death of Paolo Venini in 1959, his son-in-law Ludovico de Santillana became artistic director, and designer within the company. Many other designers have worked with Venini & Co. since the Sixties. Tobia Scarpa, Thomas Stearns, Toni Zuccheri, Tapio Wirkkala, Laura de Santillana and many young artists, many of whom were American, spent time in the furnace. In 1986, the Venini de Santillana family left the management of the company and sold their participation to the Ferruzzi Group, which continued to guarantee the refined quality of the Venini products by collaborating with new designers such as Timo Sarpaneva, Marco Zanini, Ettore Sottsass Jr., Alessandro Mendini, Mario Bellini, Barbara Del Vicario, and others. In 1998 the glassworks was acquired by the Royal Scandinavian holding company. The company changed ownership again in 2002.

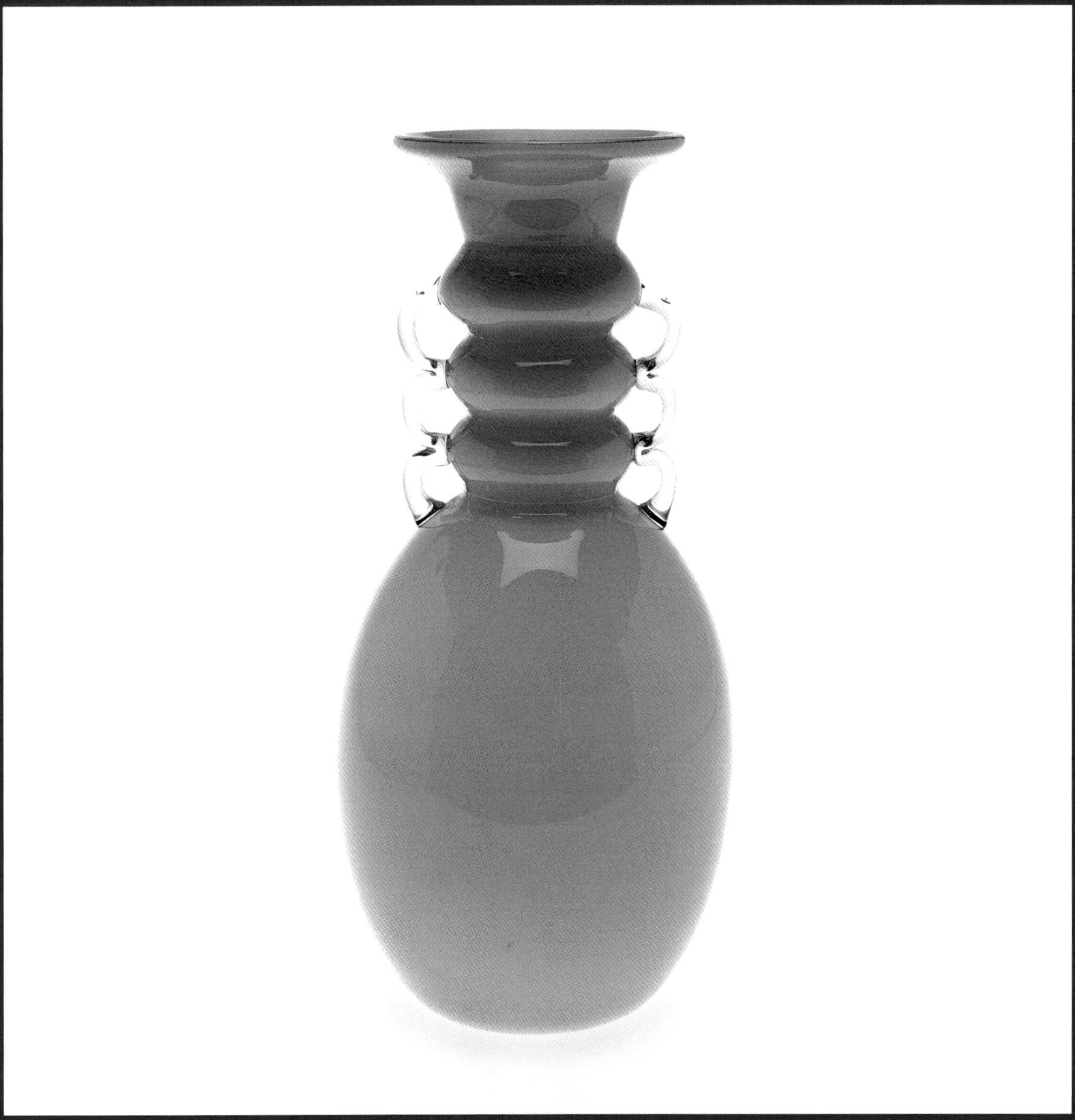

154. **Trasparente**
Vittorio Zecchin
Cappellin Venini & Co.

ca. 1924

Left: vessel from the *trasparenti* series in transparent amethyst glass with ribbed body and neck decorated with two rings. The model corresponds to No.1592 b of the Cappellin Venini Catalog, presented with the same number in the Venini Blue Catalog.

h 9.5" - 24 cm

Bibliography:
Venini Diaz de Santillana 2000, No. 14;
Murano 2001, No. 14;
Barovier, Mondi, Sonego 2002, No. 205.

Model No. 1592b, Venini Blue Catalog.

155. **Incamiciato**
Vittorio Zecchin
executed by V.S.M. Venini & Co.

ca. 1930

Top: vase in blue cased glass with three indentations on the neck decorated with small side handles in *cristallo*. The model corresponds to No.1766 of the Cappellin Venini Catalog, re-presented with the same number in the Venini Blue Catalog, in the *trasparenti* series, here executed in cased glass.
Acid-stamped: "venini murano".

h 10" - 25 cm

Bibliography: Barovier, Barovier Mentasti, Dorigato 1995, No.16; *Il vetro italiano* 1998, No. 30; Barovier 1999, p. 113; Barovier, Mondi, Sonego 2002, Nos. 165-166.

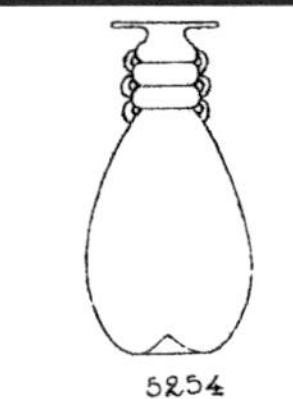

Model No. 5254, Venini Blue Catalog.

156. **Trasparente**
Napoleone Martinuzzi
V.S.M. Venini & Co.

ca. 1927-29

Sphere shaped vase from the *trasparenti* series in light green transparent glass with side handles, ring-shaped foot and neck trim in transparent green glass.

h 10.5" - 27 cm

Bibliography:
The Studio - Year Book of Decorative Art 1927, p. 142;
"Domus", January 1929;
Neuwirth 1987, No. 107.

V.S.M. Venini & Co. advertisement in "Domus", January 1929.

157. **Pulegoso**
Napoleone Martinuzzi
V.S.M. Venini & Co.

1930

Vase from the *pulegosi* series in blue glass with ribbed side handles and a ring-shaped foot finished with gold leaf applications. The series of *pulegoso* glass pieces was presented for the first time at the IV Triennale di Monza in 1930 and was produced primarily in green, blue and white. It was distinguished by its heavy archaic forms in keeping with the decorative model of the period.

h 13" - 33 cm

Bibliography:
Deboni 1989, No. 8;
Barovier 1992, No. 27;
Gli artisti di Venini 1996, Nos. 21-25;
Barovier 1999, p. 159;
Venini Diaz de Santillana 2000, Nos. 33-34;
Venetian Glass 2000, Nos. 13-14;
Murano 2001, Nos. 20-21.

158. **Incamiciato**
Napoleone Martinuzzi
V.S.M. Venini & Co.

ca. 1932

Vase in blue cased glass decorated with applications in gold leaf and serpentine handles in *cristallo*.
The model corresponds to No. 3256 of the Venini Blue Catalog, from the *pulegosi* series, made in this case in cased glass.

h 8" - 20 cm

Bibliography:
Barovier 1992, No. 18;
Deboni 1989, No. 26.

Cover page of "Domus", August 1930.

159. **Incamiciato**
Napoleone Martinuzzi
V.S.M. Venini & Co.

ca. 1931

Ribbed vase in yellow cased glass with large drops in transparent yellow glass applied at the base. This is a personal interpretation by Martinuzzi of a model designed by Vittorio Zecchin.
Acid-stamped: "venini murano MADE IN ITALY".

h 11" - 28 cm

Bibliography:
"Domus", August 1930;
Mille anni 1982, No. 541;
Barovier 1992, Nos. 62-63;
Venetian Glass 2000, No. 15;
Murano 2001, No. 28.

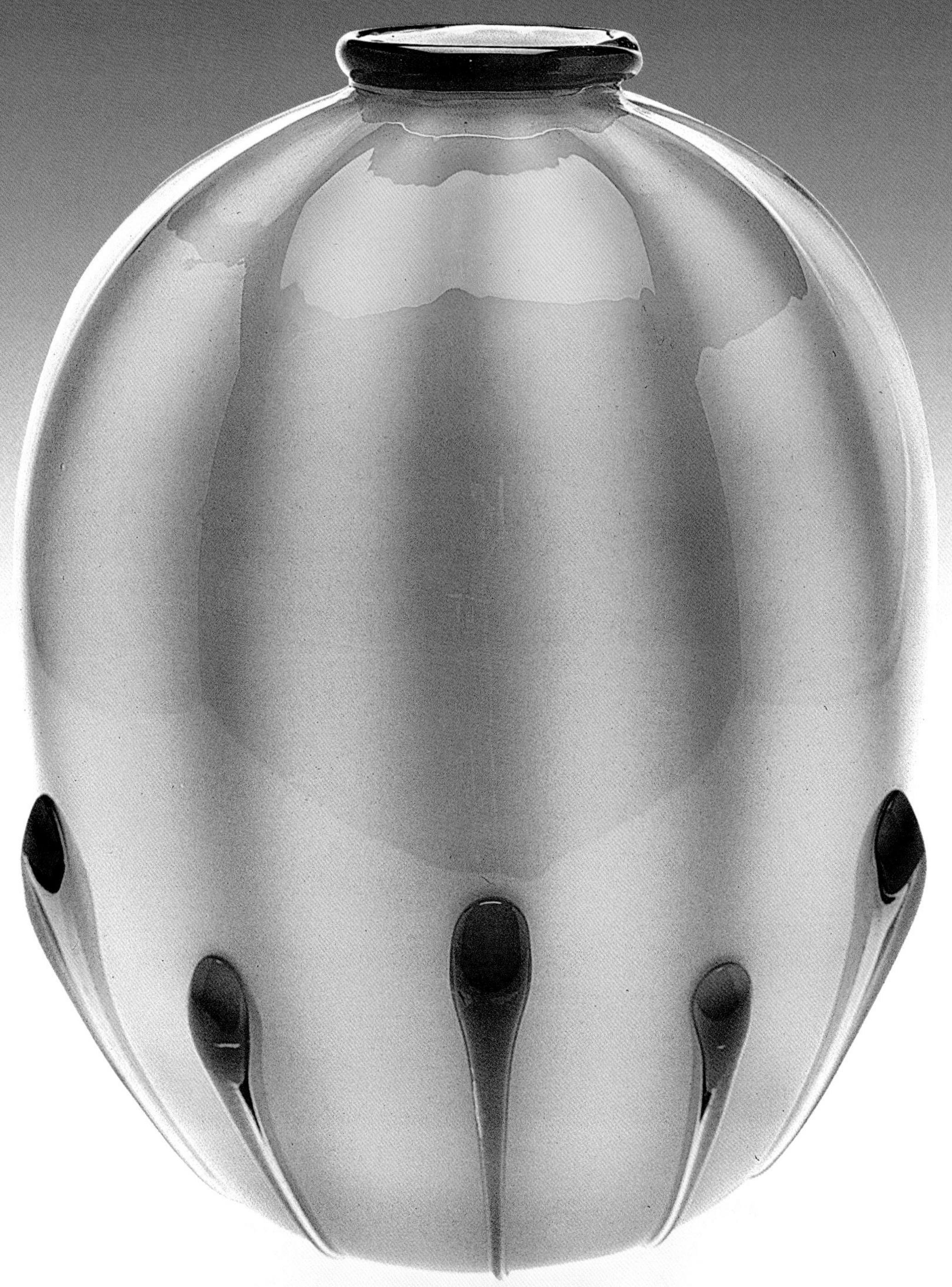

160. **Laguna**
Tomaso Buzzi
Venini & Co.

1932-33

Vase from the *laguna* series in cased glass with several layers of colored glass, finished with gold-leaf applications. Small side handles in the shape of snails are in *cristallo* with gold-leaf. The model corresponds to No. 3440 of the Venini Blue Catalog. It is part of a small series of glass pieces charmingly decorated with animals or applied ribbons, presented at the V Triennale di Milano in 1933. Acid-stamped: "venini murano".

h 6" - 15 cm

Exhibitions: 1933, Milano, V Triennale.
Bibliography: "Domus", December 1932, p. 761; "Domus", February 1933, pp. 82-83; *L'arte del vetro* 1992, No. 330; *Gli artisti di Venini* 1996, Nos. 52, 57; *Venetian Glass* 2000, No. 36; *Murano* 2001, Nos. 58-59, 63; Venini Diaz de Santillana 2000, Nos. 70-72.

Model No. 3440, Venini Blue Catalog.

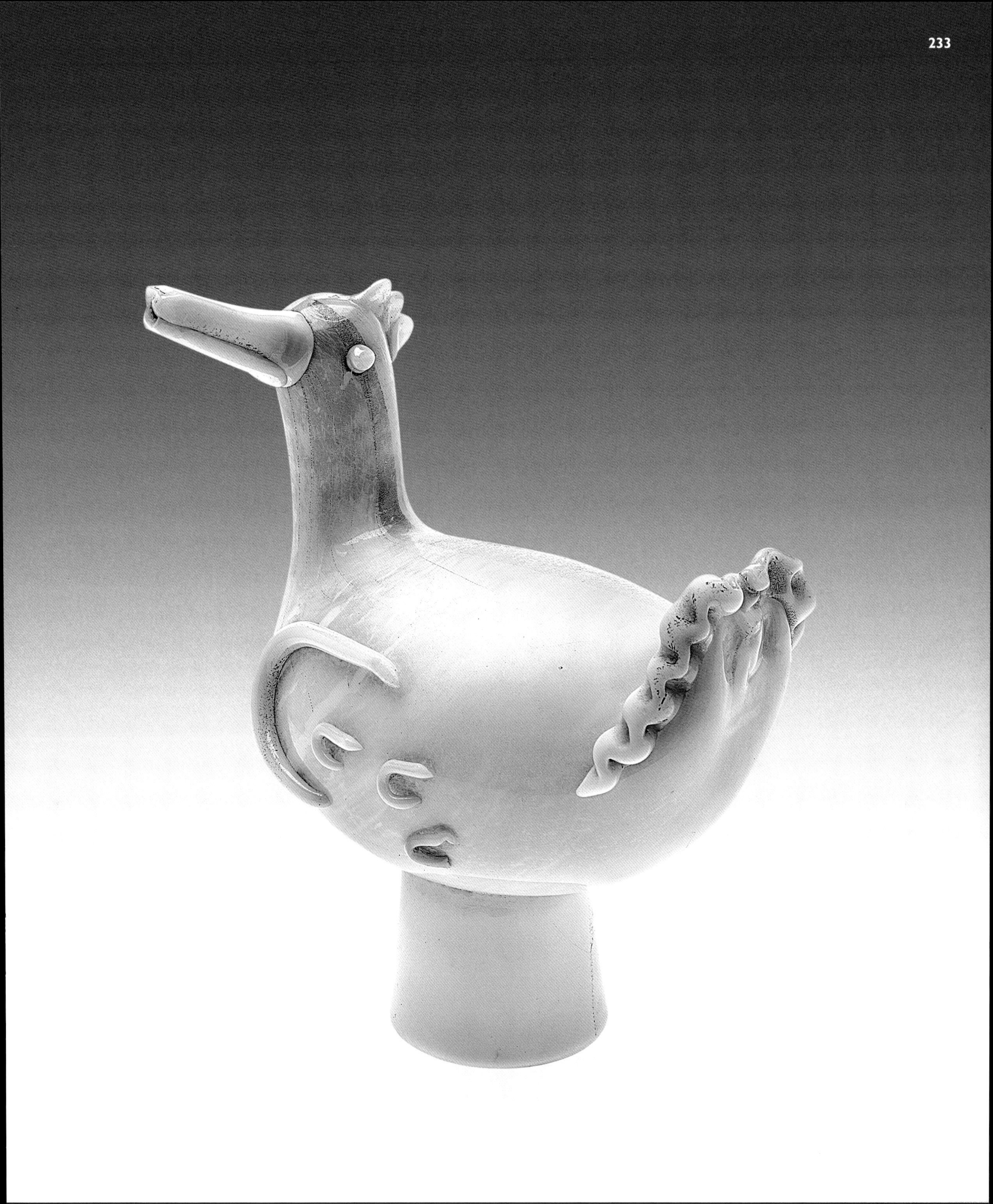

161. **Papera**
Tomaso Buzzi
Venini & Co.

1933

Duck in *lattimo* glass with applications of oxidized silver leaf.

The model corresponds to No. 2581 of the Venini Blue Catalog.
Acid-stamped: "venini murano".

h 7.75" - 19 cm

Bibliography:
"Domus", July 1933, p. 379;
Romanelli, Dorigato 1982, No. 127;
Deboni 1989, No. 49;
Cocchi 1991, No. 19;
Barovier, Dorigato 1996, No. 43;
Deboni 1996, No. 188;
Gli artisti di Venini 1996, Nos. 60-61;
Barovier 1999, p. 163;
Venini Diaz de Santillana 2000, No. 76.

Glass ducks in "Domus", July 1933.

162. **Corrosi**
Carlo Scarpa
Venini & Co.

1936

Vases from the series *corrosi a bugne* in *corroso* glass respectively in *cristallo*, green *fumé* and amethyst glass, decorated with *bugne* applied while hot and lightly iridized on the surface. The models correspond to numbers 4100, 4116, and 4101 of the Venini Blue Catalog. The series of *corrosi* glass was decorated by Scarpa not only with applied *bugne*, but also with stripes, raised patterns or irregular bases, of which a wide variety was exhibited at the XX Biennale d'Arte di Venezia and at the VI Triennale di Milano in 1936.
Acid-stamped: "venini murano MADE IN ITALY".

h 11.75" - 29 cm; h 7.5" - 19 cm; h 13 - 33 cm; h 11.5" - 30 cm; 7.5" - 19 cm

Exhibitions:
1936, Venezia, XX Biennale Internazionale d'Arte; Milano, VI Triennale.

Bibliography:
"Domus", July 1936;
"Domus", December 1936, p. 37;
"Domus", December 1938, p. 33;
Deboni 1989, No. 50;
The Venetians 1989, No. 6;
Barovier 1991, pp. 71-81;
Heiremans 1993, No. 204;
Deboni 1996, No. 26;
Barovier 1997, p. 211;
Gli artisti di Venini 1996, No. 84;
Ricke, Schmitt 1996, No. 29;
Venini Diaz de Santillana 2000, No. 96;
Murano 2001, No. 78;
Dorigato 2002, p. 285;
Formdesign-Farbdesign 2002, No. 16.

Corrosi *vases in "Domus", July 1936.*

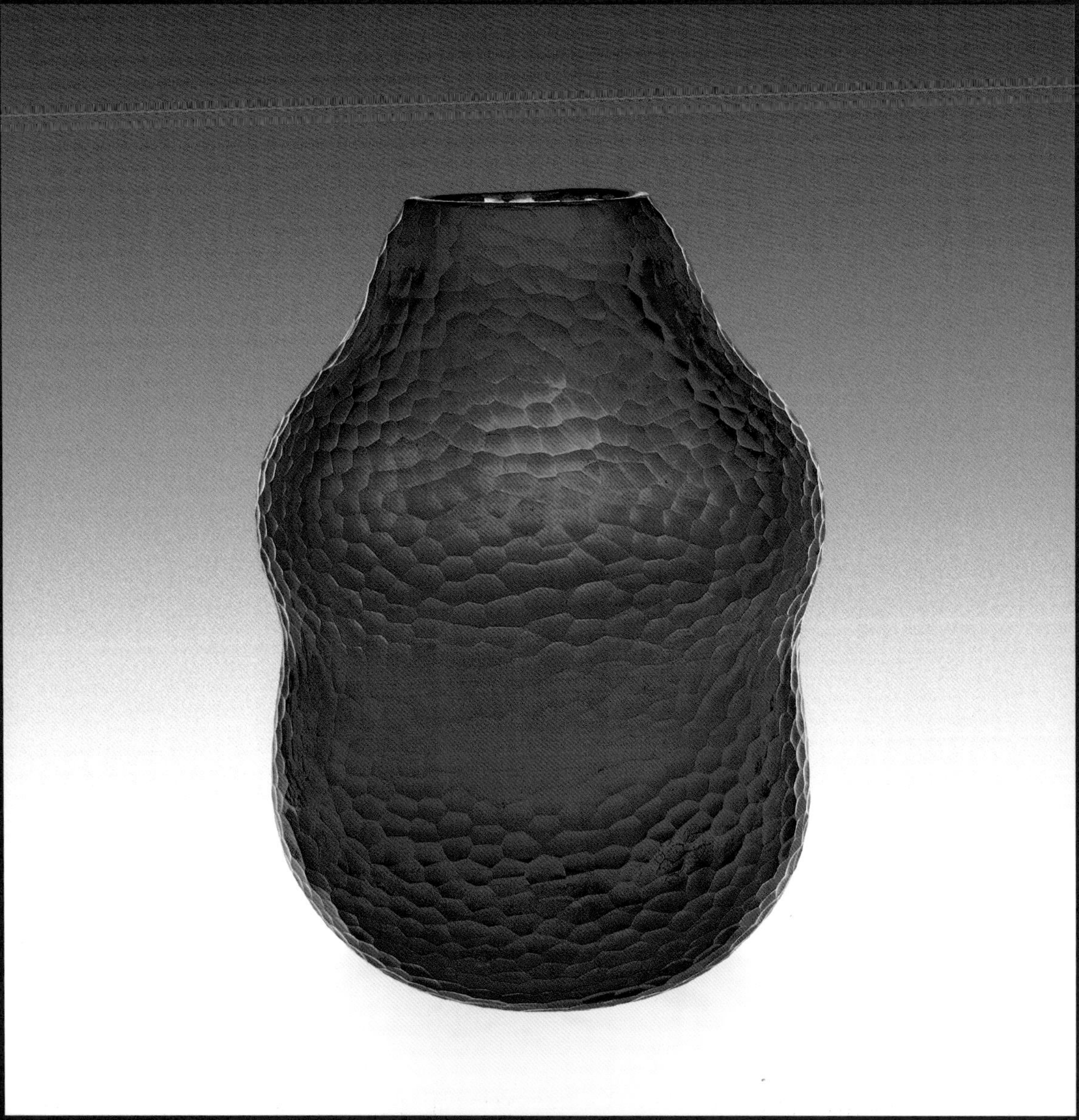

163. **Battuti**
Carlo Scarpa
Venini & Co.

1940

Top: vase from the *battuti* series in transparent red glass finished with deep irregular engraving over the entire surface.
Acid-stamped: "venini murano".

Right: bottle and bowl from the *battuti* series, respectively in amber glass and transparent grey glass, both finished with dense incisions over the entire surface. The model of the bottle corresponds to No. 3643 of the *soffiati* series, whereas the model of the bowl corresponds to No. 4118 of the *corrosi* series from the Venini Blue Catalog, in this case made in glass finished with carving at the wheel.

Bowl: acid-stamped: "venini murano MADE IN ITALY".

h 9.5" - 24 cm; h 11.75" - 29 cm; w 15.25" - 38 cm

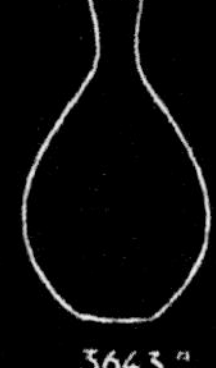

Bibliography:
Ponti 1940, p. 70;
Aloi 1945, Nos. 10, 13;
Deboni 1989, Nos. 58-63;
Barovier 1991, No. 29-32;
Barovier Mentasti 1992, No. 69;
L'arte del vetro 1992, No. 355;
Barovier, Barovier Mentasti, Dorigato 1995, No. 54;
Deboni 1996, No. 193;
Gli artisti di Venini 1996, Nos. 98-104;
Ricke, Schmitt 1996, Nos. 42-43;
Barovier 1997, p. 219;
I Barovier 1998, p. 27;
Barovier 1999, p. 187;
Venetian Glass 2000, Nos. 62, 64;
Murano 2001, Nos. 95-97, 99;
Formdesign-Farbdesign 2002, Nos. 44-46;
Heiremans 2002,Nos. 105-106.

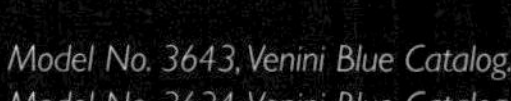
Model No. 3643, Venini Blue Catalog.
Model No. 3634, Venini Blue Catalog.

164. **Pesce**
Tyra Lundgren
Venini & Co.

1938

Fish in amethyst glass with *decoro fenicio* in *lattimo* glass, *sommerso* in *cristallo*. Trim in *cristallo*. The model corresponds to No. 2679 of the Venini Blue Catalog. In 1938 Tyra Lundgren created an interesting and diversified series of glass animals for Venini, with different vitreous patterns of which this piece constitutes a significant example.

h 4" - 10 cm, w 11" - 28 cm

Bibliography:
Barovier, Dorigato 1996, No. 60;
Formdesign-Farbdesign 2002, No. 11;
Heiremans 2002, No. 96.

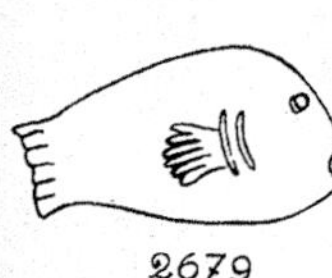

Model No. 2679, Venini Blue Catalog.

165. **Donna in crinoline**
Gio Ponti
Venini & Co.

1948

Donna in crinoline bottle in *cristallo*, transparent red, blue and red glass fit together *ad incalmo* with trim in *cristallo* and gold leaf. The model corresponds to No. 3878 of the Venini Blue Catalog.

h 11" - 28 cm

Bibliography:
"Domus", November-December 1950;
Ponti 1959, p. 40;
Neuwirth 1987, No. 218;
Heiremans 1993, No. 209;
Gli artisti di Venini 1996, No. 129;
Il vetro italiano 1998, p. 105;
Barovier 1999, p. 223;
Venini Diaz de Santillana 2000, No. 58;
Dorigato 2002, p. 304.

Donna in crinoline *vase in "Domus", November-December 1950.*

166. **A spicchi**
Fulvio Bianconi
Venini & Co.

1949-50

Large bottle from the *a spicchi* series in transparent *cristallo* with vertical stripes in amethyst, light blue, and blue. The model corresponds to No. 4891 of the Venini Catalog.
Acid-stamped signature: "venini murano ITALIA".

h 14.75" - 37 cm

Bibliography: Aloi 1955, p. 19; Ponti 1959, p. 42; Neuwirth 1987, No. 182; Deboni 1989, No. 113; Bossaglia 1993, Nos. 30-32; Barovier 1994, No. 23; *Gli artisti di Venini* 1996, No. 148; Heiremans 1996, No. 133; Venini Diaz de Santillana 2000, No. 162; *Murano* 2001, No. 120; *Formdesign-Farbdesign* 2002, Nos. 9 b, 78-81 b.

167. **Pezzati**
Fulvio Bianconi
Venini & Co.

1950-51

Vase from the *pezzati* series in glass with polychrome tesserae. The *pezzati* series was presented for the first time at the 1951 Triennale where it was highly acclaimed, and continued to be successful in the following years, remaining in production through 1969.
The model of the first vase on the right corresponds to No. 4397 from the Venini Catalog.

h 7.25" - 18 cm; h 9.25" - 23 cm

Exhibitions:
1951, Milano, IX Triennale.

Bibliography: Vetri 1952, pp. 84-85; Aloi 1955, p. 20; Ponti 1959, p. 42; Neuwirth 1987, No. 35; *La verrerie* 1988, p. 93; Deboni 1989, Nos. 107, 110, 112; Barovier Mentasti 1992, No. 103; Bossaglia 1993, Nos. 24-26, 53-54; Heiremans 1993, No. 217; Barovier 1994, Nos. 20-22; Barovier, Barovier Mentasti, Dorigato 1995, No. 104; Deboni 1996, Nos. 214-215; Ricke, Schmitt 1996, Nos. 77-80; *Gli artisti di Venini* 1996, Nos. 145-147; Heiremans 1996, Nos. 106-109; Venini Diaz de Santillana 2000, Nos. 117-119; *Venetian Glass* 2000, Nos. 86, 87; Murano 2001, Nos. 122-124; Dorigato 2002, p. 311; *Formdesign-Farbdesign* 2002, Nos. 15 a, b, 64-72; Heiremans 2002, No. 33.

168. **A fasce**
Fulvio Bianconi
Venini & Co.

1950

Vase from the *a fasce* series in transparent green glass with horizontal stripes in red glass. The model corresponds to No. 4399 of the Venini Catalog.

h 11.5" - 29 cm

Exhibitions: 1950, Venezia, XXV Biennale Internazionale d'Arte; 1954, Milano, X Triennale.

Bibliography: Aloi 1955, p. 13; Ponti 1959, p. 42; Neuwirth 1987, No. 216; Deboni 1989, No. 125; *The Venetians* 1989, No. 20; Bossaglia 1993, No. 67; Heiremans 1993, No. 221; Barovier, Barovier Mentasti, Dorigato 1995, No. 64; Heiremans 1996, No. 95; Ricke, Schmitt 1996, No. 82; *Il vetro italiano* 1998, No. 130; *Venetian Glass* 2000, No. 93; *Murano* 2001, No. 128; *Formdesign-Farbdesign* 2002, No. 11.

Venini vases in "Domus", December 1959.

169. **A fasce orizzontali**
Fulvio Bianconi
Venini & Co.

1953

Vases from the *a fasce orrizontali* series in *cristallo* with horizontal stripes in the *America* color version (stripes of *pagliesco*, yellow, black and green). The series was also made in the *Parigi* version in red, green, sapphire and *pagliesco* glass. These models correspond to No. 532.2 and 532.1 of the Venini Catalog.

h 15.5" - 39 cm; h 11.5" - 29 cm

Bibliography:
Deboni 1989, No. 117;
Cocchi 1991, No. 45;
Bossaglia 1993, Nos. 65-66;
Heiremans 1993, No. 235;
Gli artisti di Venini 1996, Nos. 156-157; Ricke, Schmitt 1996, No. 91; Venini Diaz de Santillana 2000, No. 120; *Murano* 2001, No. 127; Heiremans 2002, Nos. 122-123; Dorigato 2002, p. 310.

A fasce orizzontali *vases, Marino Barovier Archives.*

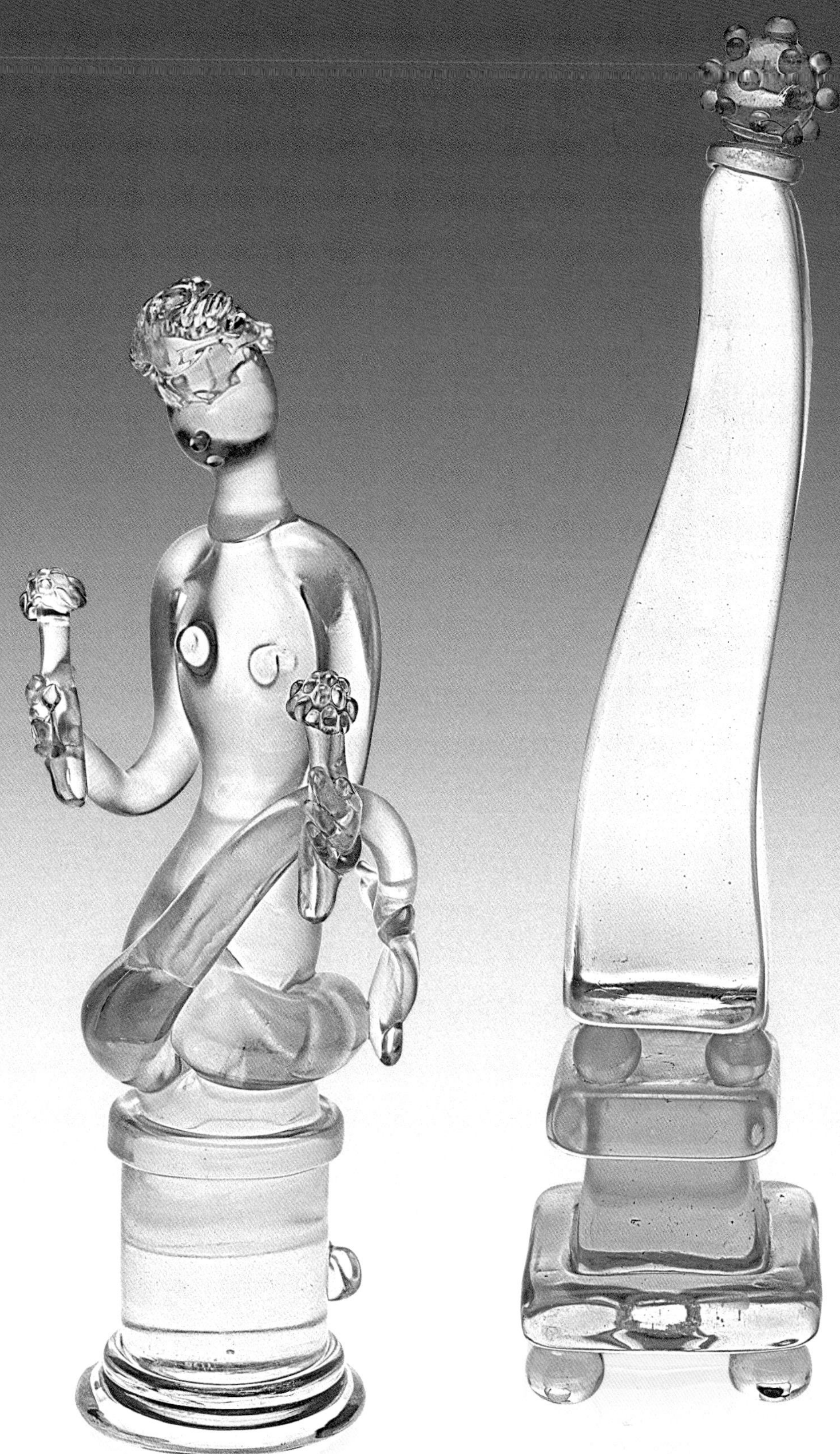

170. **Le rovine**
Eugene Berman
Venini & Co.

1951

Left: mermaid and obelisk on *cristallo* pedestal shaped while hot and lightly iridized over the entire surface. The two sculptures are part of a centerpiece entitled *Le rovine*, composed of twelve elements (five figures and seven obelisks) and inspired by ancient statues and architectural ruins.

h 10.7" - 27 cm; h 12.75" - 32 cm

Bibliography:
Deboni 1989, No. 130;
Heiremans 1993, No. 222;
Deboni 1996, p. 74;
Gli artisti di Venini 1996, Nos. 164-166;
Ricke, Schmitt 1996, No. 109;
Venini Diaz de Santillana 2000, No. 182.

Elements from the Le rovine *centerpiece, Marino Barovier Archives.*

171. **Pozzo**
Eugene Berman
Venini & Co.

h 5.5" - 14 cm

172. **Mosaico zanfirico**
Paolo Venini
Venini & Co.

1954

Vase from the *mosaico zanfirico* series in transparent blue glass with horizontal and vertical segments of *lattimo zanfirico* glass rods.

h 9.75" - 24 cm

Exhibitions:
1954, Milano, X Triennale.

Bibliography:
Ponti 1959;
"Domus", April 1955;
Neuwirth 1987, No. 69;
Deboni 1989, Nos. 126-128;
The Venetians 1989, No. 34;
L'arte del vetro 1992, No. 360;
Barovier 1994, No. 17;
Barovier, Barovier Mentasti, Dorigato 1995, p. 85;
Deboni 1996, p. 74, No. 221;
Heiremans 1996, No. 152;
Ricke, Schmitt 1996, Nos. 116-118, 120;
Il vetro italiano 1998, No. 129;
Barovier 1999, p. 231;
Venini Diaz de Santillana 2000, Nos. 84-85;
Venetian Glass 2000, No. 98;
Murano 2001, No. 135.

173. **Murrine mezzaluna**
Paolo Venini
Venini & Co.

1954

Glass vase in amethyst *murrine* with a *lattimo* half-moon design in the nucleus.

h 12" - 30 cm

Bibliography:
Aloi 1955, p. 18;
Mariacher 1967, p. 170;
Deboni 1989, Nos. 150-151;
Barovier Mentasti 1992, No. 106;
Heiremans 1993, No. 231;
Barovier 1994, No. 19;
Barovier, Barovier Mentasti, Dorigato 1995, No. 116;
Deboni 1996, p. 74, No. 220;
Gli artisti di Venini 1996, No. 178;
Ricke, Schmitt 1996, Nos. 144-145;
Il vetro italiano 1998, No. 126;
Barovier 1999, p. 231;
Venini Diaz de Santillana 2000, p. 44, No. 53.

174. **Occhi**
Tobia Scarpa
Venini & Co.

1962

Vase from the *occhi* series with *murrine* in transparent amber glass and nucleus in *cristallo* alternated with *murrine* in *lattimo pasta vitrea* and nucleus in *cristallo*.

h 5" - 13 cm

Exhibitions: 1960, Milano, XII Triennale; 1962, Venezia, XXXI Biennale Internazionale d'Arte.

Bibliography: Neuwirth 1987, No. 171; Deboni 1989, Nos. 164-166; *The Venetians* 1989, No. 18; Barovier Mentasti 1992, No. 102; *L'arte del vetro* 1992, No. 363; Heiremans 1993, No. 240; Barovier 1994, No. 43; Barovier, Barovier Mentasti, Dorigato 1995, p. 97, No. 147; *Gli artisti di Venini* 1996, Nos. 219-221; Barovier 1999, p. 261; Venini Diaz de Santillana 2000, No. 186; *Venetian Glass* 2000, No. 137; *Murano* 2001, No. 172; Heiremans 2002, Nos. 21-23.

Occhi vases in Venini advertising pamphlet.

175. **A tessere**
James Carpenter
Venini & Co.

1979

Glass vases with *lattimo* and amethyst rectangular tesserae composed in vertical and horizontal pairs, in a checkerboard pattern. Signature engraved: "Benjamin Moore Venini".

h 11" - 28 cm; h 10" - 25 cm

176. **Tessuto**
James Carpenter
Venini & Co.

ca. 1979

Left: vase in glass with a pattern of fine vertical rods in orange and black glass and in *lattimo* and black glass.

h 15.25" - 38 cm

177. **Tessuto ad incalmo**
Benjamin Moore
Venini & Co.

ca. 1979

Right: vase *ad incalmo* in green glass and with a glass texture composed of fine polychrome rods in a spiral pattern.
h 10.75" - 27 cm

Bibliography: Gli artisti di Venini 1996, No. 249; Barovier 1999, p. 289; *Venetian Glass* 2000, No. 147; *Murano* 2001, No. 185; Dorigato 2002, p.349.

Zecchin-Martinuzzi Vetri Artistici e Mosaici

Salviati & Co.

Vetreria e Soffieria Barovier Seguso & Ferro Seguso Vetri d'Arte

Zecchin-Martinuzzi Vetri Artistici e Mosaici

In 1932, Paolo Venini's two partners from Murano, the engineer Francesco Zecchin and the sculptor and designer Napoleone Martinuzzi, left the company to found Zecchin-Martinuzzi. The production, directed by Napoleone Martinuzzi and inspired by the plastic qualities of the *Novecento* style, was distinguished by the use of transparent glass and *pulegoso* glass, but was renowned for its large vases in opaque glass, its animals, cacti, and female nudes in solid glass. Some of the animals were designed by Mario Romano, and several vases by Giovanni Guerrini.
Napoleone Martinuzzi left the company in 1936, and it was definitively closed by Francesco Zecchin two years later.

Salviati & Co.

After a series of vicissitudes following the death of Antonio Salviati in 1890, in 1920 Maurizio Camerino became sole proprietor of the Salviati stores, which sold Murano glass products and Venetian crafts. After 1921, the company was supplied prevalently by the glassworks Successori Andrea Rioda, founded that same year by Camerino. In the Thirties, he began a collaboration with the native Murano painter Dino Martens, who presented unusual glass pieces at the 1932 Biennale di Venezia. For the 1936 edition of the Biennale, Salviati presented objects featuring brightly colored geometric designs, created with the mosaic technique and designed by painter Mario Deluigi, under the pseudonym of Guido Bin. In 1955, painter Luciano Gaspari became the artistic director of the company which finally opened its own furnace in 1959: until that date, in fact, its production had been entrusted to other furnaces. Sergio Asti, Claire Falkenstein, Teff and Betha Sarazin, and Heinz Oestergard have collaborated with the company. In 1987 Salviati & Co. was sold to the Ferruzzi Group and was subsequently acquired by a French company still involved in its management.

Vetreria e Soffieria Barovier Seguso & Ferro Seguso Vetri d'Arte

In 1933, several masters who had left the Vetreria Artistica Barovier, along with Archimede, Ernesto and Alberto Seguso, founded the Vetreria e Soffieria Barovier Seguso & Ferro. The artistic direction was briefly held by the native Murano painter Vittorio Zecchin, who was soon replaced by Flavio Poli in 1934. When the company was reorganized into Seguso Vetri d'Arte in 1937, Poli also became a partner. Poli worked with master Archimede Seguso, and was responsible for the thick glass animals and sculptures which were so successful in the Biennale exhibitions of that period. Following another company reorganization between 1950 and 1960, the glassworks presented a remarkable series of *sommerso* glass pieces, as well as the *valve*, and the unusual *siderali*, designed by Flavio Poli, who would remain with the company through 1963. When he retired, the position of artistic director was filled by Mario Pinzoni, who remained stylistically faithful to his predecessor. Since the Seventies, the company has been directed by Maurizio Albarelli.

178. **Pasta vitrea**
Napoleone Martinuzzi
Zecchin-Martinuzzi Vetri Artistici e Mosaici

1933

Sphere-shaped vase in green *pasta vitrea* with funnel-shaped neck and applied foot. The model corresponds to No. 2381 of the Zecchin-Martinuzzi Catalog.

h 13.75" - 35 cm

Bibliography:
Barovier 1992, No. 56;
L'arte del vetro 1992, No. 328;
Heiremans 1993, No. 259;
Barovier 1999, p. 173;
Venetian Glass 2000, No. 147;
Murano 2001, No. 23.

Model No. 2381, Zecchin-Martinuzzi Catalog.

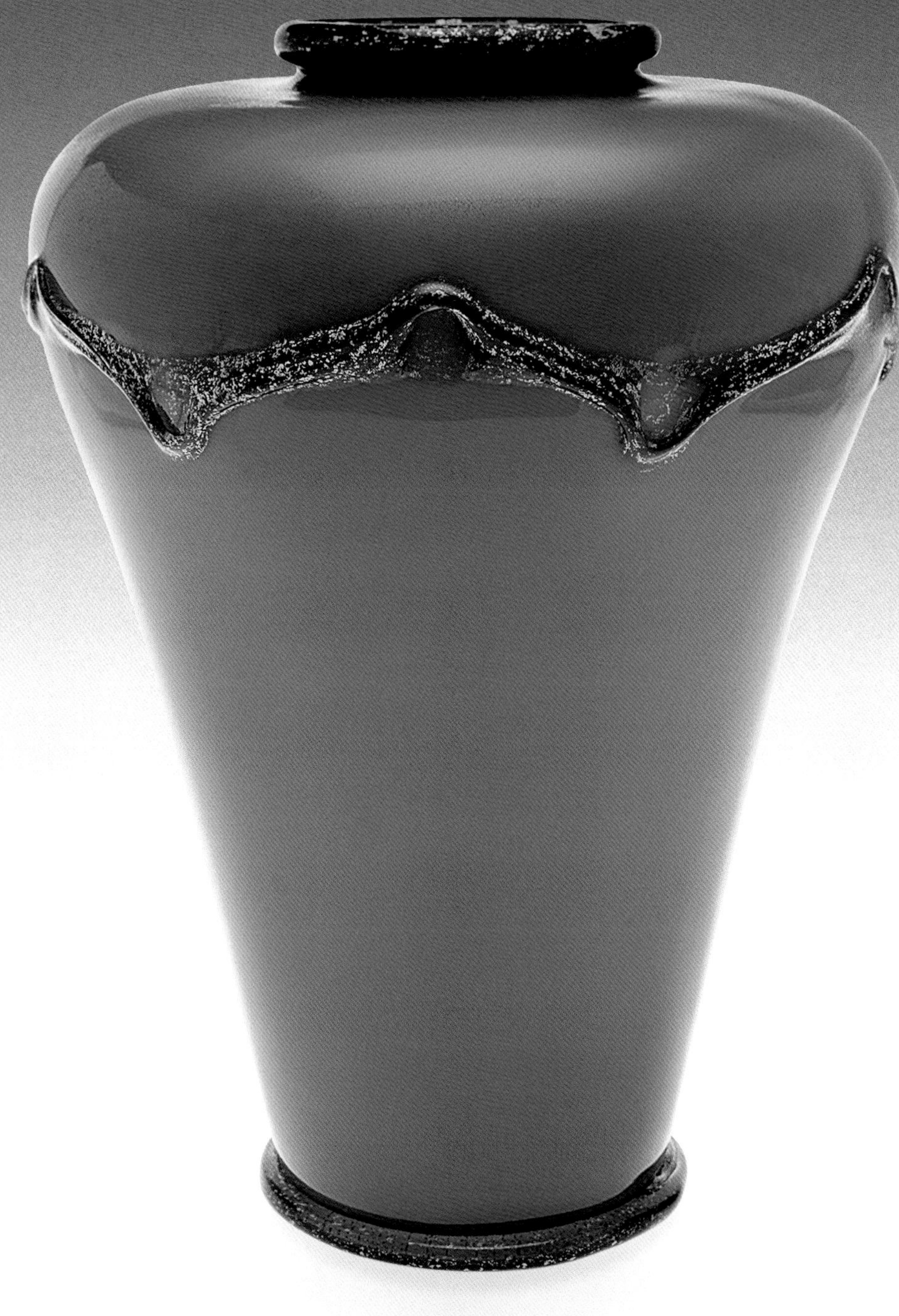

179. **Incamiciato**
Napoleone Martinuzzi
Zecchin-Martinuzzi Vetri Artistici e Mosaici

1933

foot, mouth and festoon applied on the transparent turquoise glass body with gold-leaf inclusions.

h 12" - 30 cm

Bibliography:
Barovier 1992, No. 57;
Murano 2001, No. 28.

180. **Incamiciato**
Napoleone Martinuzzi
Zecchin-Martinuzzi Vetri Artistici e Mosaici

ca. 1933

Vase from the *incamiciati* series in *lattimo* glass cased in transparent green glass with ring-shaped foot and long ribbon handles tooled at the upper edges.

h 8.5" - 22 cm

Bibliography:
Barovier 1992, No. 59.

181. **Incamiciato**
Napoleone Martinuzzi
Zecchin-Martinuzzi Vetri Artistici e Mosaici

1933

Lightly ribbed vessel from the *incamiciati* series in *lattimo* glass cased in blue glass with ring-shaped foot and long side handles tooled into waves in transparent blue glass.

h 12.5" - 32 cm

Bibliography: Barovier 1992, No. 50.

182. **Incamiciati**
Napoleone Martinuzzi
Zecchin-Martinuzzi Vetri Artistici e Mosaici

ca. 1933

Vases with slight ribbing from the *incamiciati* series, respectively in *lattimo* glass cased in transparent blue glass and in *lattimo* glass cased in transparent red glass. Both vessels have a ring-shaped foot and serpentine side handles.

h 12.5" - 32 cm; h 9" - 23 cm

Bibliography:
Barovier 1992, No. 50;
L'arte del vetro 1992, No. 329;
Heiremans 1996, No. 37;
Dorigato 2002, p. 279.

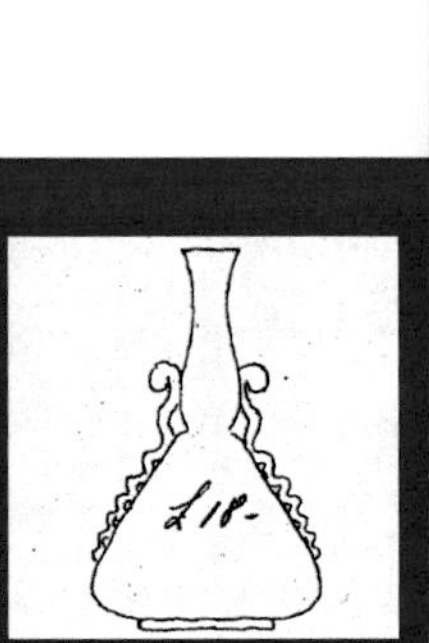

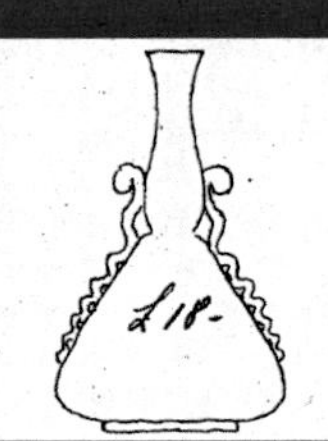

Model No. 2403, Zecchin-Martinuzzi Catalog.

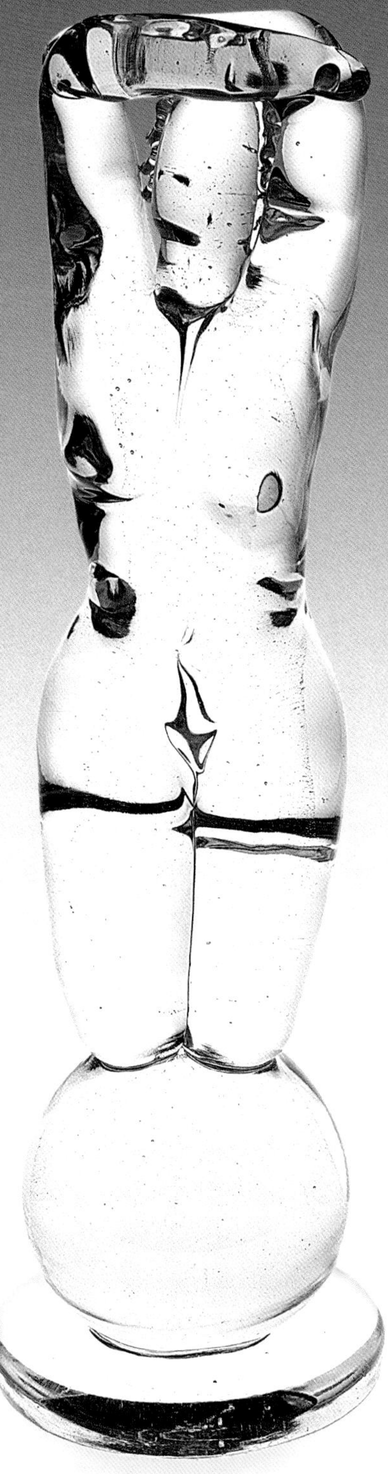

183. **Nudo**
Napoleone Martinuzzi
Zecchin-Martinuzzi Vetri Artistici e Mosaici

ca. 1933

Female nude on a sphere in *cristallo* shaped while hot.

h 14" - 36 cm

Bibliography:
"Domus", May 1933, pp. 236-237;
Barovier 1992, Nos. 111, 116;
Il vetro italiano 1998, Nos. 61, 65.

185. **Vaso**
Salviati & Co.

ca. 1932

Vase in *lattimo* glass cased in *fumé* glass with a characteristic rough surface called *ghiaccio* (ice), with small side handles and trim in black *pasta vitrea*.

h 16" - 41 cm

Bibliography:
"Domus", January 1932, plate XI.

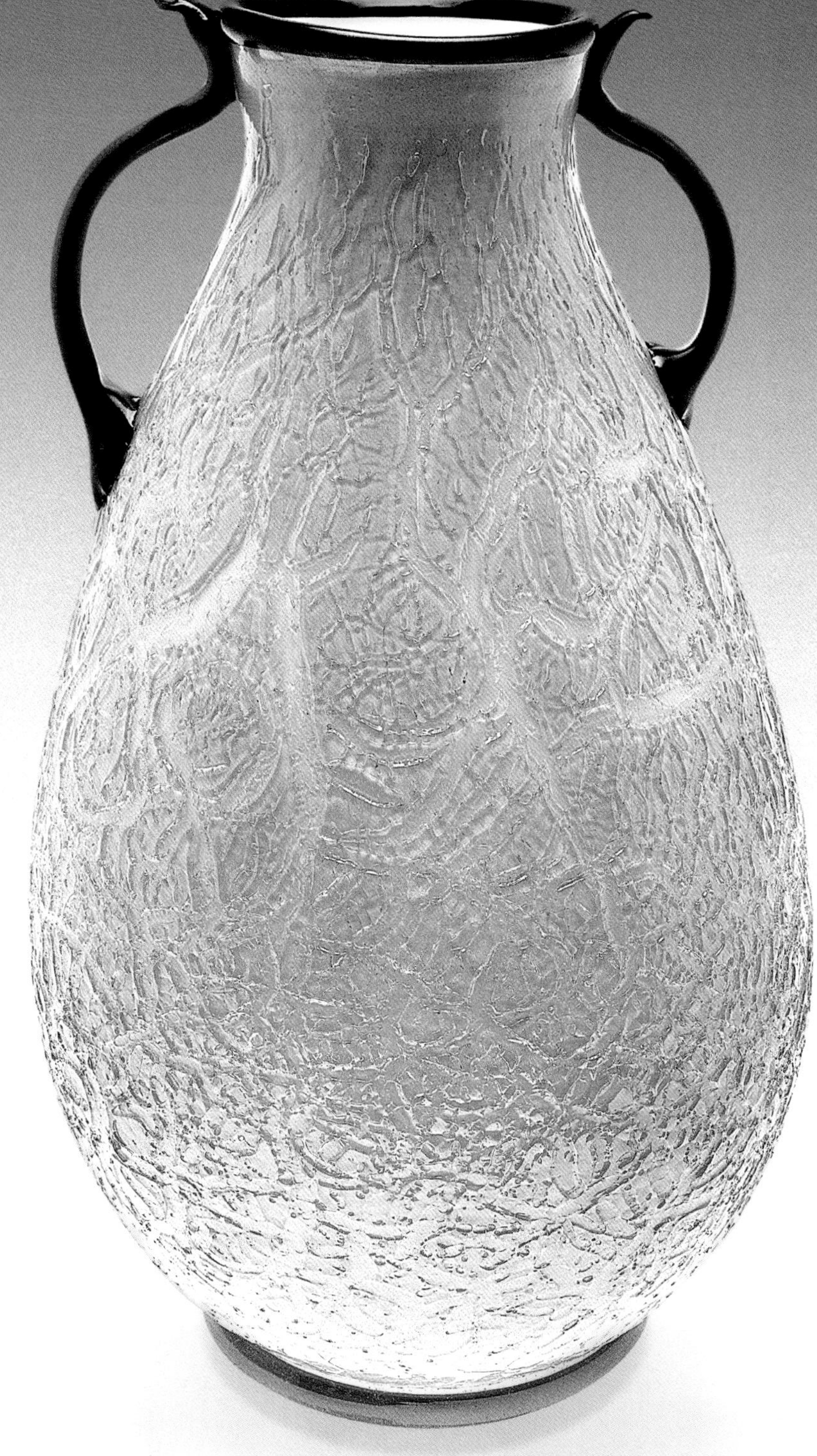

Salviati advertisement in "Domus", January 1932.

186. **Incamiciati**
Flavio Poli
Vetreria & Soffieria Barovier Seguso & Ferro

1934-36

Left: vase in grey cased glass decorated with threads in *cristallo* applied in a wavy pattern and on the neck by rings of *cristallo*. The surface is finished with gold leaf applications.
Right: vases in red cased glass with ring-shaped foot and serpentine side handles and *rostri* in *cristallo*, finished with gold leaf applications on the surface.
These vases were designed by Flavio Poli and inspired by the works of Napoleone Martinuzzi. Executed by Alfredo Barbini.

h 16" - 41 cm; h 17" - 43 cm; h 10" - 25 cm

Exhibitions:
1936, Milano, VI Triennale.

Bibliography:
Heiremans 1993, No. 132;
Il vetro italiano 1998, No. 70;
Dorigato 2002, p. 295.

Incamiciato *vase, 1934-36, Marino Barovier Archives.*

187. **Sommerso Bulicante**
Flavio Poli
Seguso Vetri d'Arte

1937

Bowl in green *sommerso* glass with bubbles and inclusion of gold leaf.

h 5" - 13 cm

Bibliography:
"Domus", November 1937, p. 51;
Franzoi 1991, Nos. 4, 7;
Barovier Mentasti 1992, No. 75;
L'arte del vetro 1992, No. 349.

188. **Con applicazioni**
Seguso Vetri d'Arte

ca. 1938

Vessel in transparent *fumé* glass with applications in gold leaf, with horizontal relief decoration and applied seashells.

h 8.5" - 22 cm

Bibliography:
Barovier Mentasti 1982, No. 281.

189. **A costolature orizzontali**
Flavio Poli
Seguso Vetri d'Arte

1937-40

Vessel in red cased glass decorated with horizontal ribbing and finished with applications of silver leaf over the entire surface. Lip wrap in black *pasta vitrea*.
Engraved on the mouth: "Seguso Vetri d'Arte".

h 13" - 33 cm

190. **Mine**
Probably Flavio Poli for
Seguso Vetri d'Arte

ca. 1938

Sphere-shaped vases in very thick transparent *fumé* glass and transparent amethyst glass, decorated with *bugne* applied while hot and heavily iridized over the entire surface.

h 11.5" - 29 cm; h 10.75" - 27 cm;
h 10.75" - 27 cm

Vetreria Archimede Seguso

Vetreria artistica rag. Aureliano Toso

Vetreria Alfredo Barbini

Vetreria Archimede Seguso

After working at Seguso Vetri d'Arte through 1942, glass master Archimede Seguso founded his own glassworks in 1946, where he re-elaborated the ancient techniques of *filigrana* to produce the remarkable *merletti*, *fili* and *piume* vases. He was a designer, experimenting with new techniques and materials, and crafted all of his own pieces, participating in several editions of the Biennale di Venezia and the Triennale di Milano beginning in 1950. Developing the *filigrana* technique became an on-going commitment for Archimede Seguso, with which he alternated *opaline* glass pieces or heavy blown works characterized by strong contrasts of color (1958-1960). Archimede Seguso died in 1999. The glassworks is currently directed by his son Gino, assisted by his grandson Antonio.

Vetreria artistica rag. Aureliano Toso

Founded in 1938 by Aureliano Toso, the position of artistic director was held through 1965 by native Murano painter Dino Martens, who at the 1940 Biennale di Venezia presented several early examples of glass *a zanfirico*, a technique he would often use in his later production.
The creations by Dino Martens brought great success to the glassworks at the most important exhibitions of decorative arts. In 1966, the artistic direction of Aureliano Toso was entrusted to designer Gino Poli, who was responsible, for example, for the pieces from the *a solchi colorati* series, glass works decorated with hot applications of polychrome stripes. The company later moved towards the production of glass for lighting which it still produces today.

Vetreria Alfredo Barbini

Born in 1912, Alfredo Barbini became a glass master at a very young age after a brief apprenticeship at S.A.I.A.R. Ferro Toso and the Società Anonima Vetrerie e Cristallerie di Murano. His encounter with sculptor Napoleone Martinuzzi at the Zecchin Martinuzzi glassworks proved decisive for his artistic training, as he devoted himself to the exploration of the plastic qualities of solid glass, making his first *Novecento* style sculptures. He went to work for V.A.M.S.A. as the *maestro di prima piazza* and pursued his figurative explorations creating animal shapes and vases in *sommerso* glass with refined chromatic effects. In 1946 he became a partner and artistic director of Gino Cenedese & Co., a glassworks with which he participated in the 1948 Biennale di Venezia, presenting a series of glass sculptures whose surface was corroded with acid. In 1950 he opened his own glassworks, where he pursued his research in the field of sculptural glass art, which became increasingly essential in its lines and material. The works he produced include some designed by Napoleone Martinuzzi. In the Sixties, his son Flavio entered the company, working as a designer as well. He revived several traditional techniques and gave them new life by producing lightweight blown pieces in *cristallo* glass and in brightly colored glass, and inventing new *murrine*. An independent artist, he still collaborates in the life of the furnace.

191. **Vittoria alata**
Unkown factory

1933

Sculpture in *cristallo* on a square base, lightly iridized over the entire surface, representing the winged Victory.

h 12.5" - 32 cm

192. **Petali filigranati**
Archimede Seguso
Vetreria Archimede Seguso

1951

Vase from the *petali filigranati* series in *fumé* glass decorated at the base with seven petals obtained applying amethyst *filigrana* rods while hot.

h 10" - 25 cm

193. **A losanghe**
Archimede Seguso
Vetreria Archimede Seguso

1951-52

Left: vase from the a *losanghe* series in *lattimo* glass cased in *fumé* glass, with decoration in a geometric pattern. Applications of gold leaf over the entire surface.

h 10.25" - 24 cm

Exhibitions:
1951, Milano, IX Triennale.

Bibliography:
Franzoi 1991, Nos. 60-61;
Barovier Mentasti 1995, Nos. 13-15;
Barovier 1999, p. 207.

194. **Merletto frastagliato**
Archimede Seguso
Vetreria Archimede Seguso

1955

Top: vase from the *merletto frastagliato* series in amethyst glass, decorated with a fine texture of *lattimo* threads obtained by using hot *zanfirico* glass rods.

h 7.75" - 19 cm

Bibliography:
Heiremans 2002, No. 66.

195. **Merletto**
Archimede Seguso
Vetreria Archimede Seguso

1952

Left: irregularly shaped bowl from the *merletto* series in *cristallo* glass composed of a tight network of *lattimo* threads, with inlays of *cristallo* and amethyst glass edges. Signed: "Archimede Seguso 1952 Biennale".

h 3.5" - 9 cm, w 9" - 23 cm

Exhibitions: 1952, Venezia, XXVI Biennale Internazionale d'Arte.

Bibliography: Mariacher 1967, p. 138; Barovier Mentasti 1977, No. 41; *La verrerie* 1988, p. 119; Franzoi 1991, No. 23; Barovier, Barovier Mentasti, Dorigato 1995, No. 91; Deboni 1996, p. 57; Ricke, Schmitt 1996, No. 189; Heiremans 2002, No. 65.

196. **Merletto a pois**
Archimede Seguso
Vetreria Archimede Seguso

1954

Center: bowl from the *merletto a pois* series in *cristallo* glass composed of a tight network of *lattimo* threads, decorated with amethyst *murrine* and trimmed along the edge with an amethyst glass stripe.

h 3.5" - 9 cm, w 8.5" - 22 cm

Bibliography: Mariacher 1967, p. 138; Franzoi 1991, Nos. 21,48; Barovier 1994, No. 31; Barovier Mentasti 1995, No. 41; Heiremans 1996, No. 131; *Venetian Glass* 2000, No. 114; *Murano* 2001, No. 154.

197. **Merletto puntiforme**
Archimede Seguso
Vetreria Archimede Seguso

1954

Right: vases from the *merletto puntiforme* series in *cristallo* glass composed of a tight network of *lattimo* threads, decorated with regular spots of amethyst glass. The pattern of *lattimo* threads, indicated with the term merletto meaning lace, was created by Archimede Seguso working with hot *zanfirico* glass rods.

h 11.5" - 29 cm; h 11.5" - 29 cm

Bibliography: Franzoi 1991, Nos. 22, 86; Barovier Mentasti 1995, No. 39; Ricke, Schmitt 1996, No. 180; *Venetian Glass* 2000, No. 115; *Murano* 2001, No. 155.

198. **Vaso**
Dino Martens
Vetreria artistica rag. Aureliano Toso

ca. 1949

Vase in glass composed of polychrome frit, *avventurina* glass and *reticello* glass inserts. Foot in *cristallo*.

h 14.5" - 37 cm

Bibliography:
Heiremans 1999, No. 15.

199. **Vasi**
Dino Martens
Vetreria artistica rag. Aureliano Toso

1949

Irregularly shaped vases in *cristallo* with inclusions of polychrome frit and *avventurina* glass. Their characteristic shapes are derived from the unusual *zucca sinfonica* vase presented at the 1948 Biennale di Venezia.

h 11.5" - 29 cm; h 9" - 23 cm

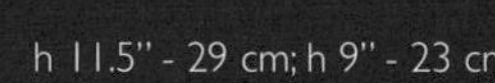

Bibliography:
Heiremans 1993, No. 154;
Heiremans 1999, No. 14.

Zucca sinfonica *vase at the XXIV Biennale Internazionale d'Arte, Venezia, 1948.*

200. **Mezza filigrana e a trina**
Dino Martens
Vetreria artistica rag. Aureliano Toso

1950-52

Top left: vase from the *mezza filigrana* series in *lattimo* and *cristallo filigrana*, and *lattimo* and amethyst *filigrana* composed in alternating stripes. The model corresponds to No. 2844 of the glassworks catalog. Top right: vase from the *a trina* series with polychrome *filigrana* composed in alternating stripes. The name of the series is given by the characteristic wavy pattern of the *filigrana* obtained by mold-shaped ribbing. These vessels are samples of the production from the Vetreria Aureliano Toso, specialized in the production of *mezza filigrana* glass.

h 13.75" - 35 cm; h 14" - 36 cm

Bibliography: mezza filigrana:
Aloi 1955, p. 32;
Heiremans 1999, pp. 160-161
Bibliography: a trina:
Heiremans 1993, Nos. 159-160;
Deboni 1996, No. 156;
Heiremans 1999, No. 69, p. 160.

201. **Zanfirico**
Dino Martens
Vetreria artistica rag. Aureliano Toso

1951

Right: vase from the *zanfirico* series in vertical glass *zanfirico* rods. The model corresponds to No. 2922 of the glassworks catalog. Martens collaborated in the creation of various *zanfirico* glass rods with unusual sections and bright colors, which he constantly used in his production.

h 10.5" - 27 cm

Bibliography:
Aloi 1952, No. 20;
Aloi 1955, p. 31;
Heiremans 1993, Nos. 156,166;
Barovier 1994, No. 26;
Barovier, Barovier Mentasti, Dorigato 1995, No. 97;
Deboni 1996, p. 63, No. 150;
Heiremans 1996, No. 103;
Heiremans 1999, Nos. 27-29;
Venetian Glass 2000, No. 109;
Murano 2001, No. 146.

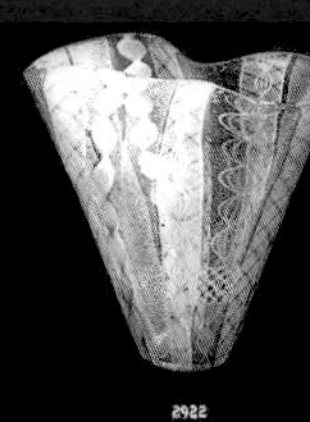

Zanfirico *vase, ca. 1951, Marino Barovier Archives.*

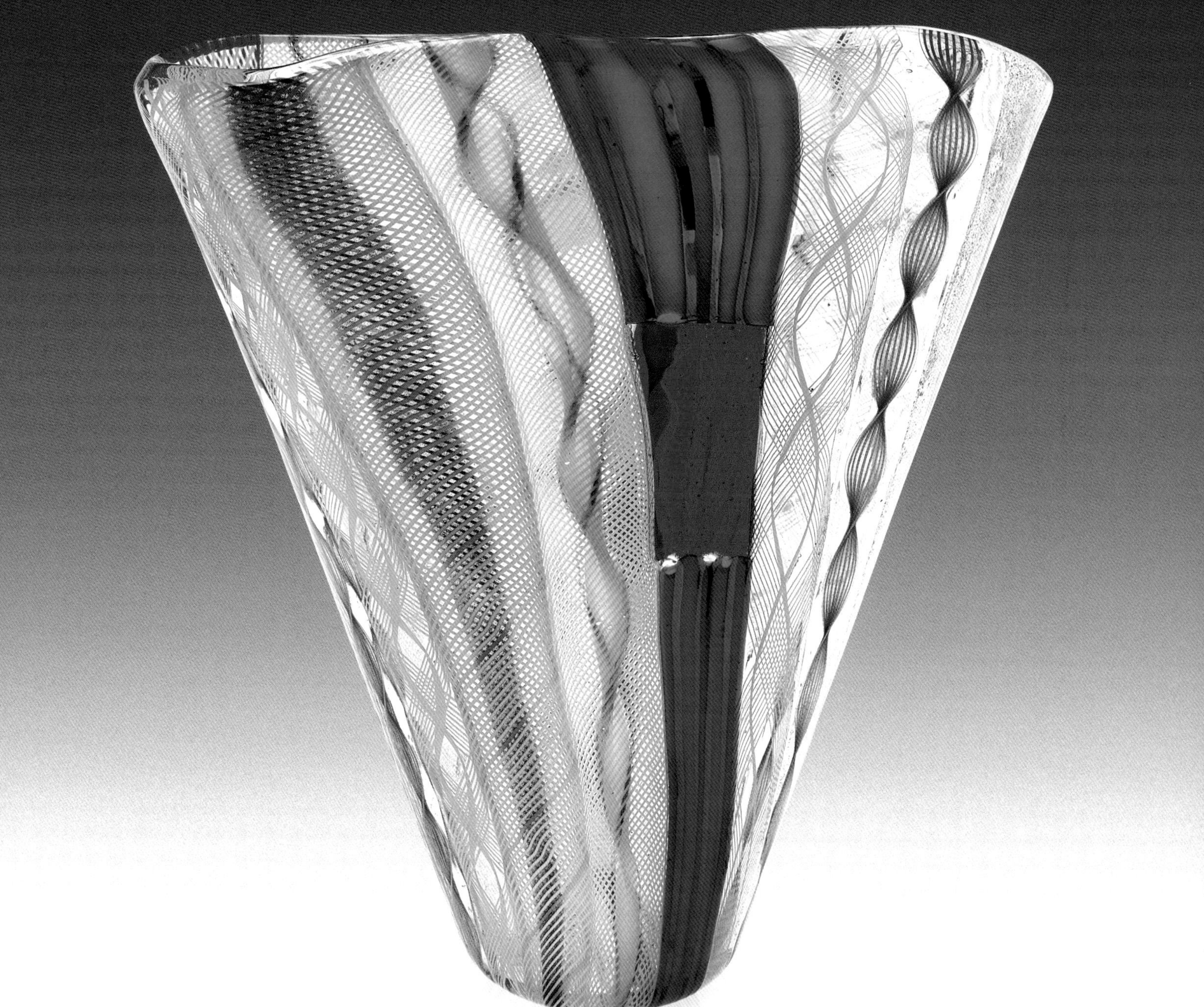

202. **Geltrude e Leandro**
Dino Martens
Vetreria artistica rag. Aureliano Toso

1952-54

Geltrude vase from the *oriente* series with patches of polychrome and *avventurina* glass, with insertions of *zanfirico* rods, of *reticello* glass and *murrine*, laid out in a characteristic design depicting a woman's face. The model corresponds to No. 5299 of the company catalog. *Leandro* vase from the *oriente* series with patches of polychrome and *avventurina* glass, and insertions of *zanfirico* and *reticello* glass rods. The vessel, with a ring-shaped foot in *lattimo* glass, is distinguished by the presence of a large stylized flower in yellow frit, *lattimo* rods and amethyst frit. The model corresponds to No.3155 from the glassworks catalog. The *oriente* was made by embedding a composition of frit and glass inclusions prepared on a refractory slab into the wall of the object, according to a design created by Martens himself. This glass series was presented for the first time at the XXVI Biennale di Venezia in 1952, drawing widespread recognition, which continued over the following years, during which the series was expanded to include many more models.

h 11.75" - 29 cm; h 7" - 18 cm

Exhibitions:
1952, Venezia, XXVI Biennale Internazionale d'Arte.

Bibliography:
Mille anni 1982, No. 615; Neuwirth 1987, No. 95; *La verrerie* 1988, p. 103; Heiremans 1989, No. 136; Cocchi 1991, No. 31; Barovier Mentasti 1992, No. 104; Heiremans 1993, Nos. 155,157-158, 161-162; Barovier 1994, Nos. 27-29; Barovier, Barovier Mentasti, Dorigato 1995, No. 95; *Venezia e la Biennale* 1995, No. 486; Deboni 1996, Nos. 152, 153; Heiremans 1996, Nos. 122-124; Ricke, Schmitt 1996, Nos. 203-206; Barovier 1999, p. 217; Heiremans 1999, Nos. 42-60, pp. 161, 166-169; *Venetian Glass* 2000, Nos. 110-111; *Murano* 2001, Nos. 147-148; Dorigato 2002, pp. 312-313; Heiremans 2002, Nos. 155-156.

Oriente *vase, ca. 1952, Marino Barovier Archives.*

203. **Oriente**
Dino Martens
Vetreria artistica rag. Aureliano Toso

1952

Left: *Nabucco* vase and long-necked vase from the *oriente* series with patches of polychrome and *avventurina* glass, with insertion of *zanfirico* rods, of *reticello* glass and a star composed with *lattimo* and amethyst rods.
The model of the *Nabucco* vase corresponds to No. 3121 of the company catalog.

h 9.25" - 23 cm; h 22" - 56 cm

Exhibitions:
1952, Venezia, XXVI Biennale Internazionale d'Arte.

Bibliography:
see No. 204.

204. **Eldorado**
Dino Martens
Vetreria artistica rag. Aureliano Toso

1953

Top: vase from the *eldorado* series with patches of transparent polychrome glass with *avventurina*, insertions of *zanfirico* glass rods, of a *reticello* glass and with a large star in *lattimo* and black glass. The model corresponds to No. 5215 of the glassworks catalog. *Eldorado* differs from *oriente* in its use of exclusively transparent frit and the constant presence of *avventurina* powders.

h 7.5" - 19 cm

Bibliography: Aloi 1955, p. 30; Heiremans 1993, Nos. 163-164; Barovier 1994, No. 25; Barovier, Barovier Mentasti, Dorigato 1995, No. 96; Heiremans 1996, Nos. 144-145; Ricke, Schmitt 1996, Nos. 207-210; Barovier 1999, p. 215; Heiremans 1999, Nos. 61-66, pp. 164-166; *Venetian Glass* 2000, No. 108; *Murano* 2001, No. 145; Dorigato 2002, p. 315; Heiremans 2002, No. 157.

Eldorado *vase, ca. 1953, Marino Barovier Archives.*

205. **Frammentati**
Dino Martens
Vetreria artistica rag. Aureliano Toso

1954

Vases from the *frammentati* series with glass pattern composed of patches of polychrome glass, inclusions of *reticello* glass, polychrome glass rods and *zanfirico*. The glass pattern was made by embedding various types of glass fragments prepared on a refractory slab, into the wall of the object.

h 11.75" - 29 cm; h 9.5" - 24 cm; h 8" - 20 cm; h 11.75" - 29 cm

Bibliography:
Heiremans 1996, No. 155;
Ricke, Schmitt 1996, Nos. 213-214;
Heiremans 1999, Nos. 107-110, p. 176.

Frammentati *vases, ca. 1954, Marino Barovier Archives.*

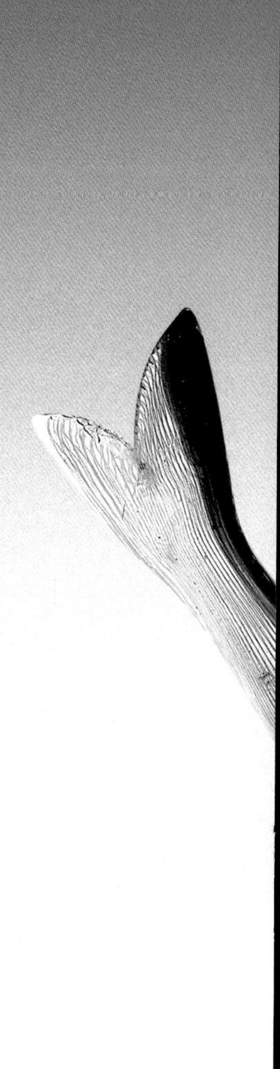

206. **Pesce**
Dino Martens
Vetreria artistica rag. Aureliano Toso

1954

Vase in the shape of a fish in polychrome glass *sommerso* under a thick layer of *cristallo*. This is a variation in *sommerso* glass, not finished at the wheel, of the *battuto Incantesimo* vase, presented at the XXVII Biennale di Venezia in 1954.

h 13.5" - 34 cm

Bibliography:
Aloi 1955, p.168;
Mariacher 1967, p. 152;
La verrerie 1988, p. 103;
Barovier Mentasti 1992, No. 97;
Heiremans 1993, No. 169;
Barovier, Barovier Mentasti, Dorigato 1995, p. 84;
Barovier 1999, pp. 218-219;
Heiremans 1999, Nos. 85-90;
Heiremans 2002, No. 166.

Polychrome sommersi *vases at the XXVII Biennale Internazionale d'Arte, Venezia, 1954.*

207. **Coppe**
Dino Martens
Vetreria artistica rag. Aureliano Toso

1957

Zoomorphic bowl in *a reticello* glass decorated along the edge with transparent blue glass frit and zoomorphic bowl in *opaline* glass and *zanfirico* glass rods.

h 5" - 13 cm; h 10" - 25 cm

Bibliography:
Heiremans 1999, Nos. 136,142-144; Heiremans 2002, No. 88.

Zoomorphic bowl, ca. 1957, Marino Barovier Archives.

208. **Zanfirico**
Dino Martens
Vetreria artistica rag. Aureliano Toso

ca. 1958

Bottle with stopper from the *zanfirico* series with vitreous texture composed of polychrome *zanfirico* rods laid out horizontally and vertically.

h 15.5" - 39 cm

Bibliography:
Heiremans 1999, No.149.

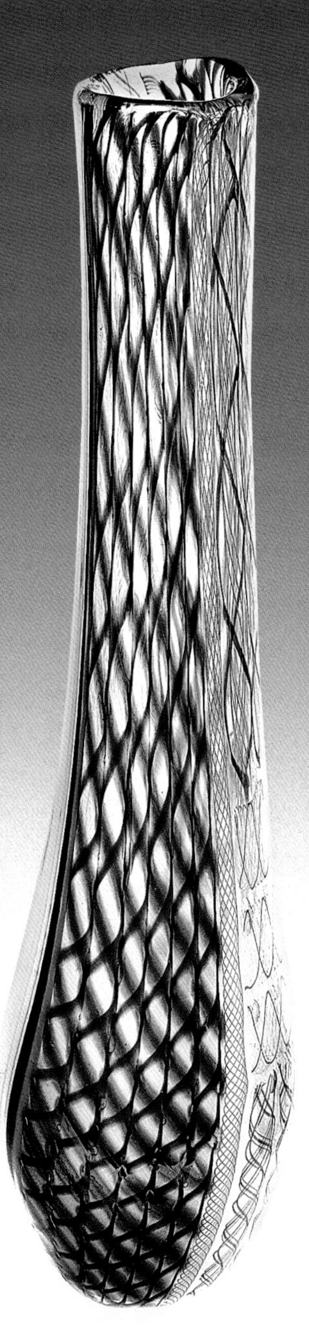

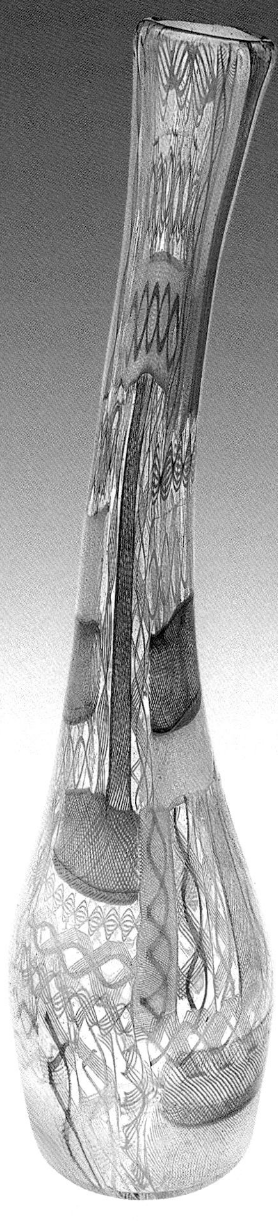

209. **Zanfirici**
Dino Martens
Vetreria artistica rag. Aureliano Toso

1957-58

Vases from the *zanfirico* series in glass with vitreous pattern consisting in polychrome *zanfirico* glass rods and *reticello*.

h 18" - 46 cm; h 23.5" - 60 cm; h 16" - 41 cm

Bibliography:
Gasparetto 1960, No. 6;
Heiremans 1993, No. 166;
Ricke, Schmitt 1996, No. 221;
Barovier 1999, p. 213;
Heiremans 1999, Nos. 145-148, p. 179.

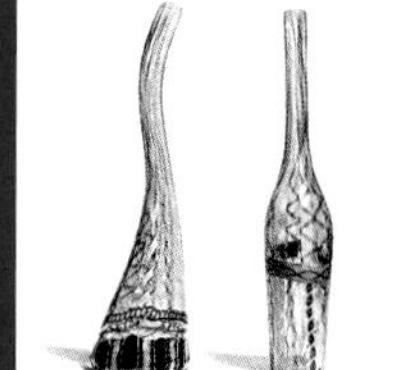
Zanfirico *vases at the XI Triennale, Milano, 1957.*

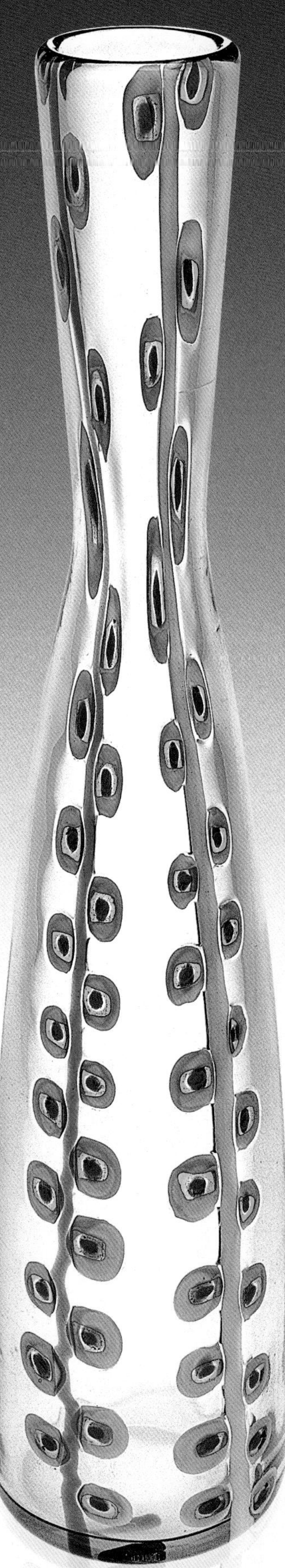

211. **A murrine**
Dino Martens
Vetreria artistica rag. Aureliano Toso

1961

Vase in *fumé* glass decorated with a vertical rod of transparent blue glass and a vertical rod of *lattimo* glass, along which *murrine* with an outer *lattimo* edge and a green and red glass nucleus are composed in a regular pattern.

h 16.5" - 42 cm

Bibliography:
Heiremans 1999, No. 164.

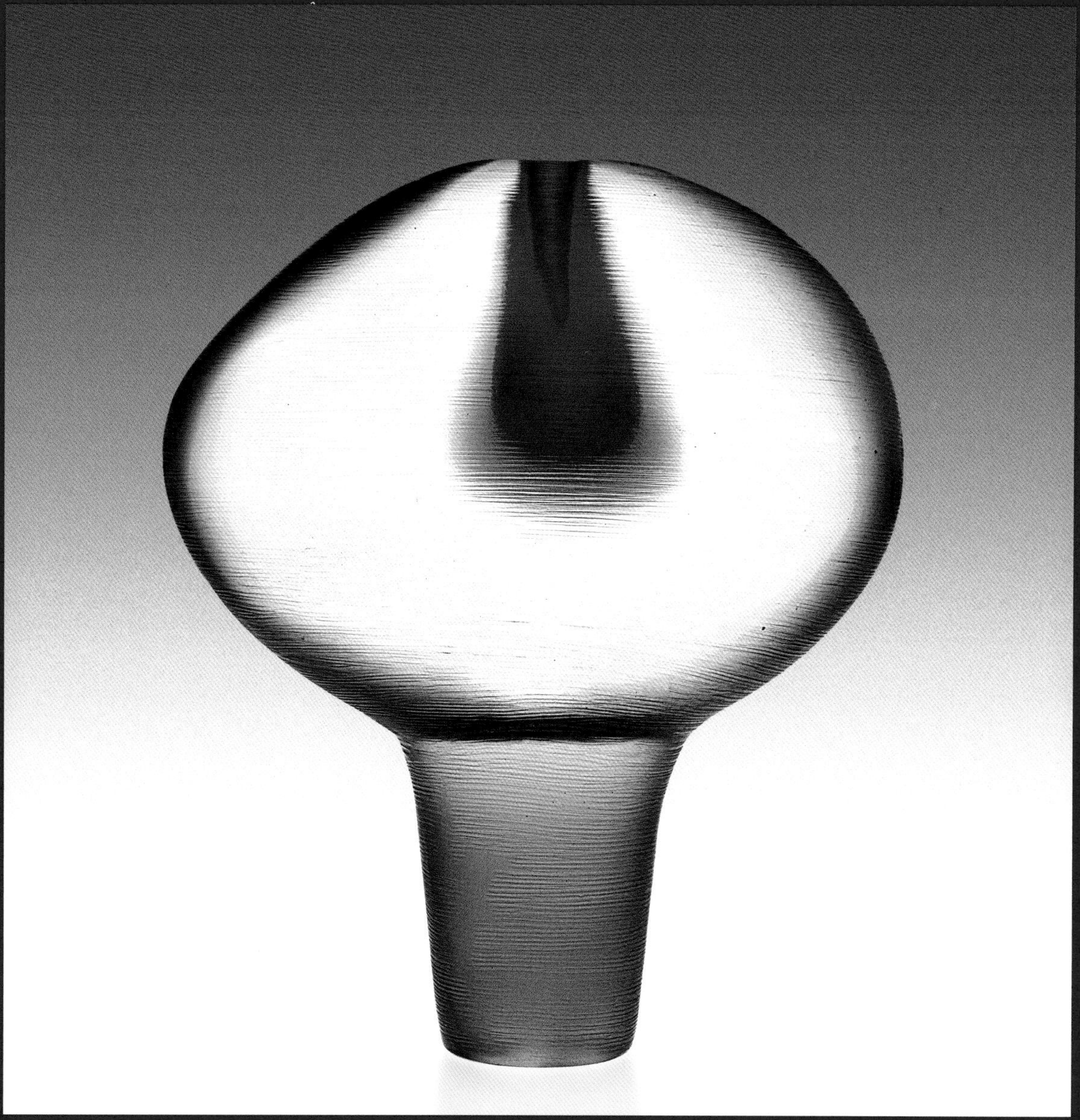

212. **Pesante**
Alfredo Barbini
Vetreria Alfredo Barbini

1962

Vessel in *sommerso* glass with mutliple layers of colored glass, finished with tight horizontal incisions carved at the wheel.

h 10.5" - 27 cm

Exhibitions:
1962, Venezia, XXXI Biennale Internazionale d'Arte.

Bibliography:
Mille anni 1982, No. 571; Heiremans 1989, No. 30; Cocchi 1991, No. 49; Heiremans 1993, No. 17; Barovier, Barovier Mentasti, Dorigato 1995, p. 95, No. 134; Heiremans 1996, No. 213; Ricke, Schmitt 1996, Nos. 252-253; Barovier Mentasti, Berengo 1997, p. 30; Barovier 1999, p. 243; *Venetian Glass* 2000, No. 133; *Murano* 2001, No. 168; Dorigato 2002, p. 335.

Pesante *vase at the XXI Biennale Internazionale d'Arte, Venezia, 1962.*

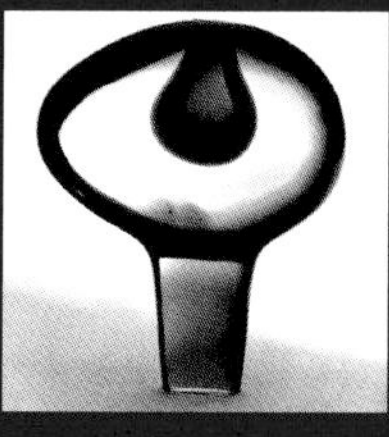

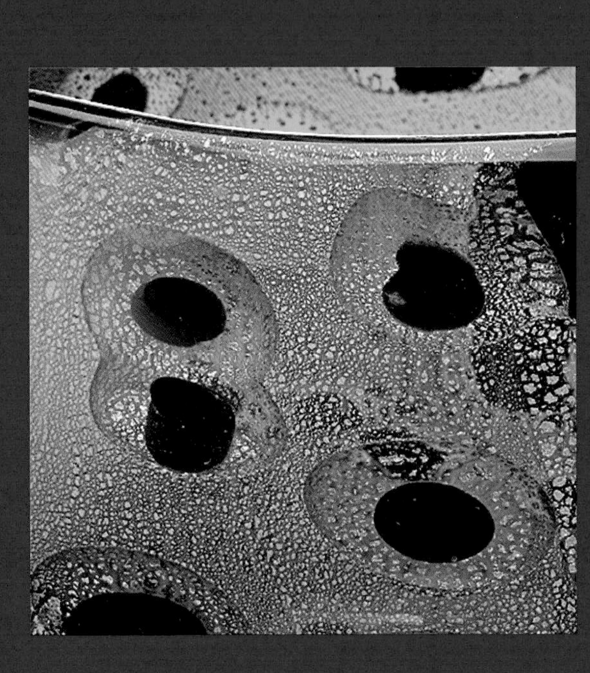

A.VE.M. (Arte Vetraria Muranese)

Gino Cenedese & Co.

A.VE.M.

In 1932 Antonio Luigi Ferro, his son Egidio and glass masters Emilio Nason, Galliano Ferro and Giulio Radi founded A.VE.M. on Murano. The furnace worked with the most exquisite techniques of Venetian glass, and during the Thirties, produced the lightweight blown pieces designed by Vittorio Zecchin and the *Novecento* style sculptures created by Emilio Nason. In the meantime Giulio Radi, who had been named artistic director in 1939, devoted himself to continuous experimentation, focusing specifically on the reactions of oxides with glass and making precious polychrome objects with gold and silver leaf. Following Radi's premature death in 1952, Giorgio Ferro succeeded him as artistic director through 1955, when he followed his father Galliano Ferro to his new glassworks. He was responsible for pieces such as the vases *ad anse volanti*. During the Fifties, A.VE.M. collaborated with painter Luigi Scarpa Croce, who designed soft *sommerso* pieces, and later with stained glass artist and designer Anzolo Fuga, who used *lattimo* and brightly colored *murrine* to create large pieces characterized by asymmetrical forms and abstract decors. Between 1966 and 1972, several models were created by glassmaster Luciano Ferro. A.VE.M. is still active today.

Gino Cenedese & Co.

In 1946, having acquired considerable furnace experience, Gino Cenedese joined forces with several Murano glass masters to found Gino Cenedese & Co.; they included Alfredo Barbini, whose works they presented at the 1948 Biennale di Venezia. During the Fifties, when Barbini left the furnace, the glassworks turned to designers such as Riccardo Licata, Napoleone Martinuzzi, Fulvio Bianconi and the painter Luigi Scarpa Croce. In 1959 Antonio Da Ros, the author of refined painterly *sommersi*, was entrusted with the artistic direction, which he still holds today. Glass master Ermanno Nason worked at Cenedese between 1965 and 1972. Since 1973, the year Gino Cenedese died, the glassworks has been directed by his son Amelio, and continues its work on Murano.

213. **A reazioni policrome**
Giulio Radi
A.VE.M.

1950-52

Top: bowls from the series *a reazione policrome* in glass with characteristic chromatic effects due to the reaction with particular metal oxydes. The bowl on the top, in black glass with gold leaf, is decorated with a pattern of embedded air bubbles obtained by using a mold with sharp points. The bowl below with gold leaf inclusions is decorated with round *murrine*.

Right: vases from the *a reazione policrome* series in *ballotton* glass with application of gold and silver leaf.

w 9.25" - 23 cm; w 12" - 30 cm;
h 4.5" - 11 cm; h 4.75" - 12 cm

Exhibitions:
1951, Milano, IX Triennale; 1952, Venezia, XXVI Biennale Internazionale d'Arte.

Bibliography:
"Domus", October 1951;
Vetri 1952, p. 41;

Dorigato, Barovier Mentasti 1981, p. 48;
Barovier Mentasti 1982, No. 296;
Mille anni 1982, No. 568-570;
Romanelli, Dorigato 1982, No.147;
Neuwirth 1987, No. 153;
La verrerie 1988, p. 113;
Heiremans 1989, No. 9;
L'arte del vetro 1992, No. 377;
Barovier Mentasti 1992, Nos. 90-91;
Heiremans 1993, Nos. 3-5;
Barovier, Barovier Mentasti, Dorigato 1995, pp. 61, 66, Nos. 88-89;
Deboni 1996, Nos. 85-87;
Heiremans 1996, Nos. 96-97;
Il vetro italiano 1998, No. 199;
Barovier 1999, p. 190;
Venetian Glass 2000, No. 107;
Murano 2001, No. 144;
Dorigato 2002, pp. 322-323;
Heiremans 2002, Nos. 7-8, 151-152.

A reazioni policrome *vases at the XXVI Biennale Internazionale d'Arte Venezia, 1952*

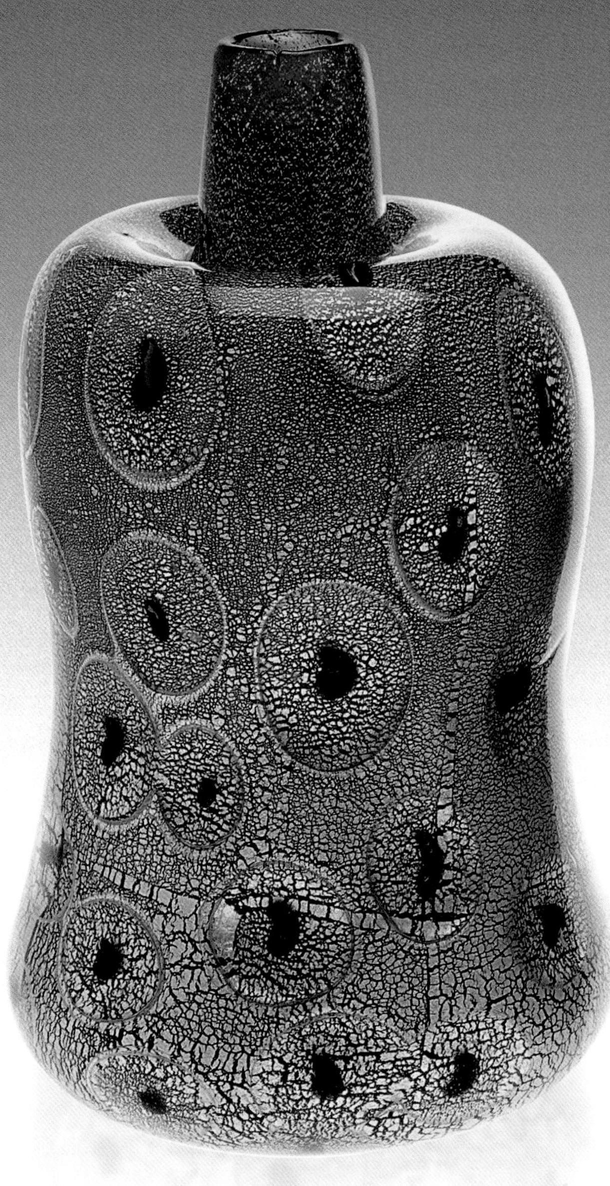

214. **A reazioni policrome**
Giulio Radi
A.VE.M.

1950-52

Irregularly shaped vase from the *a reazioni policrome* series in *cristallo* glass with applications of gold and silver leaf, decorated with round *murrine*. The characteristic chromatic effects are given by the reaction of particular metal oxides.

h 7.5" - 19 cm

Exhibitions:
1951, Milano, IX Triennale; 1952, Venezia, XXVI Biennale Internazionale d'Arte.

Bibliography:
see No. 213.

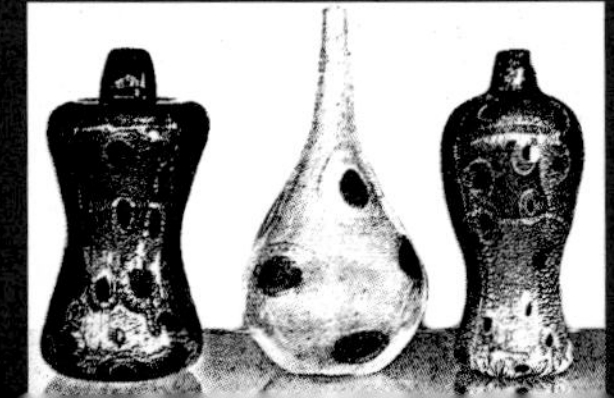

A reazioni policrome *vases at the IX Triennale, Milano, 1951*

215. **A reazioni policrome**
Giulio Radi
A.VE.M.

1950-52

Vessels from the series *a reazioni policrome* in transparent blue glass decorated with round *murrine* embedded in the wall and finished over the entire surface with particular metal oxides responsible for the characteristic chromatic effects.

h 15.5" - 39 cm; h 7.5" - 19 cm

Exhibitions:
1951, Milano, IX Triennale; 1952, Venezia, XXVI Biennale Internazionale d'Arte.

Bibliography:
see No. 213.

A reazioni policrome *vases at the XXVI Biennale Internazionale d'Arte, Venezia, 1952.*

216. **Anse volanti**
Giorgio Ferro
A.VE.M.

1952

Vessels from the series *anse volanti* in heavily iridized transparent red glass, characterized by large side handles, obtained by piercing a hole through the wall of the object.

h 4.75" - 12 cm - h 11.75" - 29 cm

Exhibitions:
1952, Venezia, XXVI Biennale Internazionale d'Arte.

Bibliography:
Nerozzi 1987, No. 53;
Neuwirth 1987, No. 201;
La verrerie 1988, p. 113;
Heiremans 1989, Nos. 3-5;
Cocchi 1991, No. 30;
L'arte del vetro 1992, No. 376;
Barovier Mentasti 1992, No. 93;
Barovier, Barovier Mentasti, Dorigato 1995, pp. 66-67, No. 90;
Venezia e la Biennale 1995, No. 469;
Deboni 1996, p. 23, No. 88;
Ricke, Schmitt 1996, No. 172;
Barovier 1999, p. 191;
Venetian Glass 2000, No. 106;
Murano 2001, No. 143;
Dorigato 2002, p. 324.

Anse volanti *vases at the XXVI Biennale Internazionale d'Arte, Venezia, 1952.*

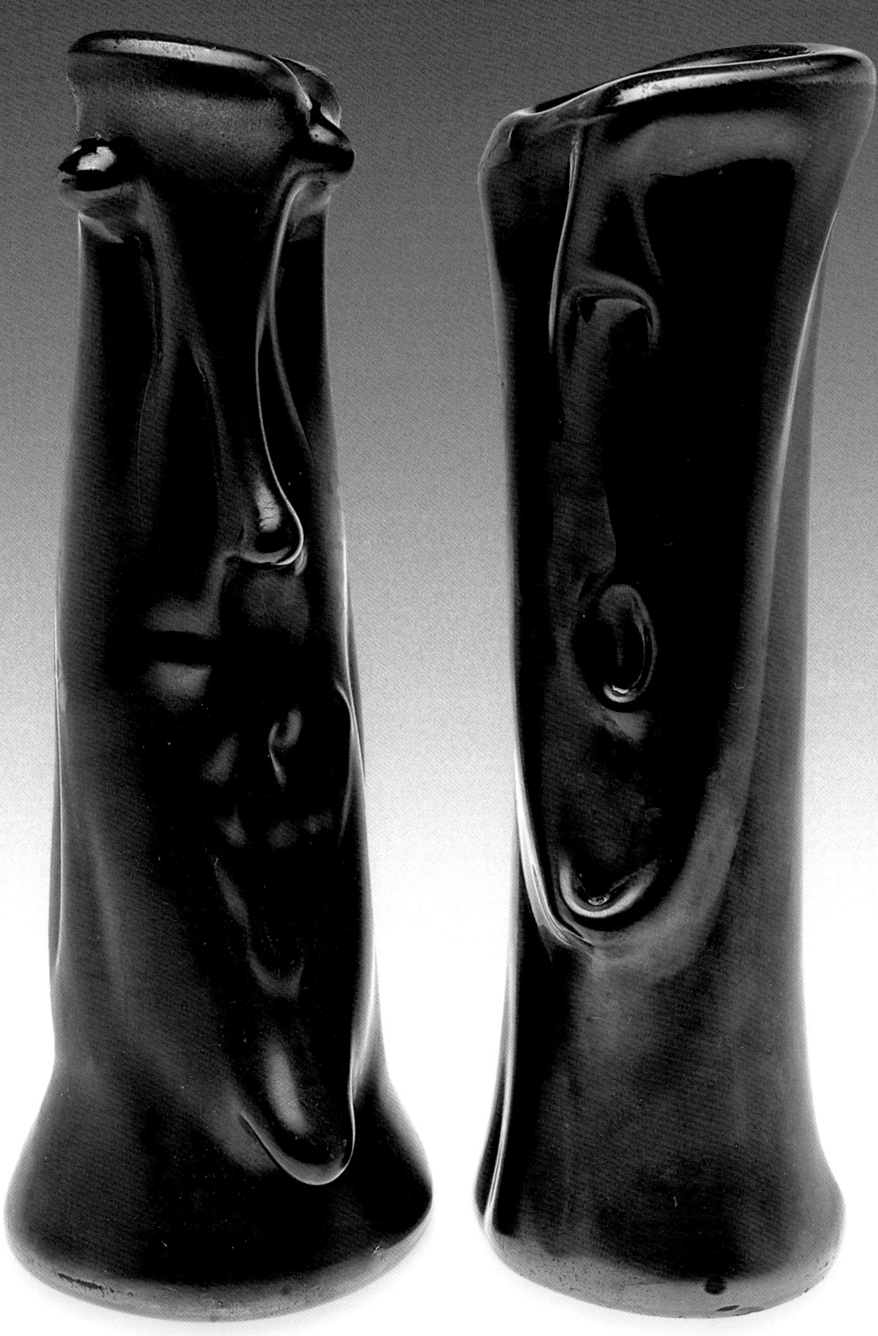

217. **Vasi**
Giorgio Ferro
A.VE.M.

ca. 1952

Vessels in blown black glass shaped while hot into faces and heavily iridized.

For this limited edition Giorgio Ferro used the same material as for the more common *Anse volanti* series (see No. 216).

h 12.5" - 32 cm; h 12.5" - 32 cm

218. **A murrine e a canne**
Anzolo Fuga
A.VE.M.

1956

Vase in *cristallo* decorated with vertical rods of *lattimo* glass and round *murrine* in transparent polychrome glass, and vessel in *cristallo* decorated with *lattimo* and green *murrine* with square inclusions composed of polychrome glass rods. Base and mouth trimmed with *lattimo* glass stripes.

h 19.5" - 50 cm; h 19.5" - 50 cm

Bibliography:
Istituto Veneto 1960, No. 89;
Heiremans 1989, No. 17;
Heiremans 1993, Nos. 1-2, 8;
Deboni 1996, No. 10;
Heiremans 1996, No. 183;
Heiremans 2002, No. 86.

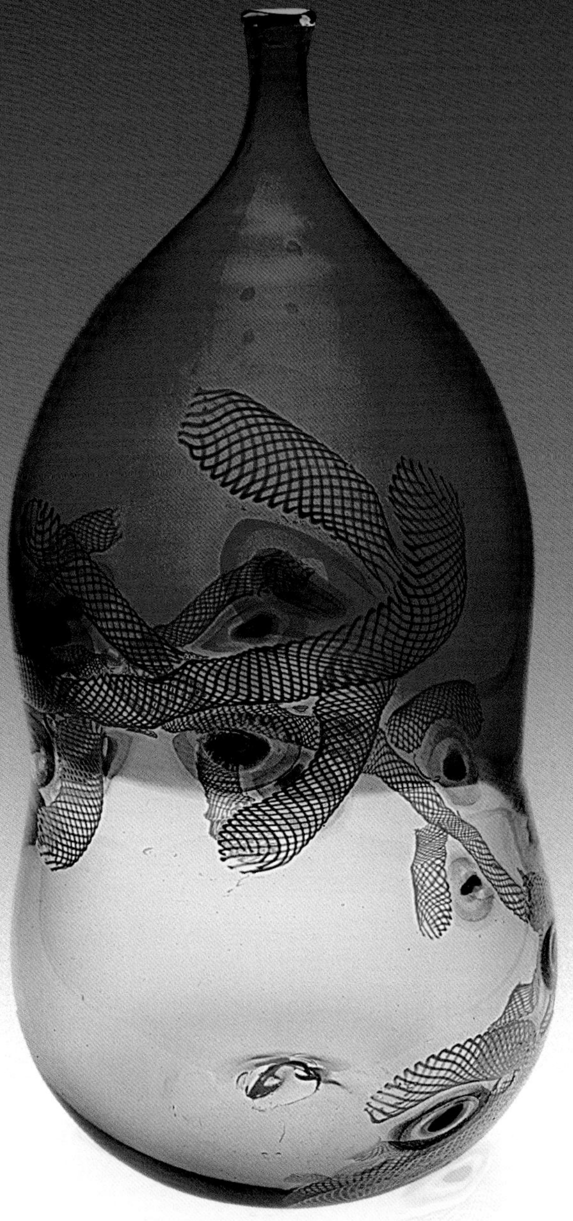

219. **A murrine e a canne**
Anzolo Fuga
A.VE.M.

ca. 1960

Vase in transparent light blue glass with a narrowing in the middle, decorated with glass rods and transparent polychrome *murrine*, and vase *ad incalmo* in transparent red and light blue glass decorated with *zanfirico* rods and round green and blue *murrine*.

h 14" - 36 cm; h 16.5" - 42 cm

Bibliography:
Gasparetto 1960, plate XXVII;
Heiremans 1989, No. 21;
Heiremans 1993, Nos. 9-10;
Deboni 1996, No. 6;
Heiremans 1996, No. 190.

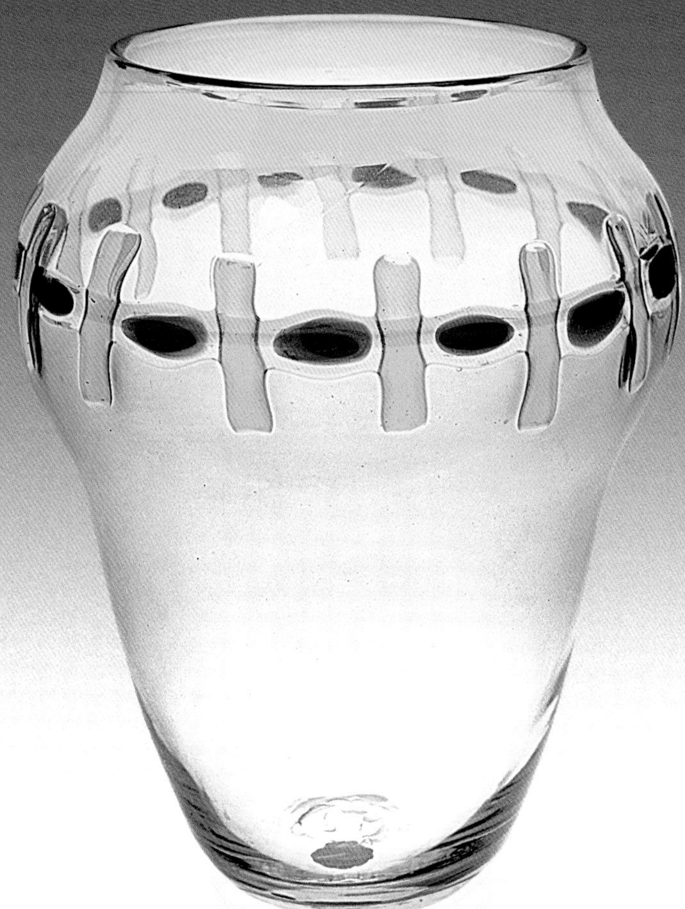

220. **A murrine**
Anzolo Fuga
A.VE.M.

ca. 1962

Vase *ad incalmo* in transparent yellow and light blue glass decorated with an irregular stripe in transparent green glass embedded with *murrine* and foot in transparent blue glass.
Vase *ad incalmo* in transparent yellow and light blue glass decorated with round red *murrine* alternating with transparent green glass rods.

h 13.25" - 33 cm; h 12" - 30 cm

Bibliography:
Heiremans 1996, No. 191;
Dorigato 2002, p. 347.

221. **Scavo**
Ermanno Nason
Gino Cenedese & Co.

ca. 1952

Left: zoomorphic vases and pitcher from the *scavo* series in glass, with irregular corroded patches obtained by applying acids and salts over the surface of the vases, at the end of the hot work. The vases in amethyst glass and in brownish-pink glass are decorated with glass applications in a floral motif. The green glass pitcher has the spout shaped into a bird's head and finished with light applications of gold leaf.

h 14" - 36 cm; h 12" - 30 cm; h 15" - 38 cm

Bibliography:
Mariacher 1967, p. 110; Deboni 1996, No. 75.

222. **Scavo**
Ermanno Nason
Gino Cenedese & Co.

ca. 1950

Top: glass vessel from the *scavo* series with irregular corroded patches obtained by applying salts and acids on the surface of the vessel during the hot work.

h 10" - 25 cm

Scavo *vase, Marino Barovier Archives.*

223. **La fornace**
Napoleone Martinuzzi
Gino Cenedese & Co.

1953-58

Tile from the *La lavorazione del vetro* series in *scavo* polychrome glass, decorated with a bas-relief made in hotwork. The same subject characterizes one of the tiles which decorate the columns of a showroom in the Cenedese glassworks, made by Martinuzzi between 1952 and 1958.

h 12" - 30 cm

Bibliography:
Barovier 1992, No. 118;
Heiremans 1993, No. 69.

Columns with scavo glass tiles in the Vetreria Cenedese on Murano.

224. **Bottiglia**
Fulvio Bianconi
Gino Cenedese & Co.

1954

Bottle with stopper in *cristallo* in the image of a female figure decorated with black glass and blue glass threads.

h 18" - 46 cm

Bibliography:
Aloi 1957, p. 63;
Mariacher 1967, p. 113;
Cocchi 1991, No. 28;
Bossaglia 1993, p. 20, No. 51.

Vases with applied threads in G. Mariacher, I vetri di Murano, *Venezia, 1967.*

225. **Vasi**
Ermanno Nason
Gino Cenedese & Co.

ca. 1965

Vase in transparent glass with irregular stripes in *cristallo* and blue glass decorated with scribbles in relief applied while hot.
Vase in *cristallo* with applied stripes in polychrome glass decorated with engraved hieroglyphics. Both vessels are corroded over the entire surface. Engraved signature: "G. Begotti A. Da Ros Cenedese".

h 19.5" - 50 cm; h 21" - 53 cm

Bibliography:
Istituto Veneto 1960, No. 100;
Mariacher 1967, pp. 111-116.

A graffiti *vase from the* scavo *series in* G. Mariacher, I vetri di Murano, *Venezia, 1967.*

226. **Scavo**
Ermanno Nason
Gino Cenedese & Co.

ca. 1970

Glass amphora and vessel from the *scavo* series with irregular corroded patches obtained by sprinkling acids and salts on the surface of the vessel, at the conclusion of the hotwork. The vessels are decorated with applied vitreous threads and their primitive shapes are inspired by archaeological models.

h 15" - 38 cm; h 10.5" - 27 cm

Bibliography:
Ricke, Schmitt 1996, No. 202.

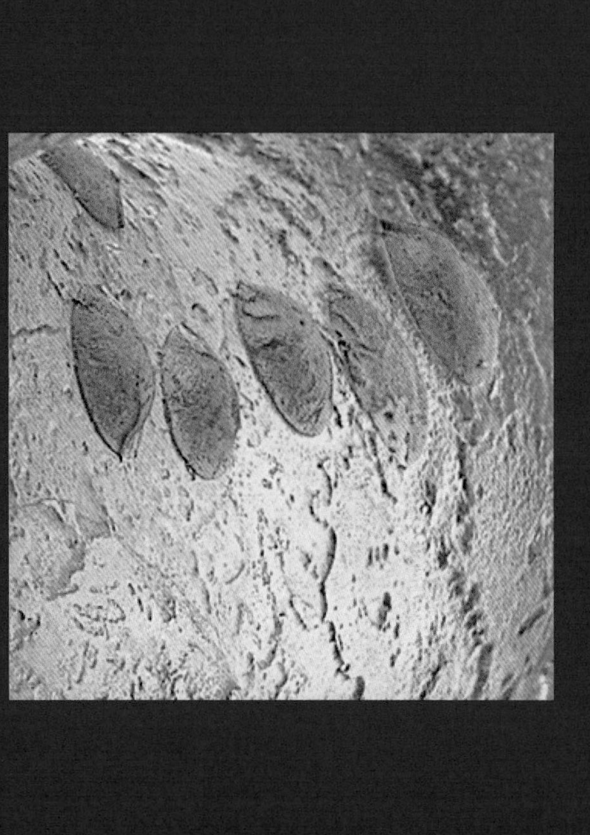

In the early Fifties the Centro Studio Pittori nell'Arte del Vetro was founded by Egidio Costantini and Venetian painters such as Virgilio Guidi, Aldo Bergamini, Bruno De Toffoli and others, to allow artists from various nations to develop their artistic expression with glass. The initiative aroused much interest and was supported by several glassworks (Ferro & Lazzarini, Dalla Venezia & Martinuzzi, I.V.R. Mazzega, etc.) and famous artists such as Braque, Chagall, Moore, Picasso, Léger, Kokoschka and Cocteau, who re-baptized the Center as La Fucina degli Angeli. During the Sixties, most of the glassworks receded from their association. After that, Egidio Costantini entrusted the execution of the pieces to individual glass masters, including Albino Carrara, Ermanno Nason and Loredano Rosin.
In the wake of this experience, other artists such as Angelo Barovier, Fulvio Bianconi or Mirko Casaril, developed these issues individually with the collaboration of many different glassworks on Murano.

227. **Vaso**
Angelo Barovier
Barovier & Toso

1952

Vessel in light green blown glass with side handle and trim in black *pasta vitrea*, decorated with applied eyes in *lattimo* and black *pasta vitrea*.

h 16.5" - 42 cm

Bibliography:
Deboni 1996, No. 44.

228. **Occhi**
Bruno De Toffoli
Dalla Venezia & Martinuzzi

ca. 1954

Occhi, a sculpture in red and yellow blown glass with applications of eye-shaped *murrine*.
Executed by: Francesco Martinuzzi.

h 15.75" - 40 cm

Bibliography:
Aloi 1955, p. 164;
Dorigato 2002, p. 331.

Occhi *in G. Aloi,* Vetri d'oggi, *Milano, 1955.*

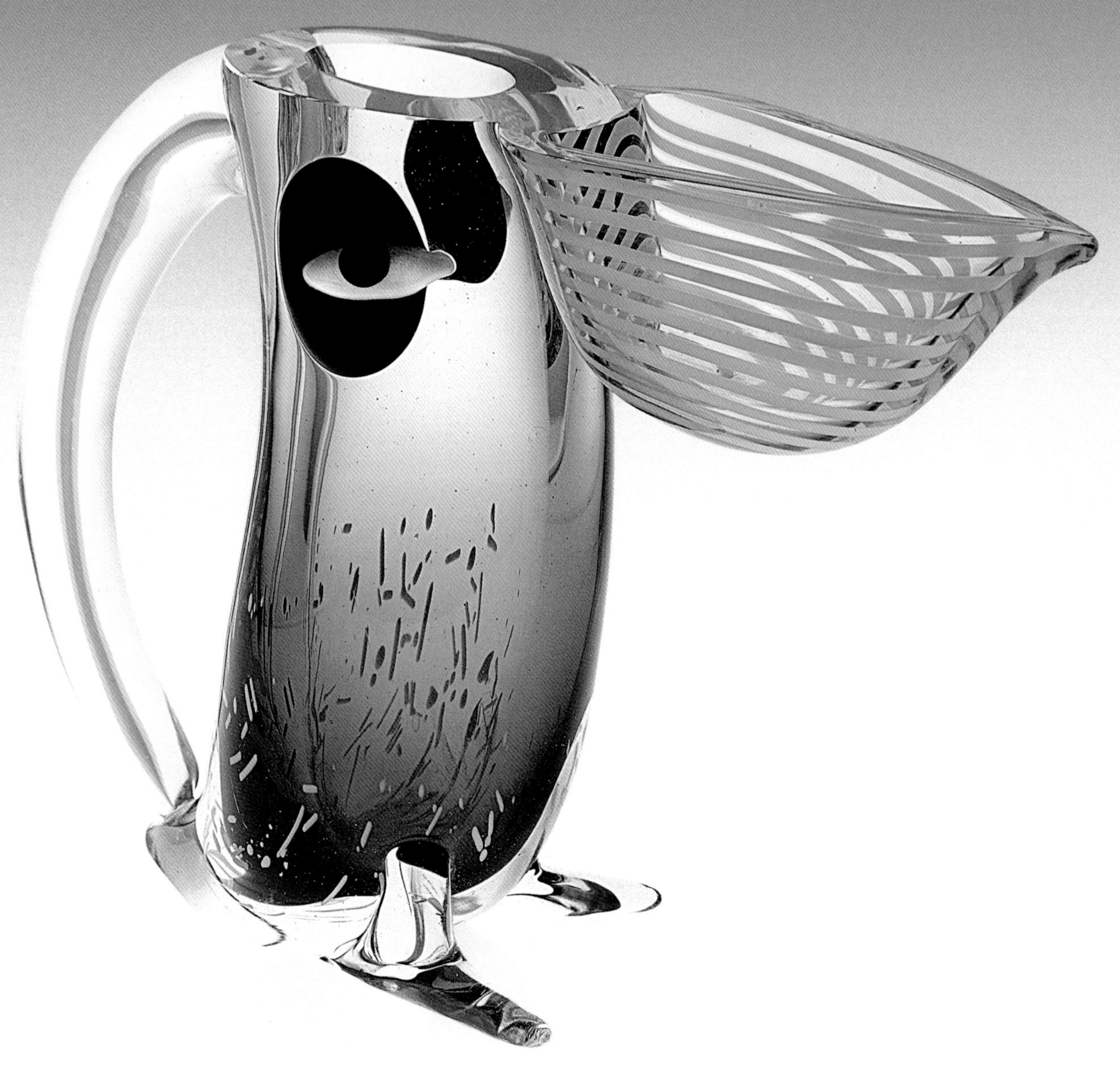

229. **Pellicano** polychrome glass.

230. **Sensazione marina**
Ezio Rizzetto
Vetreria Ferro & Lazzarini

1954

Sculpture in thick glass with stripes of amethyst glass and *lattimo* and amethyst *murrine*, and *cristallo* applications.

h 14.5" - 37 cm

Exhibitions:
1954, Venezia, XXVII Biennale Internazionale d'Arte.

Bibliography:
Barovier, Barovier Mentasti, Dorigato 1995, p. 80.

Sensazione marina *at the XXVII Biennale Internazionale d'Arte, Venezia, 1954.*

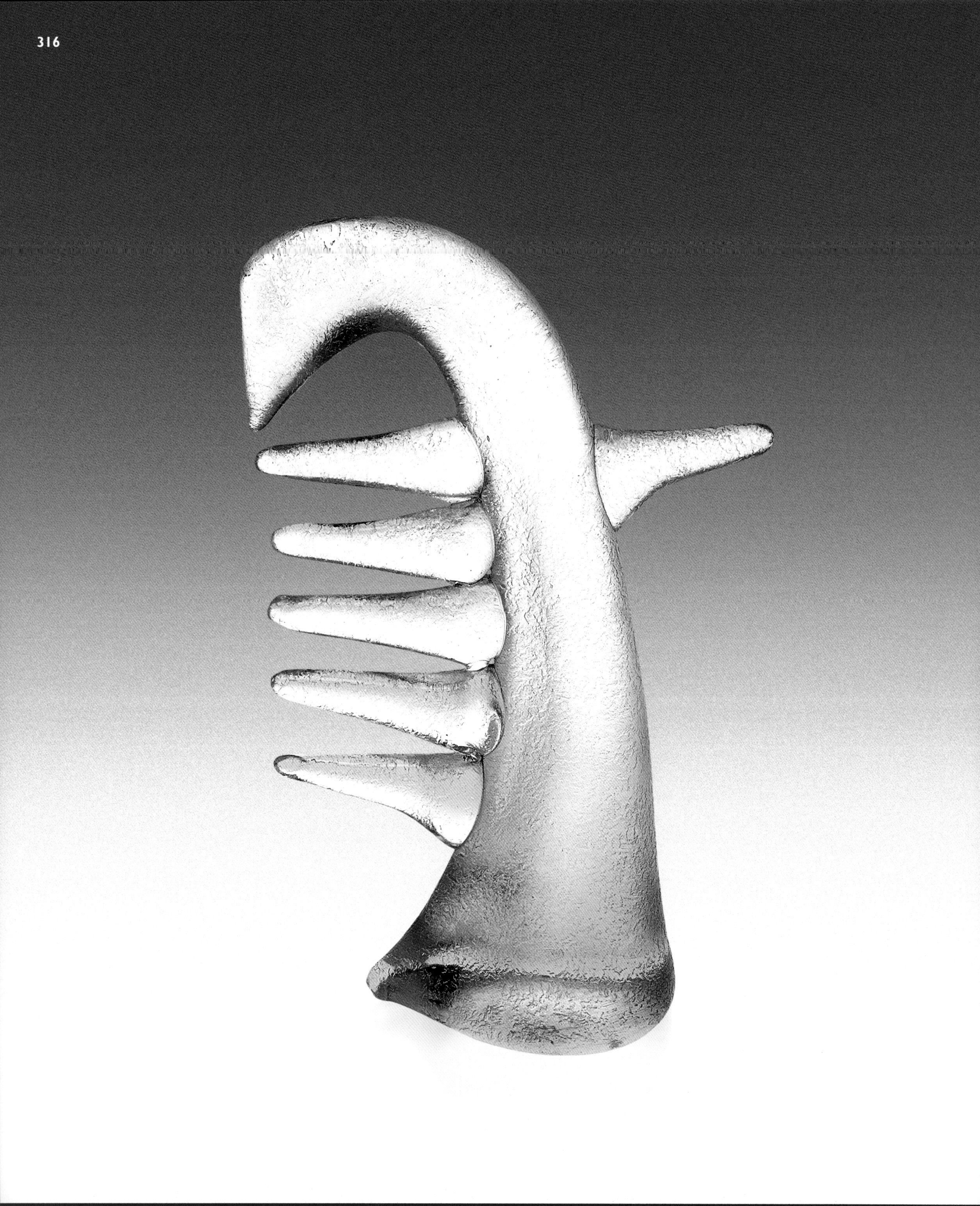

231. **Gondola**
Ezio Rizzetto
Vetreria Ferro & Lazzarini

1954

Sculpture in very thick *cristallo*, shaped while hot and finished with a superficial corrosion.

h 15.75" - 40 cm

Bibliography:
Aloi 1955, p. 165;
Barovier, Barovier Mentasti, Dorigato 1995, p. 80.

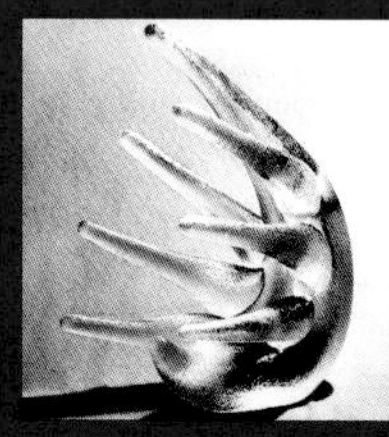

Conchiglia *at the XXVII Biennale Internazionale d'Arte, Venezia, 1954.*

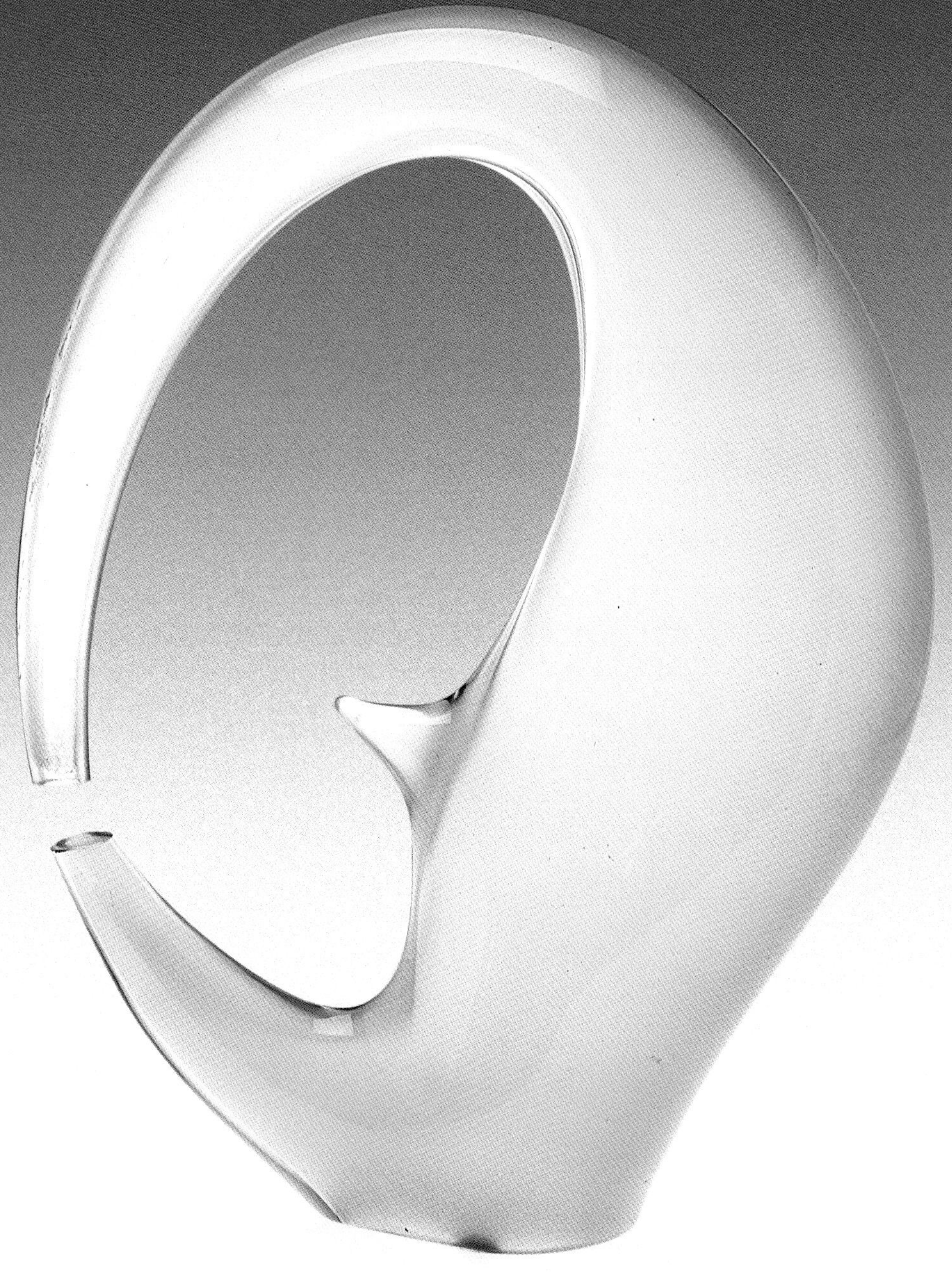

232. **Vaso circolare**
Ezio Rizzetto
Vetreria Ferro & Lazzarini

1968

Sculpture in *opaline* glass shaped while hot.

h 13" - 33 cm

Bibliography:
Barovier Mentasti 1994, No. 93, pp.108-109;
L'Art du verre 1995, p. 30;
Barovier, Barovier Mentasti, Dorigato 1995, p. 101.

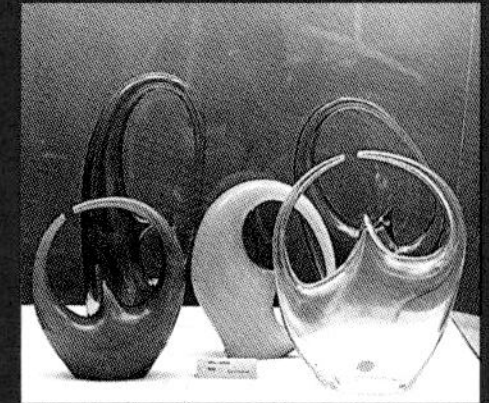

Vasi circolari *at the XXXIV Biennale Internazionale d'Arte, Venezia, 1968.*

233. **Nudo e brocca**
Aldo Bergamini
Vetreria Ferro & Lazzarini

1953-54

Vase in *cristallo* with lens-like applications in *cristallo*, lightly iridized, representing a female nude and pitcher in *cristallo* with applied patches of blue glass.

h 16.5" - 42 cm; h 10.75" - 27 cm

Exhibitions:
1954, Roma, I Mostra Internazionale del Vetro di Murano.

Bibliography:
Nudo: "Selearte", June 1953, p. 33.
Brocca: Aloi 1955, p.166.

Blown glass pitcher in G. Aloi, Vetri d'oggi, Milano, 1955.

234. **Gallinella**
Aldo Bergamini
I.V.R. Mazzega

ca. 1957

Zoomorphic vessel in *cristallo* decorated with glass threads and lens-like applications in blue glass, standing on *cristallo* legs.
Executed by: Ermanno Nason.
Engraved: "E. Nason".

h 9.5" - 24 cm

Bibliography:
"Domus", February 1957.

From Pablo Picasso
I.V.R. Mazzega

1959

Left: vessel in *cristallo* with large side handle decorated with applications in *lattimo* glass and black *pasta vitrea*, lightly iridized over the entire surface.
Executed by: Ermanno Nason.
Engraved: "Picasso Ermanno Nason 1959".

h 17" - 43 cm

Exhibitions:
1954, Roma, I Mostra Internazionale del Vetro di Murano.

Bibliography:
Egidio Costantini 1990, p. 175.

236. **Gufo**
From Pablo Picasso
I.V.R. Mazzega

1959

Right: *cristallo* vessel with side handles decorated with applications of black *pasta vitrea*, lightly iridized over the entire surface.
Executed by: Ermanno Nason.
Engraved: "E Nason 1959".

h 15.75" - 40 cm

Exhibitions:
1954, Roma, I Mostra Internazionale del Vetro di Murano.

Bibliography:
Aloi 1955, p. 155;
I Mostra 1954, p. XVIII;
"Domus", November 1955;
L'immortale 1984, p. 53;
Neuwirth 1987, No. 219;
Egidio Costantini 1990, pp. 37, 65, 156, 172-173;
La Fucina degli Angeli 1990, p. 53;
Ballarin 1992, p. 15;
Berruti, Serena 1993, p. 172;
Deboni 1996, No. 89.

Pablo Picasso and the Gufo vase, Marino Barovier Archives.

237. **Colomba**
From Pablo Picasso
I.V.R. Mazzega

ca. 1960

Vessel in *cristallo* with large side handle and applications in blue glass, lightly iridized over the entire surface.
Executed by: Ermanno Nason.
Engraved: "Omaggio a Picasso E. Nason 1960".

h 12.5" - 32 cm

Bibliography:
L'immortale 1984, p. 4;
Egidio Costantini 1990, p. 175.

238. **Burlesco**
From Jean Cocteau
I.V.R. Mazzega

1956

Cristallo vase with side handles decorated with applications of *lattimo* glass and black *pasta vitrea*, lightly iridized over the entire surface.
Executed by: Ermanno Nason.

h 15" - 38 cm

Bibliography:
L'immortale 1984, p. 50;
Berruti, Serena 1993, p. 172.

Jean Cocteau and the Burlesco *vase, Marino Barovier Archives.*

239. **Portatrice d'acqua**
From Pablo Picasso
I.V.R. Mazzega

1954

Vessel in *cristallo* with applications in black *pasta vitrea*, lightly iridized over the entire surface.
Executed by: Ermanno Nason.

h 17" - 43 cm

Exhibitions:
1954, Roma, I Mostra Internazionale del Vetro di Murano.

Bibliography:
Aloi 1955, p. 154.

Portatrice d'acqua *in G. Aloi*, Vetri d'oggi, *Milano, 1955.*

240. **Flamenco**
From Pablo Picasso
I.V.R. Mazzega

1960

Vessel in *cristallo* decorated with applications in red and amethyst glass and lightly iridized over the entire surface.
Executed by: Ermanno Nason.
Engraved: "Omaggio a Picasso E. Nason 1960".

h 16.5" - 42 cm

Exhibitions:
1954, Roma, I Mostra Internazionale del Vetro di Murano.

Bibliography:
L'immortale 1984, p. 54;
Egidio Costantini 1990, pp. 36, 171, 177;
La Fucina degli Angeli 1990, p. 52;
Ballarin 1992, pp. 23, 50;
Berruti, Serena 1993, p. 171.

Pablo Picasso and Egidio Costantini with the Flamenco vase, Marino Barovier Archives.

241. **Centauri**
From Pablo Picasso
La Fucina degli Angeli

1954

Centaur in transparent blue *corroso* glass with trim details in yellow glass and centaur in transparent yellow glass with trim details in red glass.

h 11.25" - 28 cm; h 12" - 30 cm

Exhibitions:
1954, Roma, I Mostra Internazionale del Vetro di Murano.

Bibliography:
Aloi 1955, p.153;
Egidio Costantini 1990, p. 167;
Deboni 1996, p. 40, No. 91.

Centaur *in G. Aloi*, Vetri d'oggi, *Milano, 1955.*

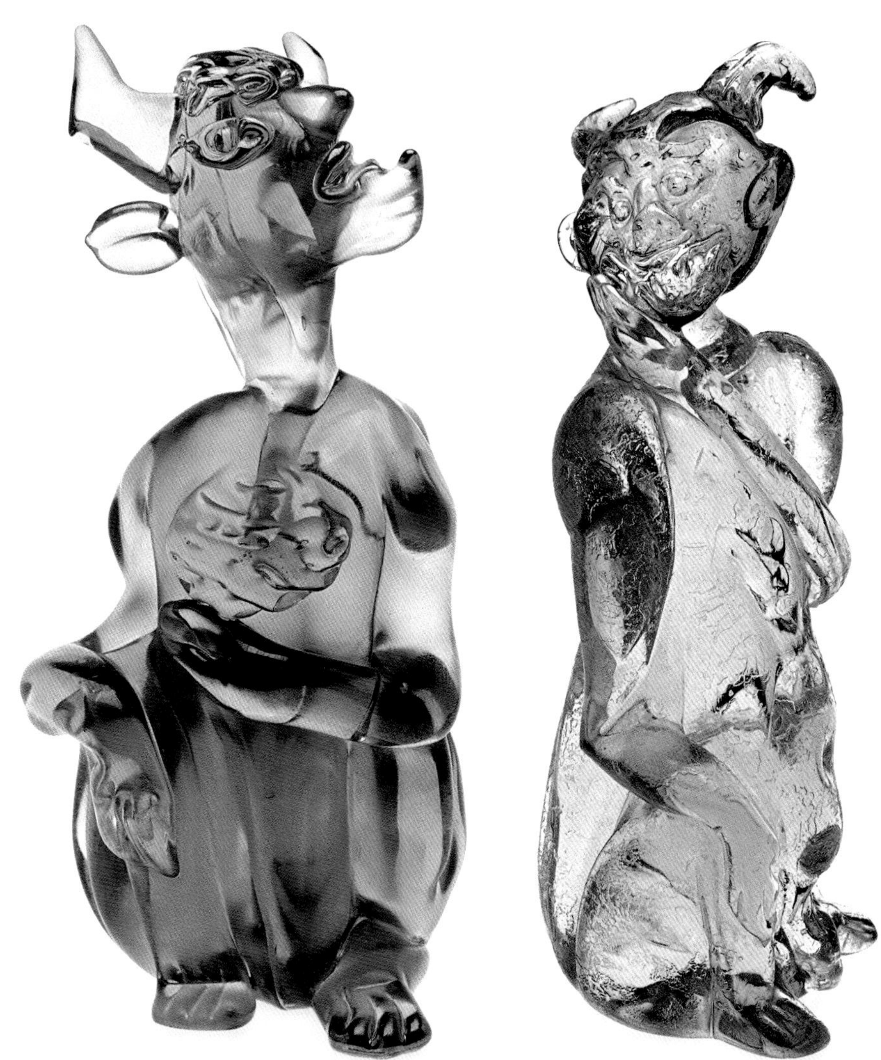

244. **Fiore Sole**
From Fernand Léger
I.V.R. Mazzega

ca. 1959

Sculpture in transparent polychrome glass on stem in black *pasta vitrea.*

Executed by: Ermanno Nason.
Engraved: "Omaggio a F. Leger E. Nason 1960".

h 17" - 43 cm

Exhibitions:
1954, Roma, I Mostra Internazionale del Vetro di Murano.

Bibliography:
I Mostra 1954, plate XIV;
"Domus", November 1955;
Egidio Costantini 1990, p. 151.

Fiore Sole *in "Domus", November 1955.*

245. **Sposi**
From Marc Chagall
I.V.R. Mazzega

with applications in polychrome glass.
Executed by: Ermanno Nason.
Engraved: "E. Nason 1960".

Berruti, Serena 1993, p. 177.

246. **Pipa pescatore**
From Anton Clavé
La Fucina degli Angeli

ca. 1957

Vase in transparent red glass with side handles and trim in *lattimo* glass and black *pasta vitrea*.

h 24" - 61cm

Bibliography:
Egidio Costantini 1990, p. 205.

Pipa Pescatore *vase, Marino Barovier Archives.*

247. **Baccanti**
From Oskar Kokoschka
Vetreria Ferro & Lazzarini

1953

Pitcher in *cristallo* decorated with copper-wheel engraving.

Engraved by: Dal Paos (S.A.L.I.R.).
Engraved: "Oskar Kokoschka Albino Carrara Ferro & Lazzarini Murano".

h 6.5" - 17 cm

Exhibitions:
1954, Roma, I Mostra Internazionale del Vetro di Murano.

Bibliography:
"Selearte", June 1953, p. 32;
I Mostra 1954, p XI, p. 15;
Aloi 1955, p. 159;
Egidio Costantini 1990, p. 144.

Baccanti *in G. Aloi*, Vetri d'oggi, *Milano, 1955.*

248. **Scultura**
Robert Willson

ca. 1975

Cristallo sculpture on square base with applications of red and *lattimo* vitreous threads.

Engraved: "Robert Willson".

h 12" - 30 cm

249. **Static moon dance**
Robert Willson

1975

Sculpture in *cristallo* glass with applications of polychrome glass, composed of two elements held together by a metal structure.
Engraved: "Robert Willson".

h 9.5" - 24 cm

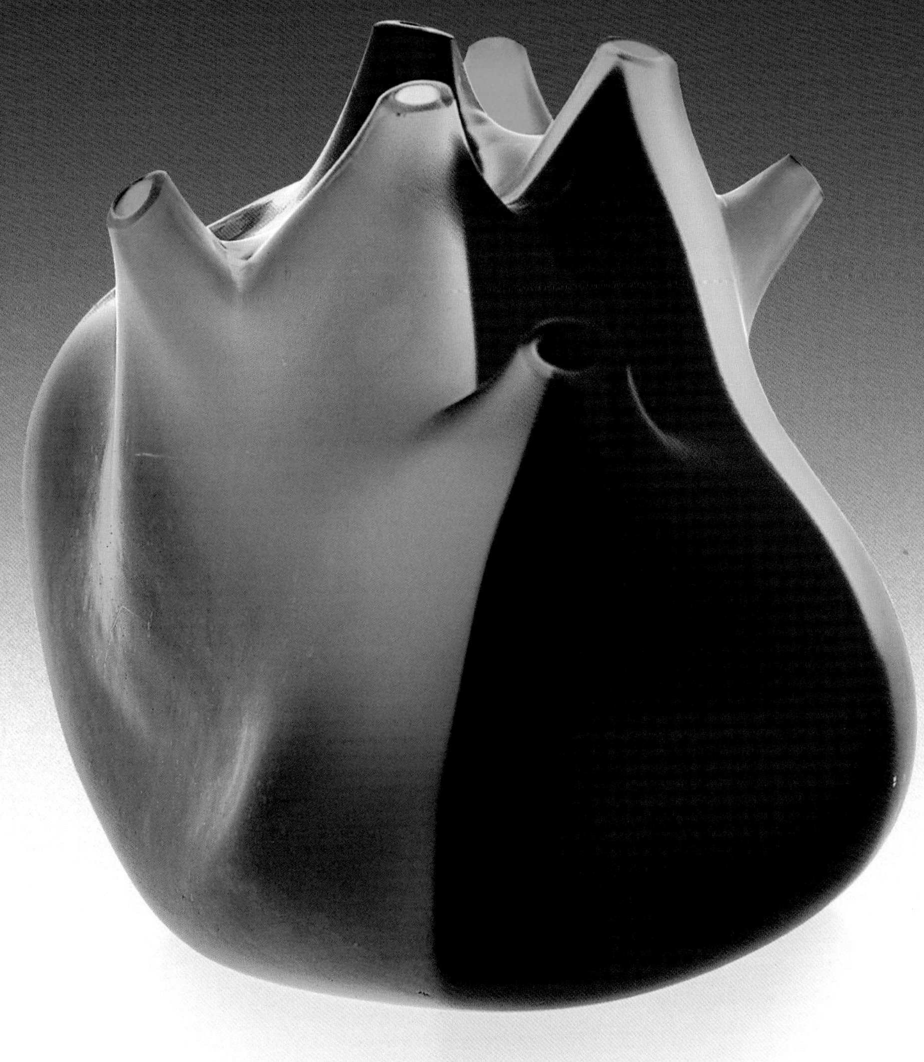

250. **Vaso**
Fulvio Bianconi
I.V.R Mazzega

ca. 1960

Vessel in polychrome glass lightly acid-finished over the entire surface.

h 7.5" - 19 cm

Bibliography:
Bossaglia 1993, No. 91;
Barovier 1999, pp. 248-249.

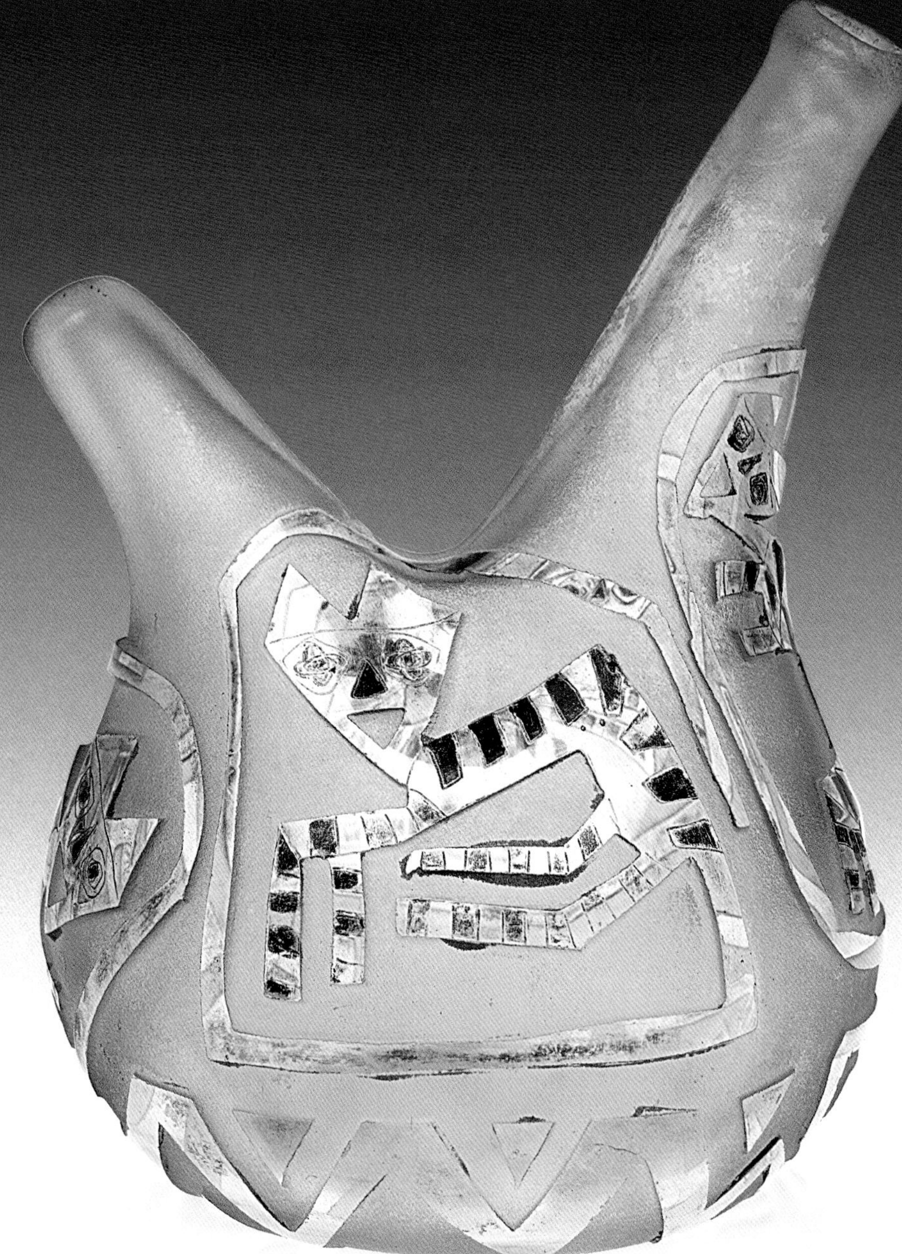

251. **Gatti**
Mirko Casaril
Pauly & Co.

ca. 1960

Vessel in *cristallo* with decorations in relief engraved at the wheel, lightly acid-finished over the entire surface.
Paper label: Pauly & Co.
Executed by: Francesco Andolfato.

h 9.5" - 24 cm

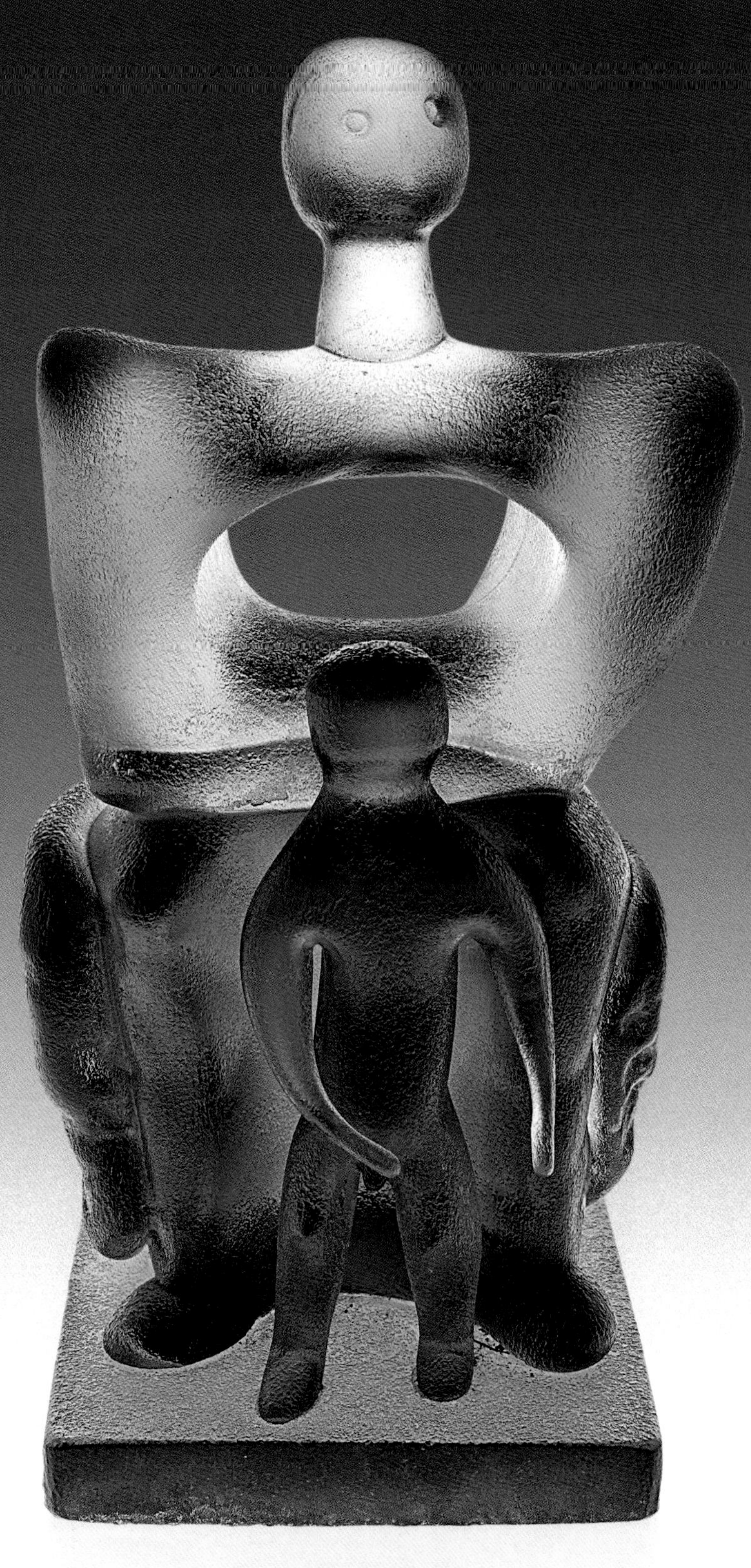

252. **Omaggio a Henry Moore**
Ermanno Nason
I.V.R. Mazzega

1974

Sculpture in blue glass with a lightly corroded surface.

Engraved: "Omaggio a Henry Moore E. Nason 1974".

h 16" - 41 cm

253. **Relax**
Loredano Rosin

ca. 1965

Grey glass sculpture on base *cristallo*.

h 29.5" - 75 cm

Bibliography:
Berndt 1989, No. 549.

254. **Scultura**
Gino Cenedese & Co.

ca. 1972

Sculpture in *fumé* glass decorated with eye-shaped polychrome glass applications and trim in transparent blue glass.
Engraved: "Cenedese 1972".

h 13" - 33 cm

255. **The Waves**
Seguso Vetri d'Arte

1960

Sculpture in *cristallo* and blue glass on base in *cristallo* glass.

h 15.25'' - 38 cm

GLOSSARY

Types of glass

Trasparente
Composed of a basic mixture similar to *cristallo* glass, it is colored by melting metal oxides during the fusion according to specific time schedules and procedures. On the basis of different chemical reactions, depending on the type of coloring agent introduced into the mixture, the glass acquires the desired chromatic characteristics.

Avventurina
Glass with a distinctive golden appearance, containing micro-crystals of copper, whose name refers to the difficulty of making it, considered an "adventure". It is produced by progressively adding the correct quantity of reducing substances to the vitreous mixture, similar to the mixture for *cristallo* glass; after a very slow cooling process, the tiny crystals of copper separate from the fusion giving the glass exceptional brilliance.

Primavera
A milky, seemingly *craquelé* glass which distinguished a limited series of objects made by the Vetreria Artistica Barovier & Co. in the early Thirties. The product of an accidental vitreous mixture, it was never reproduced again.

Lattimo
A white glass, resembling porcelain; it presents a characteristic opaque appearance and a milky color because of the large quantity of micro-particles of calcium and sodium fluoride it contains, whose refractive index is not the same as basic glass. The formation of these micro-crystals, favored by the zinc oxide, occurs when the fluoride-based components separate during the cooling process.

Pasta vitrea
Opaque colored glass with a ceramic-like consistency, obtained by mixing large quantities of pigment followed by micro-particles of white opal, or by adding tiny colored crystals to the clear or pigmented fusion. The long cooling times of this material cause the results to be uncertain, hence *pasta vitrea* is generally used for finishing details.

Opalino
Partly semi-transparent glass with a distinctive iridescent quality highlighted by the incidence of light on the surface. This phenomenon is created by adding lead arsenate to the vitreous mass.

Cristallo
This is the name given in artistic glass to clear colorless glass; its quality depends mainly on the purity of the raw materials used, which must contain the smallest possible quantity of coloring oxides.
To counteract the presence of these oxides, decolorizing substances are used during the fusion to neutralize the effect. Murano *cristallo* glass differs from lead crystal and Bohemian crystal by its long cooling times, which allow greater malleability. This is due to the high content of sodium and calcium oxides in the vitreous mixture.

Pulegoso
A transparent semi-opaque glass distinguished by a countless number of bubbles, "puleghe" in the dialect of Murano, embedded in the vitreous texture. They are liberated by the effect of the heat generated by substances (such as petroleum) added to the vitreous mass during fusion.

Types of glass

Trasparente

Pasta vitrea

Avventurina

Opalino

Primavera

Cristallo

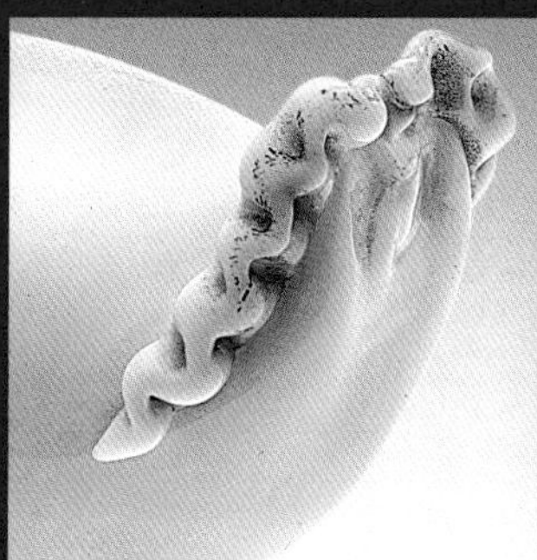
Lattimo

Pulegoso

Production techniques

Decoro fenicio
This is a vitreous texture whose decor is made by applying hot stripes or threads in colored *pasta vitrea* around the object, then "combing" them with a specific tool to produce a festoon motif.
This decor, which owes its name to the decor found on several pre-Roman Phoenician and Egyptian glass pieces, may be left in relief on the surface or be embedded into the surface at the end of the manufacturing process.

Colorazione a caldo senza fusione (glass hot-colored without fusion)
Obtained from a basic mixture similar to *cristallo* glass, it owes its characteristic irregular coloring to the addition of substances into the vitreous mass, before it is shaped, that never melt or do not have the time to do so. This technique is the product of research by Ercole Barovier, who applied it successfully from the Thirties onwards.

Incalmo
The *incalmo* technique consists of joining two blown hemispheres of the same diameter but different color along the rim when hot; they are then shaped as desired. If repeated, the operation can produce objects composed of several different colored bands.

A tessere
Glass made of tesserae in different shapes and colors, prepared before the manufacturing process. The tesserae are obtained by flattening segments of rods or by cutting sheets of colored glass into the section desired. After laying them down on a refractory surface, they are joined by firing in the kiln and fused into a single texture that may be blown and shaped.

Incamiciato
A vitreous texture made by overlaying two or more layers of glass; it is also known as cased glass. Generally transparent colored glass or in some cases *pasta vitrea* is overlaid over a base of opaque glass. This technique, which produces fine chromatic effects, was widely used starting in the Twenties, and still is today.

Vetro massiccio
A technique widely used on Murano since the Thirties for the production of thick objects and sculptures.
It consists in shaping the glass while it is still soft using specific instruments and without blowing.

Murrine
This name indicates a particular type of glass made with a complex technique previously used during the Roman era and revived in Murano at the end of the 19th Century.
It consists in joining hot sections of glass rods called *murrine*. These are obtained from polychrome rods, produced in such a way as to create a specific floral or geometric pattern in section. At the beginning of the process, the *murrine* are laid down one next to the other to form the desired decoration. They are then fired in the kiln into a single vitreous texture, which is subsequently blown and shaped by the glass master, or in other cases shaped with the use of open molds which do not require blowing. In the Forties, Carlo Scarpa made a series of *a murrine* objects for Venini, characterized by a particular finish obtained by grinding the entire surface at the wheel.

Tessuto
A polychrome glass obtained by juxtaposing thin vertical glass rods fired together. After fusing the hot canes together, generally in alternating colors, the master picks them up onto a cylinder, which he then blows and shapes. In some cases the object is completed with a light veiled finish ground at the wheel.

Sommerso
A thick-walled glass obtained by overlaying several layers of *cristallo* glass and transparent colored glass, by repeatedly immersing the object, during the manufacturing process, into different pots of molten glass. There are many variations to this technique, because some of the layers of transparent glass can be substituted with other types of glass such as glass with bubbles, with gold leaf, etc., whose inclusion creates lovely chromatic effects.

Filigrana
This is a technique dating back to the 16th Century, used to make glass pieces with a vitreous texture composed of transparent glass rods with a core in *lattimo* or colored glass. These rods are laid down one next to the other and fired together by the heat in the kiln. They are then wrapped around a cylinder of *cristallo* glass at the end of the blowpipe, which is then blown and shaped. This technique produces objects *a mezza filigrana*, *a reticello*, and *a retortoli*, whose glass texture differs depending on the type of rods or the different manufacturing techniques used. The *a mezza filigrana* and *a reticello* glass uses rods with a single thread inside, whereas the *a retortoli* is characterized by rods whose core is composed of threads wrapped in a spiral. *Mezza filigrana* is distinguished by the typical spiral decor, whereas *a reticello* features a criss-cross pattern, created by blowing inside a hemisphere of *mezza filigrana* another sphere in *mezza filigrana*, whose spiral pattern is contrary to the spiral pattern of the first blown hemisphere.
A further variation of *filigrana*, but of a more ancient origin, is the *a retortoli* technique, also known as *zanfirico* from the name of the Venetian antiquarian Antonio Sanquirico who in the first half of the 19th Century commissioned many copies of antique glass pieces made with this particular technique. In the Fifties and Sixties, glass master Archimede Seguso further elaborated the *filigrana* technique, creating new interpretations such as the *merletti*, using segments of special *a retortoli* rods which he would prepare ahead of time.

Production techniques

Decoro fenicio

Incamiciato

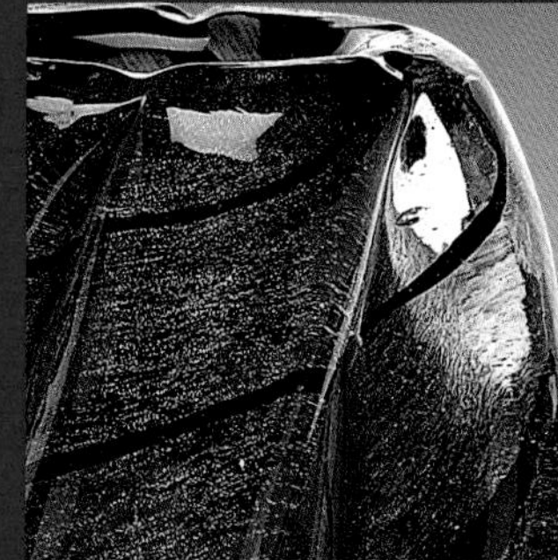
Sommerso

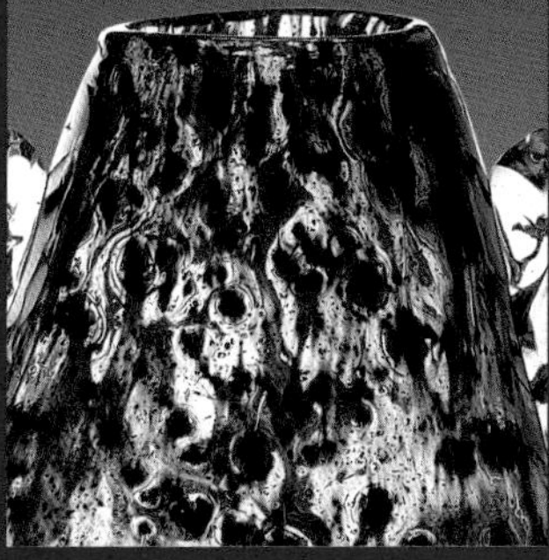
Colorazione a caldo senza fusione

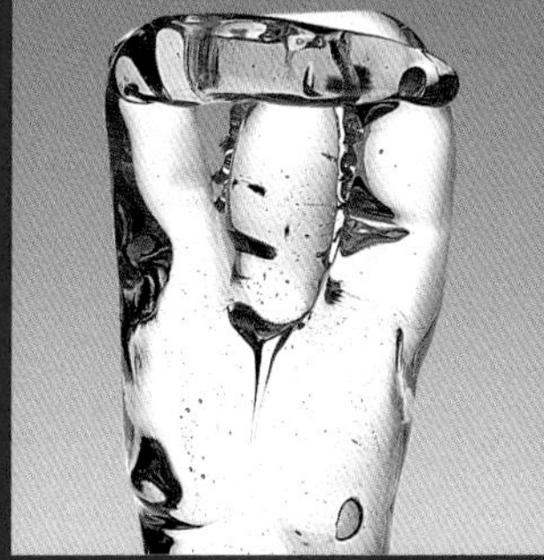
Vetro massiccio

Filigrana

Incalmo

Murrine

A tessere

Tessuto

Hot decorative techniques

Applicazioni di foglia d'oro o argento
A technique used to obtain a characteristic surface decoration of gold or silver leaf, applied during processing by gathering up very thin "leaves" of gold or silver onto the wall of the blown piece. They are then blown further to produce the characteristic fragmentation. Sometimes the pieces made with this technique are cased in a thin layer of cristallo glass.

Costolato
A technique which imprints the characteristic ribbing onto the artifact during the working process. It is achieved by inserting the incandescent ball, on the tip of the blowpipe, into a metal mold with parallel vertical blades, which are imprinted on the semi-processed material which is subsequently blown.

Iridato
It is obtained by exposing the object to tin, titanium or other metal vapors during the manufacturing process. The action of the heat on the surface of the glass forms a thin film of metal oxide which reflects the light irregularly.

Scavo
A technique used to obtain a characteristic rough finish and opaque color which is caused by the reaction or salts and oxides sprinkled over the surface of the object during the manufacturing process. To favor the reaction, the object is later brought up to high temperatures again.

Applicazioni a caldo
Applications of glass that adhere to the object. These applications can be left in relief, as in the case of *bugne*, *rostri*, *lenti*, etc., or they can be embedded into the wall by continuing the process, as in the case of threads, stripes, *pennellate*, *macchie*.

Applicazioni di foglia d'oro o d'argento

Applicazioni a caldo

Costolato

Iridato

Scavo

Cold decorative techniques

Battuto e velato
These are finishing techniques for the surface of the glass executed at the grinding wheel.
They consist in etching the surface more or less widely or deeply depending on the desired result with the help of different types of grinding wheels.
If the incisions are wide, the finish is called *battitura*, whereas the *velatura* is characterized by soft and light etchings which give the surface a satin-finished appearance.

Oro graffito
This technique involves an initial application onto the cold artifact of a thin layer of gold leaf, which is successively etched with a pointed instrument to obtain a characteristic decorative motif.

Decoro a smalti
In this technique, the glass pieces are decorated with enamels that may be melted for application with a paintbrush. The artifact is then reheated in the kiln to fix the enamels, which are composed of a very fine colored glass powder mixed with a fatty substance to ease adherence.

Inciso
This technique comes from Bohemia, and consists in the use of a small wheel made with out of abrasive stone or metal to produce lovely decorations or designs on the surface of the piece.

Corroso
A cold technique used to obtain the characteristic rough surface of glass subjected to the aggression of hydrofluoric acid.
The piece, generally made of thick glass, is sprinkled with sawdust doused in acid to cause an irregular corrosion of the outer surface.

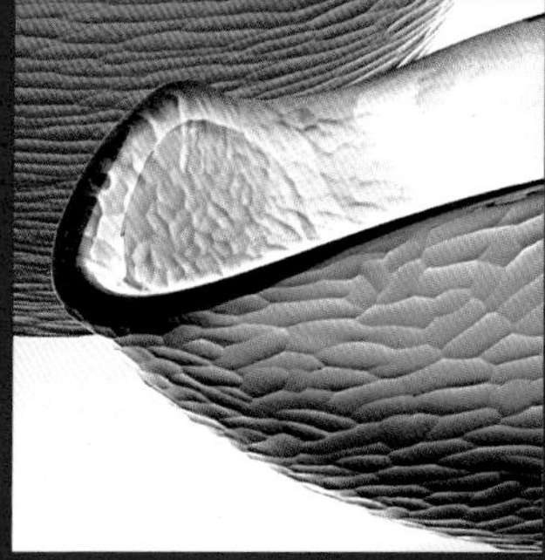
Battuto e velato

Corroso

Oro graffito

Decoro a smalti

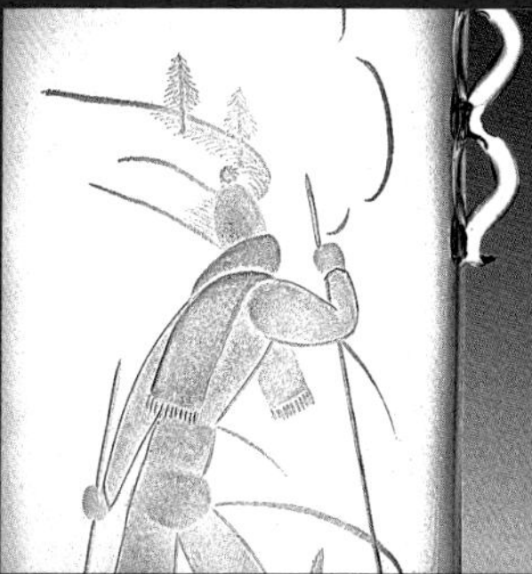
Inciso

Bibliography

1912 *Le industrie artistiche. Vetri e Vetrate*, Roma.

1921 G. Lorenzetti, *I vetri di Murano*, in "Le vie d'Italia", October.
I. Neri, *L'esposizione del Circolo artistico di Venezia*, in "Emporium", August.

1922 R. Linzeler, *Les verreries de Cappellin Venini*, in "Art et Décoration".
F. Sapori, *La XIII Esposizione d'Arte a Venezia*, Bergamo.

1923 C. Carrà, *L'arte decorativa contemporanea*, Milano.
R. Linzeler, *I vetri soffiati muranesi di Cappellin e Venini*, in "Arte pura e decorativa".
R. Papini, *Le Arti a Monza MCMXXIII*, Bergamo.
R. Papini, *La mostra delle Arti decorative a Monza*, in "Emporium", July.

1924 V. Costantini, *Maestri vetrai muranesi Cappellin*, in "Le Arti Plastiche", 16th July.
P. Du Colombier, *Le Salon d'Automne*, in "Art et Decoration", November.
A. Pozzi, *Umberto Bellotto fabbro veneziano*, Venezia.
Vetri di Murano e i vetri soffiati Venini & Co., in "Le Tre Venezie", May.

1926 U. Nebbia, *La XV Esposizione d'Arte a Venezia*, Bergamo.
XV Esposizione Internazionale d'Arte della Città di Venezia, exhibition catalog, Venezia.

1927 *Cose veneziane*, in "Le Arti Plastiche", 16th August.
G. Dell'Oro, *I veneti alla III Biennale delle Arti Decorative di Monza*, in "Le Tre Venezie", August.
G. Marangoni, *Arti del fuoco. Ceramica, vetri, vetrate. Enciclopedia delle moderne Arti decorative*, Milano.
G. Marangoni, *La terza mostra internazionale delle arti decorative nella Villa Reale di Monza. Notizie, rilievi, risultati*, Bergamo.
Le mostre di Ginevra, in "Le Arti Plastiche", 1st March.
R. Papini, *Le Arti a Monza nel 1927: gli italiani*, in "Emporium", June.
F. Reggiori, *La terza Biennale delle arti decorative a Monza*, in "Architettura e arti decorative", 1927-1928, fasc. VII.
The Studio - Year book of decorative art.
III Mostra Internazionale delle Arti Decorative, exhibition catalog, Milano.
20 Espositori a Monza, in "Le Arti Plastiche", 16th September.
E. Zorzi, *Cronache d'Arte. Mostre in preparazione. Una mostra d'Arte italiana a Ginevra*, in "Le Tre Venezie", February.

1928 G. Dell'Oro, *Le piccole industrie venete all'esposizione di Torino*, in "Le Tre Venezie", July.
Filigrane di Murano. Un'arte che riappare in forme nuove, in "Domus", January.
A. Lancelotti, *La terza mostra internazionale delle arti decorative a Monza*, in "Almanacco Italiano", vol. 33.
Murano: oggi fatto d'Arte, in "Domus", December.
A. Parini, *La Mostra piemontese dell'artigianato*, in "La Casa Bella", November.

1929 *Artisti italiani contemporanei*, catalog, Milano.
La Biennale di Monza, in "Le Arti Plastiche", 1st April.
M. Croci, *Gli italiani al Salon d'Automne*, in "La Casa Bella", December.
M. Dazzi, *Le industrie venete alla X Fiera Campionaria di Milano*, in "Le Tre Venezie", May.
"Domus", January.
L'Italie à la Foire de Paris, Paris.
Nuovi vetri di Giacomo Cappellin, in "Domus", April.
Nuovi vetri di Giacomo Cappellin, in "Domus", October.
Nuovi Vetri Muranesi, in "Domus", February.
R.S., *Le ultime settimane della mostra di Barcellona*, in "L'illustrazione italiana", December.

1930 *Alla Triennale di Monza*, in "Domus", July.
Alla Triennale di Monza, Cappellin nella galleria dei vetri d'Arte, in "Domus", September.
"La Casa Bella", May.
"Domus", August.
C.A. Felice, *Catalogo ufficiale della IV Esposizione internazionale delle Arti Decorative ed industriali Moderne*, Milano.
C.A. Felice, *I vetri alla Triennale di Monza*, in "Dedalo", fasc. V.
Guida all'arredamento, in "La Casa Bella", August.
Monza II, in "Le Arti Plastiche", 16th July.
U. Nebbia, *XVII Esposizione Internazionale d'Arte*, Venezia.
U. Nebbia, *I veneti alle arti decorative di Monza*, in "Le Tre Venezie", June.
Nuovi vetri di Giacomo Cappellin, in "Domus", January.
R. Pacini, *La IV Triennale d'arti decorative a Monza II - Le sezioni italiane*, in "Emporium", October.
R. Papini, *Le Arti d'Oggi*, Milano-Roma.
F. Reggiori, *La Triennale di Monza, IV Mostra Internazionale delle Arti Decorative*, in "Architettura e arti decorative", fasc. XI.

1931 *Catalogo della XX Esposizione dell'Opera Bevilacqua La Masa*, Venezia.
G. Dell'Oro, *Le arti decorative alla Mostra di Ca' Pesaro*, in "Le Tre Venezie", August.
Erredi, *Vetri, ceramiche e merletti alla mostra di Amsterdam*, in "Le Tre Venezie", March.
A. Felice, *Richiamo alle arti decorative*, in "Domus", October.
C.A. Felice, *Siamo nella storia*, in "Domus", January.
F. Geraci, *I veneti alla I Quadriennale Romana d'Arte*, in "Le Tre Venezie", February.
G. Lorenzetti, *Vetri di Murano*, Bergamo.
La Mostra d'Arte veneziana al Museo di Amsterdam, in "Rivista di Venezia", April.
Mostra di vetri, ceramiche e merletti d'arte moderna italiana, catalog.
U. Nebbia, *Una mostra d'arte decorativa italiana ad Amsterdam*, in "Emporium", April.
Nuova arte decorativa veneziana a Ca' Pesaro, in "Domus", July.
La pagina illustrata dell'industria artigiana, in "Le Tre Venezie", February.
I Quadriennale d'arte nazionale, exhibition catalog, Roma.

1932 *Catalogo della XIX Biennale*, Venezia.
P. Chiesa, *Il vetro alla Biennale veneziana*, in "Domus", July.
P. Chiesa, *Vetri incisi a Venezia*, in "Domus", August.
G. Lorenzetti, *Il museo vetrario di Murano*, in "Le Tre Venezie", September.
E. Motta, *Guida della XIX Biennale*, Venezia.
E. Motta, *L'Arte decorativa*, in "Le Tre Venezie", May.
U. Nebbia, *L'Arte decorativa alla Biennale*, in "Le Tre Venezie", May.
R. Papini, *Vetri di Paolo Venini*, in "Le Tre Venezie", May.
V. Querel, *Modernità e sintesi nel vetro di Murano*, in "Rassegna dell'istruzione artistica", July.
Salviati, advertisement, in "Domus", January.
Suggerimenti, in "Domus", September.
La tavola e i regali di Natale, in "Domus", December.
I tipi nei vetri d'Arte a Venezia, in "Domus", November.

1933 *Bellezze della tecnica*, in "Domus", February.

I nuovi vetri "laguna" di Venini, in "Domus", January.
I vetri d'arte alla Triennale, in "Domus", May.
I vetri d'arte italiani alla Triennale, in "Domus", July.
1934 "Domus", May.
E. Motta, *L'arte decorativa* in, "Le Tre Venezie", May.
1936 *Catalogo della XX Biennale di Venezia 1936*, Venezia.
G. Dell'Oro, *L'arte decorativa alla XX Biennale*, in "Le Tre Venezie", July.
G. Dell'Oro, *Ambienti, mobili e arredi veneti alla VI Triennale di Milano*, in "Le Tre Venezie", August-September.
E.N.A.P.I. *L'artigianato d'Italia alla VI Triennale di Milano*, Milano.
C. A. Felice, *Arti industriali oggi*, in "Quaderni della Triennale", Milano
Guida alla VI Triennale, Milano.
G. Ponti, *Considerazioni sui vetri Venini*, in "Domus", July.
Utili regali per Natale che vi consigliamo, in "Domus", December.
Venini Murano, advertisements, in "Le Tre Venezie", August-September.
1937 "Domus", April.
Seguso Murano ha realizzato questi nuovi vetri d'arte che dovete conoscere, in "Domus", November.
1938 *Alcuni vetri italiani alla Biennale di Venezia*, in "Domus", October.
Catalogo della XXI Biennale 1938, Venezia.
G. Dell'Oro, *L'Arte decorativa alla XXI Biennale*, in "Le Tre Venezie", May.
Pagine illustrate dell'Istituto Veneto per il Lavoro, in "Le Tre Venezie", May.
Regali per la signora, Regali per una giovane, in "Domus", December.
1940 *Barovier-Toso alla Triennale*, in "Domus", May.
Catalogo della XXII Biennale 1940, Venezia.
G. Dell'Oro, *Artigiani e produttori veneti alla VII Triennale*, in "Le Tre Venezie", May.
E. Motta, *Vetri e merletti*, in Le Tre Venezie, July-August.
G. Ponti, *Nuovi vetri muranesi*, in "Domus", October.
1941 *Documenti di arte decorativa italiana*, in "Domus", June.
C.A. Felice, *Contro la produzione fittizia*, in "Domus", January.
Possibilità del vetro moderno, in "Domus", February.
Produzione italiana di vetri d'arte, in "Domus", December.
"Lo Stile", special number, May.
1942 *Animali di vetro*, in "Domus", January.
Barovier-Toso, advertisment, in "Domus", March.
G. Dell'Oro, *La XXIII Biennale Veneziana, III Rassegna dell'Arte decorativa*, in "Le Tre Venezie", September-October.
Produzione italiana per l'arredamento, in "Domus", October.
1943 G. Dell'Oro, *Il rinnovamento della produzione del vetro muranese, in* "Le Tre Venezie", November-December.
"Domus", January.
Evocazione dell'Artigianato, in "Lo Stile", October.
Oggetti per la casa, in "Domus", October.
1945 R. Aloi, *L'arredamento moderno*, III serie, Milano.
1950 *Arte decorativa alla XXV Biennale*, in "Domus", October.
1951 *L'Art du verre*, exhibition catalog, Paris.
"Domus", September.
IX Triennale di Milano, exhibition catalog, Milano.
I vetri italiani alla Triennale, in "Domus", October.
1952 R. Aloi, *L'arredamento moderno*, Milano.
C. Mariacher, *Mostra storica del vetro muranese*, in *Catalogo della XXVI Biennale di Venezia*.
Murano alla Biennale, in "Domus", November.
XXVI Biennale, exhibition catalog, Venezia.
Vetri alla IX Triennale di Milano, Milano.
1953 A. Gasparetto, *Antico e moderno nella vetraria di Murano*, in "Selearte", June.
Regali di Natale, in "Domus", December.
1954 *Arti decorative alla Biennale*, in "Domus", October.
G. Mariacher, *L'arte del vetro*, Milano.
I Mostra Internazionale del vetro di Murano, exhibition catalog, Roma.
Trent'anni di Triennale, in "Domus", November.
1955 R. Aloi, *Esempi di decorazione moderna di tutto il mondo. Vetri d'oggi*, Milano.
Murano, vetri d'arte, in "Domus", November.
Piccola rassegna di Venini, in "Domus", April.
1956 *Alla Biennale, arti decorative. Breve rassegna*, in "Domus", October.
Arti decorative a Venezia, in "Domus", November.
Venini vasi, Venini lampade, in "Domus", January.
Verres Murano, exhibition catalog, Paris.
1957 *La Fucina degli Angeli*, in "Domus", February.
"Negozie Vetrine", December.
1958 *Alla XI Triennale*, in "Domus", January.
A. Gasparetto, *Il vetro di Murano dalle origini ad oggi*, Venezia.
G. Mariacher, *Venedig zeigt Glas aus Murano*, Venezia.
Rassegna Domus, in "Domus", May.
1959 G. Ponti, *Venini*, in "Domus", December.
1960 A. Gasparetto, *Vetri di Murano 1860-1960*, Verona.
Istituto Veneto per il Lavoro, *Artigianato Artistico Veneto*, Venezia.
1963 A. Gasparetto, *Mostra del vetro di Murano*, exhibition catalog, Venezia.
1964 R. Aloi, *L'arredamento moderno*, Milano.
XXXII Biennale Internazionale d'Arte, exhibition catalog, Venezia.
1965 G. Perocco, *Artisti del primo Novecento italiano*, Torino.
1967 G. Mariacher, *I vetri di Murano*, Milano.
1970 G. Mariacher, *Il Museo Vetrario di Murano*, Milano.
XXXV Biennale, exhibition catalog, Venezia.
1971 E.N.A.P.I., *Artigianato veneto*, Roma.
1977 P. Baldacci, P. Daverio, *Guido Balsamo Stella. Opera grafica e vetraria*, exhibition catalog, Milano.
R. Barovier Mentasti, *Vetri di Murano del '900*, exhibition catalog, Venezia.
1978 R. Barovier Mentasti, *Vetri di Murano dell'800*, exhibition catalog, Venezia.
S. Tagliapietra, *La magnifica comunità di Murano 1900-1929*, Verona.
1981 F. Brunello, *Arti e mestieri a Venezia nel Medioevo e nel Rinascimento*, Vicenza.
A. Dorigato, R. Barovier Mentasti, *Venezianisches Glas 19. bis 20. Jahrhundert aus dem Glasmuseum Murano/Venezia*, exhibition catalog, Berlin.
G. Perocco, *Vittorio Zecchin*, exhibition catalog, Venezia.
Vetri Murano oggi, exhibition catalog, Milano.
1982 *Antonio Salviati e la rinascita ottocentesca del vetro artistico veneziano*, exhibition catalog, Vicenza.

R. Barovier Mentasti, *Il vetro veneziano*, Milano.
A. Dorigato, G. Romanelli, *Vetro di Murano: ieri ed oggi*, exhibition catalog, Tokyo.
Mille Anni di arte del vetro a Venezia, exhibition catalog, Venezia.
S. Tagliapietra, *Cronache muranesi II. Murano veste la divisa 1926-1950*, Venezia.
1983 A. Dorigato, *Murano: Il vetro a tavola ieri e oggi*, exhibition catalog, Venezia. *Murano Glass in the Twentieth Century*, St. Peterburg.
1984 *L'immortale. I capolavori di Egidio Costantini della Fucina degli Angeli*, Parma.
Mercato e travestimento. L'artigianato d'arte a Venezia fine '800 inizi '900, Venezia.
M. Miani, D. Resini, F. Lamon, *L'arte dei maestri vetrai di Murano*, Treviso.
Mostra del vetro italiano 1920-1940, exhibition catalog, Torino.
Venini & the Murano Renaissance, exhibition catalog, New York.
1985 Cerutti, *Arti decorative del '900. Liberty*, Novara.
I. De Guttry, M.P. Majno, M. Quesada, *Le arti minori d'autore in Italia dal 1900 al 1970*, Roma.
A. Dorigato, *Il vetro mosaico muranese*, in "Bollettino dei Musei Civici Veneziani".
S. Tagliapietra, *Cronache muranesi: l'Ottocento*, Venezia.
1986 A. Dorigato, *Il Museo Vetrario di Murano*, Milano.
1987 *Gli anni di Ca' Pesaro 1908-1920*, exhibition catalog, Milano.
R. Bossaglia, M. Quesada, P. Spadini, *Secessione Romana 1913-1916*, Roma.
B. Nerozzi, *Impronte del soffio. Tradizioni e nuovi percorsi a Murano*, Venezia.
W. Neuwirth, *Vetri Italiani 1950-1960*, exhibition catalog, Wien.
1988 R. Bossaglia, M. Quesada, *Gabriele D'Annunzio e la promozione delle arti*, exhibition catalog, Roma.
La verrerie Européenne des années 50, Marseille.
1989 L. E. Berndt, *Loredano Rosin. Sculture in vetro*, Venezia.
F. Deboni, *I vetri Venini*, Torino.
A. Dorigato, *Ercole Barovier 1889-1974, vetraio muranese*, Venezia.
G. Duplani Tucci, *Venini 1921*, Milano.
M. Heiremans, *Murano glass 1945-1970*.
H. Ricke, *Reflex der Jahrhunderte*, Leipzig.
The Venetians, Modern Glass, 1919-1990, New York.
1990 *Egidio Costantini. Il Maestro dei Maestri*, Bruxelles.
La Fucina degli Angeli. Da Chagall a Max Ernst. Magia di Vetri, Milano.
G. Sarpellon, *Miniature di vetro, murrine 1838-1924*, exhibition catalog, Venezia.
1991 M. Barovier, *Carlo Scarpa. I vetri di Murano 1927-1947*, Venezia.
M. Cocchi, *Vetri di Murano del '900, 50 capolavori*, Milano.
U. Franzoi, *I vetri di Archimede Seguso*, exhibition catalog, Venezia.
1992 *L'arte del vetro. Silice e fuoco: vetri del XIX e XX secolo*, Venezia.
R. Ballarin, *Egidio Costantini: Vetro, un Amore. La Fucina degli Angeli 1948-1992*, Venezia.
M. Barovier, *Napoleone Martinuzzi vetraio del '900*, Venezia.
R. Barovier Mentasti, *Vetro Veneziano 1890-1990*, Venezia.
1993 M. Barovier, *L'Arte dei Barovier vetrai di Murano 1866-1972*, Venezia.
N. Berruti, M.A. Serena, *Vetro, un amore. Biografia di Egidio Costantini*, Trento.
R. Bossaglia, *I vetri di Fulvio Bianconi*, exhibition catalog, Torino.
M. Heiremans, *Art Glass from Murano 1910-1970*, Stuttgart.
S. Lutzeier, *Modernes Glas von 1920-1990*, Augsburg.
H. Newman, *Dizionario del vetro*, Milano.
1994 M. Barovier, *Fantasie di vetro*, exhibition catalog, Venezia.
R. Barovier Mentasti, *Vetri veneziani del '900*, Venezia.
1995 *L'Art du verre a Murano au 20ème siècle*, exhibition catalog, Paris.
M. Barovier, R. Barovier Mentasti, A. Dorigato, *Il vetro di Murano alle Biennali 1895-1972*, Milano.
R. Barovier Mentasti, *I vetri di Archimede Seguso 1950-1959*, Torino.
E. Baumgartner, *Verre de Venice et "façon de Venice"*, Genève.
La Biennale di Venezia, 46. Esposizione Internazionale d'Arte, Venezia.
Glas, Band II, Zürich.
H. Lockwood, *Vetri: Italian Glass News*, April.
Maestri vetrai creatori di Murano del '900, exhibition catalog, Milano.
H. Ricke, *Glaskunst. Reflex der Jahrhunderte*, München-New York.
Venezia e la Biennale. I percorsi del gusto, exhibition catalog, Milano.
1996 *Gli artisti di Venini. Per una storia del vetro d'Arte veneziano*, exhibition catalog, Milano.
M. Barovier, A. Dorigato, *Il bestiario di Murano*, exhibition catalog, Venezia.
F. Deboni, *Murano '900*, Milano.
M. Heiremans, *20th Century Murano Glass*, Stuttgart.
H. Ricke, E. Schmitt, *Italienisches Glas Murano - Mailand 1930-1970*, München-New York.
M. Quesada, *Hans Stoltenberg Lerche (1865-1920)*, Venezia.
1997 M. Barovier, *Carlo Scarpa, I vetri di un architetto*, exhibition catalog, Milano.
M. Romanelli, M. Laudani, *Design: Nordest*, Milano.
1998 M. Barovier, *Het Venitiaans glaswerk van Carlo Scarpa*, Bruxelles.
I Barovier: una stirpe di vetrai, Hakone.
S. Barr, *Venetian Glass*, New York.
A. Bova, R. Junck, P. Migliaccio, *Murrine e Millefiori 1830-1930*, Venezia.
New Glass, exhibition catalog, Venezia.
Tra creatività e progettazione. Il vetro italiano a Milano 1906-1968, Milano.
Venini Venetian modern glass, exhibition catalog, Riihimäki.
1999 M. Barovier, *Il vetro a Venezia, dal moderno al contemporaneo*, Milano.
A. Bova, R. Junck, P. Migliaccio, *The colours of Murano in the XIX Century*, Venezia.
M. Heiremans, *Dino Martens*, Stuttgart.
Vetri in tavola, I vetri di Murano per la tavola dell'800, Venezia.
2000 *Kiku. Meraviglioso mondo delle Murrine*, Kotaki.
Venetian Glass. The Olinck-Spanu Collection, New York.
Venini Diaz de Santillana, *Venini. Catalogo ragionato 1921-1986*, Milano.
2001 M. Barovier, *Il Liberty a Murano*, in F. Benzi, *Il Liberty in Italia*, Milano.
C. Moretti, *Glossario del vetro veneziano*, Venezia.
Murano. Vetri dalla Collezione Olinck-Spanu, Milano.
Vetri veneziani dal Rinascimento all'Ottocento, Napoli.
2002 M. Barovier, M. Mondi, C. Sonego, *Vittorio Zecchin 1878-1947*, Venezia.
M. Cisotto Nalon, R. Barovier Mentasti, *Suggestioni colori e fantasie. I vetri dell'Ottocento muranese*, Milano.
A. Dorigato, *L'Arte del Vetro a Murano*, Venezia.
Le età del vetro, Storia e tecnica del vetro dal mondo antico ad oggi, Milano.
Formdesign-Farbdesign. Finnisches und italienisches Glas der Sammlung Losch, Düsseldorf.
M. Heiremans, *Murano Glass, themes and variations*, Stuttgart.
2003 E. Baumgartner, *Venise et façon de Venise*, exhibition catalog, Paris.
2004 M. Barovier, *Il Déco a Murano*, in F. Benzi, *Il Déco in Italia*, Roma.

Index of objects by artist

The numbers refer to pagination

Index of objects by manufacturer

The numbers refer to pagination